OUTLAW MARRIAGES

OUTLAW
MARRIAGES

The Hidden Histories of Fifteen
Extraordinary Same-Sex Couples

...

Rodger Streitmatter

Beacon Press, Boston

Beacon Press
25 Beacon Street
Boston, Massachusetts 02108-2892
www.beacon.org

Beacon Press books
are published under the auspices of
the Unitarian Universalist Association of Congregations.

15   14   13   12   8   7   6   5   4   3   2   1

This book is printed on acid-free paper that meets the uncoated paper
ANSI/NISO specifications for permanence as revised in 1992.

Text design by Wilsted & Taylor Publishing Services

For photo credits and permissions,
please see Photography/Illustration Credits on page 211.

Library of Congress Cataloging-in-Publication Data
Streitmatter, Rodger.
Outlaw marriages : the hidden histories of fifteen
extraordinary same-sex couples / by Rodger Streitmatter.
p. cm.
Includes bibliographical references.
ISBN 978-0-8070-0334-3 (alk. paper)
1. Same-sex marriage—United States. I. Title.
HQ1034.U5S77 2012
306.84'8—dc23   2011048309

CONTENTS

PROLOGUE

The couples who come to life in the following chapters were social insurgents. That is, each pair of men and each pair of women defied the social order by creating sub-rosa same-sex marriages long before such relationships were legally sanctioned.

Tennessee Williams and Frank Merlo, for example, began their outlaw marriage in 1948—spending every day and night together, while loving and supporting each other to a degree fully comparable to that of any husband and wife. Their partnership continued until Merlo died of cancer in 1963.

Outlaw Marriages tells Williams and Merlo's story, along with those of fourteen other same-sex couples who combined their lives either as husband and husband or wife and wife during eras when no legal institution and no church approved of such a union.

The other trait that these renegade couples have in common is that they all fully qualify as, in a word, *extraordinary.*

In many instances, that powerful adjective fits because of the remarkable contributions a particular couple made to the culture—the fields ranging from literature to modern art to filmmaking. The achievements of other couples include opening graduate education to American women and pioneering a new form of journalism in the pages of the *New Yorker* magazine.

With Williams and Merlo, their gift was creating some of the most memorable plays in the history of American theater. Williams was addicted to drugs and promiscuity when he met the rock-solid Merlo. The World War II vet then saw to it that the playwright regained his emotional and physical equilibrium, allowing him to write such theatrical masterpieces as the Pulitzer Prize–winning *Cat on a Hot Tin Roof.*

A few of the other extraordinary contributions that unfold in this book are

- Walt Whitman and Peter Doyle reinventing American poetry
- Jane Addams and Mary Rozet Smith revolutionizing the field of social work
- Greta Garbo and Mercedes de Acosta taking the lead in transforming Hollywood into the celebrity capital of the world

When reading the statements above, you probably recognized only one of the two names in the pairings. That's because the achievements of one partner often became widely known, while those of the other partner stayed hidden—until the publication of this book.

Outlaw Marriages is an apt title on two levels.

First, all fifteen couples created unions that defied the laws and mores of their day. Many of these de facto partnerships survived and thrived, despite their lack of support by church or state, for thirty or forty years—in some cases, *fifty*.

Second, these couples flouted convention. Aaron Copland was thirty-two years old when he met and instantly fell in love with a drop-dead gorgeous violinist named Victor Kraft, who was only seventeen. The composer's friends and family didn't take the relationship seriously, convinced the couple wouldn't survive the dramatic age difference. Copland and Kraft proved them wrong. The men not only stayed together but also jointly created a distinctly American style of music that critics today, eighty years later, are still praising.

That the couples were willing to bend the marital rules doesn't mean they all succeeded in creating relationships that were made in heaven—far from it. A regrettable scenario that plays out in several chapters begins with the lesser-known partner being absolutely essential to the better-known partner's rise to success, but then . . . the high-achieving partner getting what might be called the "twenty-year itch." Martha Carey Thomas set the standard back in the 1890s, summarily dumping her partner of two decades, Mamie Gwinn, for another woman. Janet Flanner went a similar route in the 1930s, as did Audre Lorde in the 1980s.

In the instances listed above as well as in others where the outlaw marriage eventually falls apart, readers hear the whole story—which typically includes infidelity, deceit, and betrayal. These unfortunate factors are revealed in full detail, as they're the realities that often confront any long-term relationship, gay or straight.

To help the various outlaw marriages come alive in the reader's mind, I've included photos of all fifteen couples. Tracking down these images was often a challenge, especially in the instances when one or both members of a couple—as with Greta Garbo and Mercedes de Acosta—didn't publicly acknowledge their relationship. And so, in some cases, I've had to use two separate photos of the partners, since a single photo of them together either didn't exist or wasn't available. There are also instances—as with Jane Addams and Mary Rozet Smith—when I've used a photo of poor quality because it shows the partners together, even though higher-quality photos of the two individuals separately could have been used.

Whether a chapter begins with a single image or a pair of them, each story that follows is a page-turner. Sometimes the most compelling element in it is the contribution the couple made; other times, it's the internal dynamics of their relationship. But one theme runs through them all:

Two people joining together to create an outlaw marriage plays a central role not only in the couple's extraordinary achievements, but also in each individual partner's very being.

Chapter 1

Walt Whitman & Peter Doyle

1865–1892

Revolutionizing American Poetry

...

Many literary scholars consider Walt Whitman this country's most influential poet. Widely referred to as the father of free verse, he liberated poetry from rhyme and meter, opening it up to the flexible rhythms of feeling and voice. The works collected in Whitman's *Leaves of Grass* pay homage to the freedom and dignity of the individual while celebrating democracy and the brotherhood of man, even though early critics condemned his references to same-sex love as being obscene.

Peter Doyle was a twenty-one-year-old conductor on a horse-drawn streetcar when he and Whitman, who was forty-five at the time, began their romantic relationship. During their quarter-century outlaw marriage, Doyle became Whitman's muse. In that role, the younger man inspired some of his partner's best-known works and also caused the general tone of Whitman's poetry to become more optimistic.

...

Walter Whitman was born into a working-class family on Long Island, some fifty miles east of New York City, in 1819. His father was a carpenter and sometime farmer, and his mother cared for the couple's eight children.[1]

Whitman left school at the age of eleven. One of his first jobs was as a printer's apprentice for a newspaper, and he then read dozens of books so he could become a schoolteacher. By his late teens, his focus had shifted to journalism, and, in his early twenties, he was editing New York's *Brooklyn Daily Eagle.*[2]

At the same time that Whitman was working at his various jobs, he was also jotting down poetic phrases in a notebook he carried with him. The lines came spontaneously in flashes of emotion and were written in the loose way that people talked rather than in a formal structure. The subjects he wrote about ranged widely, from nature to city life and religion to sexual mores.[3]

In 1855, Whitman gathered together twelve of his poems and used what he'd learned as a printer to self-publish a volume titled *Leaves of Grass.* The punctuation was erratic, with few commas or periods but an abundance of ellipses, and the content was unconventional, with some lines being straightforward—such as, "The regatta is spread on the bay . . . how the white sails sparkle!"—while others were a challenge for a reader to understand—such as, "And am stucco'd with quadrupeds and birds all over."[4]

Reviewers who critiqued the poems condemned both them and their author. The critic for the *Boston Intelligencer,* for example, called the book a "mass of bombast, egotism, vulgarity, and nonsense," speculating that the author must be "some escaped lunatic, raving in pitiable delirium."[5]

Whitman soon produced two more editions of his book, adding new poems each time. Scholars who've studied these early editions note that they communicated a sense of desperation. In one poem, Whitman spoke of "dark patches" in his soul brought on by feelings of "guile, anger, lust, hot wishes I dared not speak." In another, he made the violent statement, "Let him who is without my poems be assassinated!" The pessimistic tone reflected the struggles in Whitman's personal life. After his father died, he assumed financial responsibility for his mother and two brothers.[6]

In the third edition of *Leaves of Grass,* published in 1860, Whitman added the "Calamus" poems. These works included erotic passages describing homosexual affection. One poem read, "But the two men I saw to-day on the pier, parting the parting of dear friends / The one to remain hung on the other's neck and passionately kissed him—while the one to depart tightly prest the one to remain in his arms."[7]

When the Civil War broke out, Whitman moved to the nation's capital to volunteer as a nurse for injured Union soldiers. He supported his family by working as a clerk for the federal government, initially in the Bureau of Indian Affairs and later in the attorney general's office.[8]

Peter Doyle was born into a working-class family in Limerick City, Ireland, in 1843. When Pete was eight years old, the Doyles boarded a ship and came to the United States, settling in northern Virginia, just a few miles south of Washington, D.C. His father worked as a blacksmith, and his mother took in sewing while also caring for the couple's eight children.[9]

Little is known of Doyle's early years beyond the fact that his formal education was minimal. When he was seventeen, he enlisted in the Confederate Army. He saw heavy action in several battles and was wounded at Sharpsburg in 1862. Early the next year, he was taken captive and imprisoned for about a month before being released on the condition that he leave the military.[10]

Doyle then moved to the nation's capital, initially working as a blacksmith's helper at the Washington Navy Yard. His father had died by this point, so he became the head of a household that included his widowed mother and several younger siblings. By 1865, Doyle had landed a job as a conductor on the Washington and Georgetown Railroad line, which traveled along Pennsylvania Avenue.[11]

CREATING AN OUTLAW MARRIAGE

Walt Whitman and Peter Doyle met in early 1865 when the older man was a passenger on the streetcar where the younger man sold tickets. "Walt had his blanket—it was thrown round his shoulders—he seemed like an old sea-captain," Doyle later recalled of their first encounter. "He was the only passenger, it was a lonely night, so I thought I would go in and talk with him. Something in me made me do it, and something in him drew me that way. He used to say there was something in me that had the same effect on him. Anyway, I went into the car."[12]

According to Doyle's account, the two men made physical contact within a matter of minutes after they'd met. "We were familiar at once—I put my hand on his knee—we understood. He did not get out at the end of the trip—in fact went all the way back with me," Doyle said. "From that time on, we were the biggest sort of friends."[13]

Whitman going "all the way back with me" meant that the poet stayed on the streetcar until Doyle ended his shift and the two men then spent their first night together. Doyle recalled, "It was our practice to go to a hotel on Washington Avenue after I was done with my car. I remember the place well—there on the corner." The Union Hotel was at the intersection of what today is 30th and M Streets in the city's Georgetown neighborhood.[14]

Whitman and Doyle being drawn to each other was, in several respects, a classic example of opposites being attracted. Whitman was forty-five years old, six feet tall, and heavyset, while Doyle was twenty-one years old, five feet eight inches tall, and slender. Whitman also was a highly literate man, while Doyle had no more than a rudimentary education—the poet soon began tutoring him in spelling, arithmetic, and geography. On top of these other differences, Whitman supported the Union cause, while Doyle had fought for the Confederacy.[15]

Despite the men being attracted to each other, family circumstances kept them from living together. Whitman repeatedly told his young partner that he wanted them to set up housekeeping as a couple, but Doyle insisted that it was his duty, as the oldest unmarried son, to live with and care for his widowed mother. And so, Whitman had to be satisfied with spending most nights with Doyle, either at the hotel or at the poet's rooming house, while the two men maintained separate residences.[16]

ENJOYING AN INTIMATE LIFE TOGETHER

Beginning the night they met and continuing for the next eight years, Whitman and Doyle were inseparable. The poet wrote his friends about Doyle, describing the younger man as a "hearty full-blooded everyday divinely generous working man: a hail-fellow-well-met." Flattered by such words, the high-spirited Doyle took to calling himself "Pete the Great."[17]

The couple's favorite activity was hiking. "We would walk together for miles and miles, never sated," Whitman told one biographer. "Often we would go on for some time without a word, then talk—Pete a rod ahead or I a rod ahead. It was a great, a precious, a memorable experience." Doyle also spoke of these hikes, saying Whitman was "always whistling or singing" to express his pleasure. "We would talk of ordinary matters. He would recite poetry, especially Shakespeare—he would hum airs or shout in the woods."[18]

Their most frequent destinations were in or near Alexandria, Virginia. This meant they walked south from downtown Washington, crossed over the Potomac River via the Navy Yard Bridge, and then continued south for a total distance of between five and ten miles, depending on their exact starting and ending points.[19]

The couple also spent time together while the younger man was working. After Whitman finished his clerk's job for the day, he'd climb aboard Doyle's streetcar and ride along for the rest of the route, positioning himself as close to "Pete the Great" as he could. One observer later described Whitman as "resting against the dash, by the side of the young conductor—evidently his intimate friend."[20]

Whitman didn't have much extra money at this point in his life, but Doyle had even less. So the poet sometimes had clothes made for his young partner. There were also occasions when Whitman surprised Doyle by bringing him bouquets of fresh-cut flowers, much as a doting husband might bring his wife.[21]

ASSUMING THE ROLES OF POET AND MUSE

Whitman falling in love had a powerful impact on his writing. Literary scholars have identified several poems—and specific lines from many others—that they attribute to Doyle having become the poet's muse.

The most famous of the works credited to Whitman's relationship with Doyle is his tribute to Abraham Lincoln, "O Captain! My Captain!" This poem became extremely popular soon after Whitman wrote it, the only one of the poet's works to appear in anthologies while he was still alive. Scholars say Whitman wrote the piece largely because "Pete the Great" had been an eyewitness to Lincoln's assassination in Ford's Theatre on Good Friday, April 14, 1865. Doyle later shared his recollections of that night with one of Whitman's biographers:[22]

"I heard that the President and his wife would be present and made up my mind to go. There was a great crowd in the building. I got into the second gallery. I saw everything on the stage and was in a good position to see the President's box. I heard the pistol shot. I had no idea what it was, what it meant—it was sort of muffled. I really knew nothing of what had occurred until Mrs. Lincoln leaned out of the box and cried, 'The President is shot!' I needn't tell you what I felt then, or saw. It is all put down in Walt's piece. That piece is exactly right."[23]

Whitman's poem portrays Lincoln as a ship captain who dies just as the craft he's piloted safely through a storm—the poet's metaphor for the Civil War—is arriving at its harbor. Literary scholars believe that Whitman chose the sea-journey approach to describe Lincoln's death in an effort to please Doyle, referring back to the Irishman's journey to America. The ship that Doyle and his family were aboard had almost wrecked during a violent storm on Good Friday night.[24]

A second poem that clearly shows Doyle's influence is the one titled "Come Up from the Fields Father." The work is unique among the hundreds that Whitman created in that it's the only one that uses a first name—"Pete"—to identify a fictional hero.[25]

More evidence of Doyle inspiring Whitman can be found in works that appeared in the 1867 edition of *Leaves of Grass*, the first published after the men began their outlaw marriage. Among the specific lines that scholars point to is one about an old soldier burying his "son of responding kisses"—the old soldier is thought to be Whitman, while the son who's being kissed is

Doyle. Another line is "Many a soldier's kiss dwells on these bearded lips"—
with "these bearded lips" alluding to the facial hair that Whitman wore. A
third line that scholars cite is one that tells of a young man in camp being valued "more than all the gifts of the world"—the phrasing speaks to Whitman's
love for Doyle being more important to him than worldly goods.[26]

For some scholars, the strongest impact of Whitman's relationship with
Doyle isn't found in the poems he added to *Leaves of Grass,* but in the works
he chose to delete from the 1867 edition. That is, Whitman removed a number of poems that had appeared in the previous edition and that critics char-
acterize as expressing the poet's earlier "self-doubt and despair." They say that
Whitman eliminated these works because he'd now found the love of his life
and therefore was in a "more optimistic mood." In the words of one scholar,
"Walt's new-found confidence in love was, in large measure, a result of his satisfying relationship with Pete."[27]

COMMUNICATING THEIR LOVE IN LETTERS

Whitman and Doyle began writing to each other in 1868, the first time they
were apart after beginning their outlaw marriage. The men were separated
because Whitman visited his family in New York, while "Pete the Great" had
to stay in Washington to work. Their correspondence continued, off and on
whenever they were apart, for almost two decades.[28]

In the first surviving letter, Doyle exclaimed, "I could not resist the inclination to write to you this morning it seems more than a week since I
saw you." Whitman then responded, "I think of you very often, dearest
comrade—I find it first rate to think of you, Pete, & to know that you are
there, all right, & that I shall return, & we will be together again."[29]

In the six weeks that the men were apart that first time, Doyle wrote at
least seven letters and Whitman wrote at least eleven.[30]

During that period as well as during later ones, Whitman routinely began
his letters with the words "My darling" and ended them with phrases such as
"Love to you, my dearest boy" or "So long, dear Pete—& my love to you as always." Doyle ended his letters by writing "Pete the Great" or "Pete X X," using
the X's to represent the kisses he sent his partner.[31]

The men filled most of their letters with descriptions of the small events in
their daily lives, but they also sometimes spoke of their love for each other. In
one letter, Whitman told Doyle, "I think of you very often. My love for you is
indestructible," and in another he wrote, "I don't know what I should do if I
hadn't you to think of & look forward to."[32]

Many letters included erotic passages in which Whitman talked about
kissing his young lover. In one instance, "Pete the Great" had complained in a
previous letter about his job. The older partner then proposed, in his next let-

ter, how he'd like to take Doyle's mind off his troubles. "All I have to say is—to say nothing—only a good smacking kiss, & many of them—& taking in return many, many, many from my dear son—good loving ones too—which will do more credit to his lips than growling & complaining."[33]

Whitman's correspondence to Doyle also reflected the fact that the poet's literary stature was growing. In 1872, he boasted to his partner that "my books are beginning to do pretty well." The progress was largely due to the smattering of positive reviews that appeared in the press, such as the *New York Galaxy* stating that Whitman's poetry "means power, health, freedom, democracy, self-esteem, a full life in the open air, an escape from old forms and standards."[34]

SHIFTING TO A LONG-DISTANCE RELATIONSHIP

In January 1873, Whitman suffered a stroke. He was then confined to his bed and had to hire a nurse to care for him.[35]

Doyle had changed jobs by this point and was now working the evening shift as a brakeman for the Pennsylvania Railroad. Every day he stopped by to see his ailing partner before going to his job. Many years later, Whitman reminisced about those visits. "Pete, do you remember, during my tedious sickness ('73) how you used to come to my solitary garret room and make up my bed, and enliven me and chat for an hour or so—before you went on duty?"[36]

By the spring, Whitman could no longer afford a nurse, but he still needed someone to care for him. Doyle couldn't do the job because he had to work, so Whitman moved in with his brother George and sister-in-law Lou in Camden, New Jersey. "I think about you every night," Whitman wrote Doyle once he'd settled in. "I do not miss any thing of Washington, but *your visits.*"[37]

Doyle applied for a new job as a baggage handler on the railroad line that served New York, so he could move closer to Camden. The baggage job came through, but he wasn't assigned to the New York line but to the one that traveled from Washington to Baltimore, so he continued living with his family in Alexandria.[38]

"Pete the Great" was determined to keep the outlaw marriage a central part of his life, so he made frequent journeys to New Jersey—sometimes two or three weekends in a row—to see his ailing partner. After one such trip, Whitman wrote gleefully to a friend of how he'd enjoyed seeing the younger man. "Peter Doyle has paid me a short visit of a couple of days—the dear, dear boy—& what good it did me!"[39]

The couple experienced a major setback in 1874 when a new attorney general was appointed, and Whitman, who'd been on leave from his clerk's job since his stroke, was officially discharged. He tried to reassure Doyle that they'd survive the continued separation. "My darling son, you must not be unhappy about me—I hope & trust things may work so that we can yet be with each other, at least from time to time—& meanwhile we must adapt ourselves to circumstances," Whitman wrote. "You keep on, & try to do right, & live the same square life you always have, & maintain as cheerful a heart as possible—& as for the way things finally turn out, leave that to the Almighty."[40]

What the poet didn't write was that a new love interest had entered his life. Whitman met Harry Stafford, who was forty years his junior and worked as an errand boy at a Camden printing shop, in 1876. Stafford never became as important to Whitman as Doyle was, but the aging poet was clearly smitten by the eighteen-year-old who he referred to as his "darling boy."[41]

And yet, Whitman continued to send his long-time partner letters that expressed his love. "I ought to have written to you before—but I believe lazy & listless fits grow stronger & frequenter on me as I get older," the poet wrote in December 1876. "But I often, often think of you, boy, & let that make it up." Whitman ended his letter by saying, "My loving boy, I underscore the words, for I know they will make you feel good to hear."[42]

Whitman's correspondence during this period included erotic passages that spoke of his longing to have physical contact with Doyle. By the summer of 1877, the poet's feelings for Stafford had faded and he told "Pete the Great" that he was spending many of his days at a farm near Camden. Whitman wrote, "I have a fine secluded wood & creek & springs, where I pass my time alone, & yet not lonesome at all (often think of you, Pete, & put my arm around you & hug you up close, & give you a good buss—often)."[43]

In the fall of 1880, Whitman and Doyle went on a holiday together to Niagara Falls. They'd both been looking forward to the trip, and it met their expectations in full measure, as Whitman wrote a friend that having been with Doyle made him feel "as fresh as a lark."[44]

As the years passed, Whitman continued to revise *Leaves of Grass,* with the version dated 1882 ultimately becoming the most significant. That edition, which had grown to three hundred poems, was published by a prominent Boston firm. When Massachusetts state officials declared the book "obscene" and blocked its distribution, a Philadelphia publisher stepped in and took on the project. The obscenity charge attracted national attention, resulting in a plethora of flattering reviews—the *Chicago Tribune* called the book "brilliant" and "remarkable," and *Critic* magazine lauded the poet as "an aggressive champion of democracy and the working-man." From that point on, *Leaves of Grass* sold extremely well. In the words of one biographer, "Whitman emerged from the controversy well paid and famous."[45]

THE OUTLAW MARRIAGE WANES

Doyle continued to visit Whitman in Camden in the early 1880s, but their times together grew less frequent as the poet's schedule became increasingly filled with the many lectures and readings he was asked to give.[46]

Now that the intense period of the men's relationship was behind them, Whitman wrote longingly of their bygone days. In one letter, he reminisced, "Pete do you remember—(of course you do—I do well) those great long jovial walks we had at times for years, out of Washington City—often moonlight nights, or Sundays, up and down the Potomac shores, one side or the other, sometimes ten miles in a stretch? Or when you work'd on the horse-cars, coming home late together?"[47]

A major change in Doyle's life came in 1885 when his mother died. Now that he didn't have the responsibility of caring for her, he relocated to Philadelphia, so he lived just across the river from Camden. After the move, the men's correspondence ended because of their close geographic proximity to each other.[48]

By this point, however, a new complication made Doyle's visits to Whitman infrequent. The problem was that the poet, now having enough money to buy his own house, had both a housekeeper and a nurse working for him. "In the old days," Doyle later complained, "I had always open doors to Walt—going, coming, staying as I chose. Now, I had to run the gauntlet of [the housekeeper] Mrs. Davis and a nurse and what not. Somehow, I could not do it." So Doyle sometimes didn't see Whitman for several months in a row. "We loved each other deeply," Doyle continued. "I should have gone to see him, I know it now. I did not know it then, but it is all right. Walt realized I never swerved from him—he knows it now—that is enough."[49]

In early 1892, soon after Doyle expressed his regrets for not having visited more often, Whitman lapsed into a coma. The seventy-three-year-old poet remained in this condition until he died, in March, of pulmonary emphysema. Doyle was among the mourners who stood over the body as it rested inside an oak coffin and then was buried in Camden.[50]

America's major newspapers published lengthy obituaries and tributes to Whitman. The *Washington Post* called him "a poet for humanity," and the *New York Times* lauded him as a "champion of democracy" and "remarkable" literary figure who "had the courage to speak out." None of the articles made any reference either to the poet's homosexuality or to Peter Doyle.[51]

GOING PUBLIC WITH THE INTIMATE CORRESPONDENCE

By the time Whitman died, Doyle had matured into a handsome man of forty-nine, and yet he never entered into another romantic relationship. Instead, "Pete the Great" dedicated his life to a project involving the man he'd loved for twenty-seven years.[52]

That undertaking had its roots back in 1880 when a physician named Richard Maurice Bucke had contacted Doyle. Bucke was writing a biography of Whitman, and the poet told him that his life story wouldn't be complete unless it included information about his intimate relationship with Doyle. After traveling to Washington to meet with the poet's long-time partner, Bucke was particularly excited when he learned that Doyle had kept the letters that Whitman had written to him.[53]

Bucke stayed in touch with Doyle over the next several years, ultimately deciding that the letters—along with those from Doyle that Whitman had kept—deserved a book all their own. It wasn't until after the poet died, however, that Bucke moved forward with the project. When *Calamus, A Series of Letters Written During the Years 1868–1880 by Walt Whitman to a Young Friend (Peter Doyle)* was published in 1897, it not only caused a sensation in literary circles but also transformed Doyle into a celebrity among Whitman's many followers.[54]

Reviews of the book were decidedly mixed. *Literature* magazine praised the letters as "positively delightful," but the *Nation* condemned them for "their unvarying puerility."[55]

Within the community of Whitman admirers, one quotation from "Pete the Great" that was published in the book of letters brought him enormous affection. Doyle's poignant passage involved a sweater of his partner's that he'd kept. "I now and then," Doyle said, "put it on, lay down and think I am in the old times. Then Walt is with me again. When I get it on and stretch out on the old sofa, I am very well contented. It is like Aladdin's lamp. I do not ever for a minute lose the old man. He is always nearby."[56]

Whitman devotees saw the quotation as capturing Doyle's enduring love for his partner. So the baggage handler became a welcome guest at gatherings of the Walt Whitman Fellowship, a group founded in 1893. He was repeatedly asked to give speeches or share his recollections from his outlaw marriage, and he also became a source for additional Whitman biographers.[57]

Peter Doyle continued to live in Philadelphia and work for the railroad until he contracted kidney disease in early 1907. He died later that year, at the age of sixty-three. Doyle's sister wrote the brief death notices that appeared in Philadelphia and Washington newspapers, neither of them making any reference to Walt Whitman.[58]

Chapter 2

Martha Carey Thomas & Mamie Gwinn

1878–1904

Opening Graduate Education to American Women

...

In 1885, Martha Carey Thomas made history by creating the first graduate program in the United States that admitted female students. She took that unprecedented step in her position as dean of the faculty at Bryn Mawr College, going on to become president of that institution and to be widely recognized as one of the most admired women in America.

In 1879, however, Thomas had been in a very different place. At that point in her life, she had earned a bachelor's degree and wanted to continue her education, but no college or university in the country would allow her—or any woman—to enroll in a graduate program. It was at this point that Thomas enlisted the help of Mamie Gwinn, who would become her same-sex partner and play an instrumental role in her successful efforts to make history.

...

Martha Carey Thomas was born into an upper-class Baltimore family in 1857. Her father was a physician, and her mother devoted her time to raising the couple's eight children. The Thomas family belonged to the Society of Friends, or Quakers, and so they didn't participate in activities involving music, art, or drama.[1]

Carey—the name that Martha Carey was known by—was described, from an early age, as being plain in appearance, with a large nose and a "squarish body." By her teens, she exhibited such strong intellectual abilities that her parents took the unusual step of sending her to a boarding school that emphasized academics rather than social skills. While at Howland Institute, Carey spent two years studying the classics.[2]

At seventeen, Carey enrolled at Cornell, one of the few American universities that admitted female students. She didn't have any trouble competing with the men, thanks to her strong intellect and extremely disciplined nature. "The more I study, the more I care about it," she wrote her aunt.[3]

After earning her bachelor's degree, however, Thomas faced a brick wall vis-à-vis her education, as no college or university in the United States accepted women as graduate students.[4]

Mamie Gwinn was born in 1861 into a Baltimore family that was both wealthier and more prominent than the Thomases. Her father was Maryland's attorney general, and her grandfather had served in the U.S. Senate. Her mother oversaw Mamie's upbringing and was active in the Episcopal Church.[5]

During her early years, Mamie was groomed in the refinements of being a lady of the highest social class. Her mother taught her how to dress and comport herself, while private tutors came to the family home to develop her appreciation for music, art, and literature.[6]

Mamie took a particular liking to modern British poets, with her favorite being Algernon Swinburne. Her parents indulged their teenage daughter by buying her all of Swinburne's works, including his controversial *Poems and Ballads,* which praised the lesbian poet Sappho.[7]

Mamie possessed the pale skin and delicate frame that defined her, by the standards of the era, as the epitome of feminine beauty. Her relatives and friends described the girl, by her teenage years, as "brilliant" but also as "moody," "restless," and "not easily satisfied."[8]

BEING ATTRACTED—FOR VERY DIFFERENT REASONS

From the moment a mutual friend introduced Martha Carey Thomas to Mamie Gwinn, the older girl was smitten. "Mamie is the cleverest girl—damnably clever—I ever had anything to do with," Thomas wrote in her diary in 1878, when she was twenty-one and Gwinn was seventeen. "She is fantastic in so many ways."[9]

Gwinn wasn't initially attracted to Thomas, finding her unladylike because she spoke in a "sledge-hammer voice," was "ill dressed," and had a habit of "being highly animated when she talked." But after learning that Thomas had an independent nature and a college degree, Gwinn was drawn to the slightly older woman. She offered the potential, as Gwinn wrote in her diary, "for me to escape alike a husband's and my parents' rule."[10]

A few months after the women met, Thomas devised a plan that had two benefits. First, the arrangement would further her efforts to earn a graduate education. Second, it would allow her to live with the woman she'd fallen in love with. In her diary, Thomas wrote, "Mamie is lovely. I am wrapped up in her," and in a letter to Gwinn, she vowed, "I cannot do without you."[11]

The first element of Thomas's plan emerged because a handful of European universities gave some rights to women graduate students. Among these schools was the highly regarded University of Leipzig, where women could sit in on lectures, although they weren't allowed to earn degrees.[12]

The second part of the plan began with Thomas knowing her parents wouldn't let her study in Germany on her own, but speculating that they'd agree to let her live abroad if she were accompanied by another young woman of high social standing.[13]

Gwinn embraced Thomas's plan because she wanted to see Europe and get out from under the watchful eye of her highly protective parents. She made her motivations clear to Thomas, bluntly writing to her, in early 1879, "I do not love you."[14]

Gwinn's parents initially didn't agree to let their daughter live in Germany, fearing for her safety. But Mamie was accustomed to getting her way, so she persisted, feigning illness and telling her parents that it was because they didn't trust her. The Gwinns then relented.[15]

CREATING AN OUTLAW MARRIAGE

And so, in the fall of 1879, Thomas and Gwinn moved into an apartment some four thousand miles away from their parents. They continued this arrangement for the next four years, while also going on holidays together to other parts of Europe.[16]

Thomas's typical day began with attending four lectures—all in German—in the morning and then reading independently in the afternoon. Her area of specialty was literature, with a focus on linguistics. "I feel head and shoulders above my former self," she wrote her mother a few months after arriving in Leipzig. "I am so happy."[17]

She also wrote her mother that she wished she and Gwinn could marry. "If it were only possible for women to elect women as well as men for a 'life's love,' I would do so with Mamie in a minute," Thomas wrote in 1880. She repeated the same thought in another letter two years later, this time saying that her fondest dream was that "Mamie and I could go through the marriage ceremony together."[18]

Although Thomas didn't tell her mother the details of her relationship with Gwinn, entries in her diary show that the women were physically intimate. "When I kiss her, it as if I am in a trance—so blissful do I feel," Thomas wrote. More references to the sexual dimensions of the outlaw marriage came in the letters the two women wrote to each other. When Gwinn made a brief trip to Berlin by herself, for example, she wrote to her partner in Leipzig, "'Tis 11:30 but I am awake, and longing for you. I lie on the sofa and don't undress because I am miserable undressing without you."[19]

One by-product of the two women spending time together was that Gwinn taught her partner how to behave in a more ladylike manner. The more refined woman persuaded Thomas to speak more softly, dress more fashionably, and use more nuanced gesturing by moving only her fingers rather than flinging her entire arm. Gwinn also exposed Thomas, for the first time, to the ballet and the opera.[20]

FACING COMPLICATIONS
The university calendar consisted of eight months of study followed by four months of vacation, and the two women took full advantage, during their first year, of the opportunity to leave campus by spending the entire summer in Italy. "Rome, Naples, Capri, Pompeii—we have seen them all," Thomas wrote a friend.[21]

After the women returned to Leipzig, however, their priorities diverged. Thomas was increasingly focused on her studies, while Gwinn preferred to while away her days reading the authors she most admired—for her own enjoyment rather than to pursue a degree.[22]

During the academic year, the differing priorities weren't a problem, as each woman spent her time as she chose without disrupting the other's activities. But the situation grew more difficult when it came to deciding what they'd do during their summer vacations. Thomas wanted to study, while Gwinn wanted to travel.[23]

By year three, Thomas had a plan for how she could earn her doctorate, despite the University of Leipzig's policy against awarding graduate diplomas to women. To secure the degree, she'd have to work with the University of Zurich, a less prestigious institution but one that was open to granting graduate degrees to women.[24]

MAKING HISTORY FOR MARTHA CAREY THOMAS
It was at this point that Thomas and Gwinn devised a strategy that would give both of them what they wanted. The couple developed their plan in response

to the combination of Thomas facing stringent requirements to earn her degree and Gwinn wanting to see as much of Europe as she could during the four years that her parents had stipulated was the maximum she could live away from home.[25]

The University of Zurich faculty told Thomas she'd have to complete four steps: write a dissertation based on original research in the field of linguistics, spend one semester in Zurich, pass a series of exams, and submit an analytical paper demonstrating her expertise in a field of literature other than linguistics. Thomas could fulfill the first three requirements on her own, but she needed Gwinn's help on the fourth.[26]

As her first step, Thomas submitted her dissertation, a linguistic comparison of twelfth-century French poetry with the fourteenth-century English poem "Sir Gawain and the Green Knight." The Zurich faculty accepted the manuscript, giving its content their highest praise, although not being as impressed with how the work was written.[27]

Thomas then went to Zurich to fulfill the residency requirement and take her exams, while Gwinn stayed in Leipzig and worked on a poetry paper for her partner. When Gwinn finished the paper, Thomas submitted it to the faculty, identifying herself as the sole author.[28]

Gwinn's contribution to her partner's academic advancement made practical sense, as it meant that Thomas completed her degree requirements soon enough that the couple had several months to travel, as Gwinn wanted. At the same time, however, the couple's action violated standards of academic authorship—Zurich faculty members weren't aware of that breach when they accepted the paper.[29]

Regardless of Thomas and Gwinn's impropriety, their plan succeeded. In late 1882, Thomas received her degree summa cum laude, becoming the first woman of any nationality to earn that distinction. Thomas and Gwinn then traveled to France during 1883.[30]

MAKING HISTORY FOR AMERICAN WOMEN

When Thomas returned to the United States, she was hired as dean of the faculty at Bryn Mawr College, a new Quaker institution for women that was scheduled to open near Philadelphia in the fall of 1885. She then set out to fulfill the formidable responsibilities of her new job, which included creating admissions requirements, developing the curriculum, and hiring the faculty.[31]

At the same time that she was setting these myriad processes in motion, Thomas found the time to make sure influential newspapers reported on what she was doing. In a story about Bryn Mawr's upcoming opening, for example, the *New York Times* wrote, "Martha Carey Thomas, Dean of the Faculty and

Professor of English, will adopt standards of admission and instruction equal to the highest in existing colleges."[32]

The reason Thomas took the step of publicizing her work at the college became clear when she announced to the board of trustees that she wouldn't continue in her position unless they supported one specific proposal from her: Bryn Mawr must become the first college in the country to offer graduate degrees to female students.[33]

The board members then faced the threat that their chief academic officer would resign—a development they knew would be widely reported in the press—unless they agreed to her demand. Although several of the men grumbled about Thomas's calculated tactics, they approved the history-making policy.[34]

BEING CREATIVE ON A PERSONAL LEVEL

On a less positive note, Thomas and Gwinn's relationship had been disrupted as Gwinn's parents had insisted that when their daughter returned to the United States, she had to live with her family in Baltimore. Gwinn quickly tired of this arrangement, writing Thomas that she found the circumstances "monotonous" and "life-sucking."[35]

By the time Bryn Mawr opened its doors, the two women had come up with a plan that improved Gwinn's quality of life—as well as Thomas's. As dean, Thomas decided which graduate students would be admitted as well as which would receive financial support through fellowships. For the first graduate fellow in English, she took the highly unusual step of selecting an applicant who would enter graduate school without a bachelor's degree: Mamie Gwinn.[36]

In addition, the dean invited that student to live with her. That is, Thomas and Gwinn both moved into the eight-room cottage located on campus, called the Deanery, that the college provided for its chief academic officer. And so the two women again began sharing a home, as they had in Germany. This time, though, the arrangement continued for more than two decades.[37]

COLLABORATING IN THE CLASSROOM

Thomas quickly found, when the school opened, that her duties as dean of the faculty were onerous because the trustees required her, in addition to fulfilling her administrative responsibilities, to teach the introductory Western literature course that every undergraduate was required to take. Thomas didn't see how she could do it all, so she persuaded Gwinn to help with her teaching.[38]

Specifically, Gwinn took care of all the behind-the-scenes preparation. She chose which works Thomas's students were required to read, put together the exams, assigned the research papers, and wrote out—word for word— every lecture that Thomas then delivered as her own. And when students submitted their exams and research papers, Gwinn read and graded them.[39]

Meanwhile, the couple's outlaw marriage appeared to be progressing smoothly. In return for helping with the course, Gwinn asked her partner to spend most evenings at home. A letter that Gwinn wrote to Thomas while they were apart for a few days provides a glimpse into how the women spent those quiet times. "I am starved for our nightly ritual," Gwinn wrote, "of you in your red dressing gown and me in my black Antwerp silk with the lace and cherry ribbons, you reading and me with my head nestled serenely on your lap."[40]

During the three years that Gwinn was a student, she stayed in the couple's bedroom when Thomas entertained dinner guests at the Deanery. After Gwinn finished her doctoral degree and Thomas hired her as a professor in 1888, however, the two women hosted social events as if they were husband and wife. Likewise, when members of the board of trustees invited Thomas to dinner, she took Gwinn with her.[41]

CLIMBING TO NEW HEIGHTS

The early 1890s marked a period of continued triumph for Thomas, as other colleges followed her lead and opened their graduate programs to women. Many of those institutions paid tribute to Thomas for her role in advancing the cause of female students. When the University of Pennsylvania, for example, made its graduate programs coed in 1892, Thomas was asked to give the keynote address at the ceremony celebrating the new policy.[42]

And then, in 1894, Bryn Mawr president James Rhoads retired. Thomas was the logical choice to replace him, but several trustees were reluctant to name a woman to such a powerful position. If they made the appointment, the thirty-six-year-old Thomas would become only the second woman in the country's history to serve as a college president—Alice Freeman of Wellesley had been the first in 1882.[43]

The board eventually agreed to promote Thomas, but only after abolishing the position of dean of the faculty. This meant that she now had to fulfill all the duties that Rhoads had been responsible for, while giving up none of the duties she already had.[44]

Thomas's primary mission upon becoming president was to increase Bryn Mawr's enrollment from the current 325 students to a target figure of 875. This growth was essential, the board believed, to transform the college from a tiny liberal arts school into a major force in American higher education.[45]

SUCCEEDING AT ACADEMIC MARKETING

Thomas's strategy to increase enrollment was to establish herself as a nationally recognized educational leader, thereby raising Bryn Mawr's profile—as well as her own. So she began traveling around the country speaking to civic and educational groups, often asking Gwinn to help her write the speeches.[46]

The most frequent theme in the addresses was that educators were doing a disservice by teaching female students nothing but manners and domestic skills, which was the practice in the majority of American colleges and universities. Thomas told New York University alumni in 1896, for example, that limiting the education of female students caused long-term damage because those young women grew up to become the classroom teachers in charge of educating the next generation of boys as well as girls. "Our women are uneducated, and yet the education of this nation's children are in the hands of those very women," Thomas protested.[47]

Newspapers around the country reported on Thomas's speeches, partly because it was a novelty for a woman to address crowds containing both men and women. Eye-catching headlines that ran above the stories included "Women Merely Man's Drudge, Says the President of Bryn Mawr College" and "Mental Reach of Girls Fully Equal to Mental Reach of Men, Carey Thomas of Bryn Mawr Opines."[48]

Thomas had, by the late 1890s, achieved her enrollment goal and also had become one of the nation's best-known female educators. When the *New York Times* published a story about higher education for women, Thomas was highlighted. "Reference would naturally be made to M. Carey Thomas first in any discussion of the present-day leaders in the education of women," the *Times* reported.[49]

Despite these professional successes, a letter that Thomas wrote in 1896 suggests that her personal life wasn't going so smoothly. Gwinn was preparing to take over the Western literature course that Thomas had been teaching, so she asked her partner to publicly acknowledge that the lectures she'd been giving weren't entirely her own but, in fact, were a collaborative effort between the two women. Thomas responded to the request by letter, telling Gwinn, "I am not willing to say that we worked over them together, as I have been giving them as mine for eleven years, and it will surely be misunderstood." Thomas also said, later in the letter, "The fact that you helped me out is a secret that must be kept."[50]

MARTHA CAREY THOMAS CULTIVATING A NEW RELATIONSHIP

Bryn Mawr's growth brought Thomas a new challenge because the physical size of the campus hadn't kept up with the increase in students. And so, in an era before colleges had development staffs, Thomas added fund-raising to her myriad other duties.[51]

When she began identifying wealthy individuals who might make major gifts to Bryn Mawr, Thomas focused on Mary Garrett, a friend from her early years in Baltimore. The Garrett family had amassed a fortune valued at $20 million through investments in the Baltimore & Ohio Railroad, which meant that Mary, whose parents were now dead, had become one of the wealthiest women in the country.[52]

Mamie Gwinn didn't support Thomas's plan to ask Garrett, who wasn't married, for donations. Gwinn had known Garrett when the three women were all in their twenties, and she'd insisted that Thomas distance herself from the other woman because, Gwinn said in letters she wrote at the time, Garrett was "in love with" Thomas and the physical affection that Garrett wanted from Thomas "belongs not to Mary Garrett but to me."[53]

Thomas was determined to raise money for the college, however, so she ignored Gwinn's objections and appealed to Garrett, who began giving Bryn Mawr $10,000 a year, which was more than 10 percent of the annual budget.[54]

It's not clear exactly when the relationship between Mary Garrett and Martha Carey Thomas became intimate, but they definitely had crossed that line by the turn of the century. In 1901, Thomas wrote Garrett a letter laying out her plans for a trip to her lover's house in Baltimore. "Let us have a bottle of champagne for dinner and a mince pie and broiled lobster," Thomas wrote. "And let us sleep in your bedroom."[55]

MARTHA CAREY THOMAS BALANCING TWO RELATIONSHIPS
When Thomas began her affair with Garrett, she didn't end her relationship with Gwinn. Indeed, for several years, Thomas simultaneously maintained intimate relations with both women. During the week, she and Gwinn lived together in the Deanery, while on many weekends when Gwinn visited her widowed mother in Baltimore, Garrett moved in.[56]

Meanwhile, Garrett's gifts to Bryn Mawr kept coming. She endowed various scholarships and set aside $100,000 for Thomas to spend however she wanted. Garrett gave another $100,000 to the college to expand the Deanery.[57]

Thomas tried to keep her affair with Garrett a secret, but Gwinn soon figured out what was going on. She wrote Thomas, while visiting her mother, that "Carey Thomas and Mary Garrett have become as familiar as Carey Thomas and I are. I have been positioned in the role of the first wife, and the first wife these days is frequently feeling forgotten."[58]

Even though Gwinn was angry that her partner was having an affair, she didn't end the relationship. Gwinn stayed with Thomas at least partly because she knew that if she ended the outlaw marriage, Thomas had the power to remove her from the faculty. And if Gwinn left Bryn Mawr, her mother would demand that her daughter return home, in keeping with the expectations for an unmarried woman at the time. Gwinn adamantly opposed that idea.[59]

And so, Mamie Gwinn began to explore the possibility of taking her personal life in a dramatically new direction.[60]

ENDING THE OUTLAW MARRIAGE

Alfred Hodder had joined Bryn Mawr's literature faculty after earning his doctorate from Harvard. When Gwinn discovered that her same-sex partner was romantically involved with Mary Garrett, she set her sights on seducing the handsome and charming Hodder. "He is exactly the person that I have been looking for," Gwinn wrote in her diary. She saw marriage to Hodder as a path that would allow her to leave Thomas but avoid having to live with her mother.[61]

By 1902, Thomas and Gwinn were both having affairs with other people while continuing their long-standing relationship with each other. Thomas was happy with the arrangement, writing Garrett that, "It is such great fortune for me to love two people like you and Mamie." Gwinn, however, had other plans. In early 1904, she announced that she and Hodder were engaged to be married.[62]

Thomas arranged that she and Garrett were vacationing in Europe on Gwinn's wedding day, so she had an excuse for not attending the ceremony. When Thomas returned to Bryn Mawr, Garrett moved into the Deanery as a full-time resident.[63]

After Gwinn and Alfred Hodder married, they left Bryn Mawr as well as academic life and moved to New York City. He took a job in city politics, and she read poetry.[64]

The marriage ended up being short lived, as Alfred Hodder died of an intestinal ailment a mere three years after the wedding. Social mores of the time then allowed Mamie Gwinn Hodder, as a widow, to live by herself rather than with her mother.[65]

Martha Carey Thomas's relationship with Mary Garrett also ended sooner than the women had expected. In 1912, Garrett was diagnosed with leukemia. She died three years later.[66]

Garrett left the bulk of her estate to Thomas, who committed much of that money to constructing several buildings at Bryn Mawr. Indeed, the campus became one of the country's leading showplaces for Gothic-style architecture.[67]

Thomas's transformation of the campus was one of the reasons the *New York Times* named her, in 1922, one of the country's dozen most admired women. To create the high-profile story, the *Times* asked each of twenty national leaders to make a list. Thomas was one of three women that the *Times* spotlighted—along with social reformer Jane Addams and suffragist Carrie Chapman Catt—as "being mentioned on every one of the lists."[68]

SPIRALING DOWNWARD

Despite Thomas's many accomplishments, the final decades of her life were unhappy ones. Her personal maid said in an interview several decades later, "There was a constant sadness about her."[69]

One development that contributed to Thomas's sorrow came in 1922 when she reached the college's mandatory retirement age of sixty-five. She appealed to the trustees to make an exception in her case. When the college's senior faculty, however, complained that she'd fired at least seven faculty members not because of poor performance but merely because she didn't like them, she was forced to leave her position.[70]

It wasn't long after her retirement, although the exact year is uncertain, that Thomas tried to reconcile with Gwinn. She wrote her former partner that she'd made a grave mistake in becoming intimate with Mary Garrett, attributing her error to being attracted to Garrett's fortune. "Now I have everything that money can give," Thomas wrote Gwinn, "but I realize I loved you—and still love you—more than anything in the world." Thomas said that because of the hurt she'd caused Gwinn, "My heart is broken."[71]

Gwinn rejected the overture, refusing to respond to her former partner. In the draft of a memoir Gwinn never published, she wrote a bitter assessment of Thomas's character. "She was created—so it seems to me in retrospect— as being as incapable of an altruistic feeling as my cat is." Gwinn also wrote, speaking of the time she lived with Thomas at Bryn Mawr, "Those were years in which I was a prisoner in the dwelling of an ogress."[72]

And so, Thomas and Gwinn never saw each other again after 1904.

Martha Carey Thomas died in 1935 at the age of seventy-eight, and Mamie Gwinn Hodder died in 1940 at the age of seventy-nine. The nation's leading newspapers reported on Thomas's passing in prominent obituaries and tributes. The *New York Times* described her as "one of the world's foremost women educators" and the *Chicago Tribune* as "one of the most brilliant leaders of her sex," while the *Washington Post* stated, "Higher education for women owes a debt of permanent gratitude to this great educator." None of Thomas's numerous obituaries included any reference to Gwinn. Likewise, when Mamie Gwinn Hodder died, her single published obituary made no mention of Thomas.[73]

Chapter 3

Ned Warren & John Marshall
1884–1927

Building the Collections of America's Art Museums

...

Most people who stroll through the classical antiquities sections of this country's finest art museums—filled with marble sculptures, terra-cotta vases, and other objects from Greek and Roman civilizations—don't think about exactly *how* these magnificent items found their way out of Europe and into the United States. And so, it's only by digging into the archival records of these institutions that a person can gain a sense of the enormous debt the nation owes to the same-sex couple John Marshall and Ned Warren.

From the 1890s through the 1920s, these two men devoted their lives to locating high-quality antiquities, buying the items, and placing them on display in the Museum of Fine Arts in Boston and the Metropolitan Museum of Art in New York City. During their forty-three-year partnership, the men blended their complementary skills and aptitudes to build the core antiquities collections that millions of visitors now enjoy. "The great collections of Marshall and Warren," one scholar has written, "remain one of the most significant collecting feats of all time."[1]

John Marshall was born in Liverpool, England, in 1860. His father built a successful business as a wine merchant, and his mother devoted much of her time and energy to the local Anglican parish. He was a quiet and introspective boy as well as an excellent student.[2]

After completing his public education, Marshall enrolled at Liverpool College and immersed himself in the classics, with plans to become a priest. His mother was pleased with the boy's choice of study, but his father was concerned that he was spending too much time in the rarefied world of academics. And so, Marshall was required to work part-time in his father's business, dealing both with the journeymen who made wine and the wealthy clients who bought it.[3]

Marshall performed so well as an undergraduate that he was awarded a classics scholarship that allowed him to continue his studies at the prestigious Oxford University. He excelled in that highly competitive environment as well, ranking as the top student in his class.[4]

In addition to earning a reputation as a gifted scholar, Marshall also was known as one of the most popular students at the university. His classmates praised his congenial nature and his ability to get along with everyone who came into contact with him.[5]

Edward Perry Warren was born in Waltham, Massachusetts, just outside of Boston, in 1860. His father had made a sizable fortune in the paper industry, and his mother collected Old World paintings and Chinese porcelain.[6]

When Ned—as he was known throughout his life—was three years old, the Warrens moved to a mansion in the exclusive Beacon Hill section of Boston. His early years weren't happy ones, as his four siblings as well as other children ridiculed him for walking around the neighborhood dressed in a Roman toga.[7]

Warren would later recall that his most pleasant childhood memories were of the times he was able to sneak pieces of his mother's china out of the parlor and into his bedroom where he could admire them more closely. Other highlights came when the family traveled to Europe when Ned was eight years old and again when he was thirteen.[8]

By the time Warren entered Harvard College in 1879, he'd already developed a series of romantic crushes on several male classmates, although none of the boys felt the same way about him. "My friends were affectionate," he later wrote, "but their affection did not pass beyond a certain point." Warren didn't excel in his classes, but he managed to earn a bachelor's degree so he could enroll in graduate studies at Oxford.[9]

Upon arriving at the university, Warren embraced all things English. He exhibited so many mannerisms of his adopted country, in fact, that most other students didn't realize he was from the United States. First among those affectations, according to Warren's classmates, was an annoying sense of superiority similar to that displayed by many British aristocrats.[10]

CREATING AN OUTLAW MARRIAGE

Ned Warren's fellow students also described him as making no secret of his eagerness to become romantically involved with other men. Unlike his earlier efforts to find a lover, however, those at Oxford were successful. He first had a relationship with a lad four years his junior, and then he set his sights on the most intellectually gifted student in his class.[11]

John Marshall and Ned Warren began their romantic relationship in 1884, when they were both twenty-four years old. Warren told a friend that he was attracted to Marshall because his lover was "unpretentious and very touching in his affections."[12]

After the two young men had been together for almost four years, Warren's father died. Now independently wealthy, Warren decided to devote his life to collecting classical antiquities that he'd send to Boston so the country of his birth would begin to understand the importance of the Greek and Roman cultures.[13]

Warren wanted his lover to join him in this work, but Marshall wasn't so sure. His reluctance came mainly from the fact that Marshall's parents expected him to spend his life as an Anglican priest and scholar, not as an antiquities collector.[14]

Warren then set out to change Marshall's mind. The wealthy young man knew that his lover dreamed of living in a historic manor house, so he tried to find such a home for them to share. After Warren bought an eighteenth-century residence in the Sussex area on the southeastern coast of England in 1889, Marshall agreed to join him in the collecting venture, writing, "Now everything you say and do seems inseparable from my love for you."[15]

The couple then settled into Lewes House. Interior features of the impressive residence included a flagstone entrance hall and a grand staircase. The imposing structure was surrounded by several acres of gardens and pastures. One visitor would later say, "The grounds of Lewes House rolled away toward Brighton. When we rode our horses up there on a fine day, we could see the English Channel glistening in the distance like a great silver shield."[16]

BEGINNING THE BOSTON COLLECTION

After settling into their home, the men were now prepared to begin, in earnest, their life as antiquities collectors. Their timing was perfect, as it coincided with the directors of the Museum of Fine Arts in Boston deciding to assemble the best collection of Greek and Roman objects in the United States. Because the original building on Copley Square wasn't large enough to house such a collection, the directors built a larger facility on Huntington Avenue. The new museum had seven times as much display space as the original, so there was plenty of room for additional items.[17]

Marshall and Warren traveled to Boston in 1891 to meet with the museum's new curator of antiquities, Edward Robinson. He initially opposed the men's proposal that they buy works of art and then sell them to the museum for the price they'd paid plus 20 percent to cover their expenses. Robinson was fine with the financial part of the plan, but he wasn't willing to let Marshall and Warren decide which items would make up the museum's collection.[18]

It was at this point that Marshall demonstrated one of the strengths he brought to his professional partnership with Warren. Specifically, after the curator rejected the men's proposal, Marshall went back to talk with Robinson by himself. The congenial Marshall was willing to negotiate and compromise—two things Warren refused to do. In this instance, Marshall persuaded Robinson to give the two men a chance to prove their abilities as collectors and then revisit his decision about the terms of their arrangement with the museum.[19]

The test that Marshall suggested was one involving a French estate. In 1892, he and Warren traveled to Paris and examined items that had belonged to the Van Branteghem family. Despite competition from several other collectors, the couple came away with the best of the Greek terra-cotta pieces. The Boston curator then inspected the purchases, confirmed their high quality, and immediately put them on display at the museum. Most significant among the items was a large drinking cup that dated back to the sixth century B.C. and was signed by Euphronios, widely recognized as "the Michelangelo" of terra-cotta painting. After Marshall and Warren's initial success, the curator agreed to let the two men purchase whatever objects they wanted.[20]

The duo's next major acquisition was of several ancient bronze statues and terra-cotta vases from Italy's Count Tyskiewicz—this time, they had to outbid agents of the Russian czar who wanted the items for the Hermitage Museum. This purchase revealed another signature trait of the two men's professional partnership. Warren had highly refined taste and an exceptional aesthetic eye, instinctively knowing which items would look good in the museum setting where they'd eventually be displayed. He didn't, however, have either the patience or the scholarly aptitude that were needed to undertake the research necessary to determine the exact age and origins of such works. Marshall did.[21]

Although Marshall and Warren's initial acquisitions were from members of wealthy families, later ones moved them into what were labeled "gray areas." That is, they bought directly from men who worked outside the law to unearth ancient artworks and then sell them to the highest bidder, while always steering clear of European authorities. "The material on the market came mostly from illegal excavations," one scholar noted. "The antiquities market of the late nineteenth and early twentieth centuries was a complicated and treacherous world." Marshall and Warren used their combined skills to overcome the challenges.[22]

SETTING A NEW STANDARD AS ANTIQUITIES COLLECTORS

By 1894, the two men had become so immersed in collecting that they set up a second home in Rome so they could be closer to the Italian middlemen who were unearthing and selling antiquities. It was also at this point that the couple decided to focus most of their attention on securing ancient marble sculptures, which they believed were the dazzling items that could establish the Boston museum, without question, as the premier one in the United States.[23]

Among the purchases the couple soon made were a large Greek lion that dated back to the fourth century B.C., a Roman torso of Hermes that dated back to A.D. 30, and the bust of a Roman woman that dated back to the second century A.D.—the couple gave the last item as a donation rather than charging the museum for it. Another of their notable acquisitions was the Boston Throne, which consisted of three panels and dated back to the fifth century B.C.[24]

Marshall and Warren's most significant acquisition of all was the head of a Greek goddess that dated back to the fourth century B.C. and became known as the Chios Head. Many critics would come to identify this piece, with its exquisitely detailed facial features, as the finest item in the museum's entire collection of artwork.[25]

The backstory about another marble piece speaks to Marshall's ability to detect forgeries. While on a trip to Greece, the men heard about a marble sculpture of the Greek god Apollo that a dealer had for sale. When they saw the item, Warren instantly wanted to buy it, but Marshall questioned the item's authenticity, writing to a friend that the statue had no patina "save a yellow stain here and there—such as forgers add to their work." Marshall had to beg his partner to reject the statue, but he ultimately triumphed and they didn't buy it. Scholars later determined that the item was, indeed, a fake.[26]

Not only were the two men very good at collecting, but it also brought them great pleasure. Warren wrote his brother Henry, "As we get behind the scenes, and into the intrigues—for the antiquity business is full of intrigues—we have something to laugh at every day. We learn the polite evasive answer, the wily silence. It is so entertaining that if we were dealing in pig-iron, instead of in beautiful things, the work would still be enjoyable."[27]

Within a decade after they'd entered the field, the couple had become the most widely respected antiquities collectors in the world, with Warren receiving most of the recognition because of his wealth and the prominence of his family. For example, Charles Eliot Norton, the most widely regarded art historian of the time, wrote of Warren, "There is not and never has been in America or in Europe a man with such capacities, will, and circumstances for collecting, and the Museum of Fine Arts is entirely dependent upon him."[28]

On the final point in that statement, by 1902, officials in Boston had decided that the section of their museum devoted to classical works was complete, with 90 percent of the items having been secured by Marshall and Warren.[29]

ENDURING LIFE'S CHALLENGES

In the early 1900s, family matters became a high priority in Warren's life. His mother died in 1901, and soon after that he became increasingly concerned about his oldest brother's management of the estate, which had a value of about $5 million.[30]

Warren went to Boston in 1902 and hired a lawyer to look into the financial aspects of how Samuel D. Warren Jr. was running the family's paper business. Although Marshall initially supported his partner going to the United States, he soon became frustrated because he was living in Europe while Warren was making lengthy trips to Boston. Marshall refused to stay in the United States for more than a few days at a time, telling Warren, "The place is dreadful and the people worse." But Marshall also quickly tired of Warren spending so much time away from him. "I am sick of being alone and, Puppy dear, it is bad for me," he wrote to Warren during one separation. "I would sooner do anything than live alone."[31]

Marshall's displeasure with Warren escalated as the trips to Boston sometimes stretched into several months. In one letter, Marshall complained to his partner, "You run your own affairs and expect me to follow like a slave any move you make. You think your duty lies in Boston, and I know you too well to try to stop you."[32]

Part of Marshall's frustration came from the fact that he questioned his partner's motivation for spending so much time in Boston. Warren claimed it was solely to take care of family business, but Marshall suspected that his partner also relished the celebrity status that his work with the Museum of Fine Arts gave him among wealthy Bostonians.[33]

In 1903, Marshall decided to busy himself by becoming involved in a new collecting project. He traveled to New York City and visited the Metropolitan Museum of Art, finding that the institution was "hopeless with respect to antiquities." He then returned to Europe and began an effort to persuade the museum's directors to hire him to improve their holdings of Greek and Roman pieces.[34]

Marshall was also becoming involved in a platonic relationship that would evolve into a huge element of his life. Since 1901, Warren's unmarried cousin, Mary Bliss, had been living at Lewes House. Determined to rid herself of the stigma that came with being labeled a "spinster," Bliss soon announced that she wanted to marry Marshall. When the Met hired Marshall to be its European purchasing agent, Bliss set about becoming—in the words of one observer—"just the right help-mate John Marshall needed to meet his new challenge."[35]

BUILDING THE NEW YORK COLLECTION

Mary Bliss knew that her major bargaining chip was her aesthetic eye. That is, she had the ability to select which antiquities would create an attractive museum exhibit—a talent that Marshall had failed to develop. In 1907, she gave Marshall an ultimatum, saying she'd no longer help him with his collecting unless he married her. Marshall then agreed to make her his wife, although he stipulated that the marriage wouldn't involve sexual activities of any kind. The wedding soon followed.[36]

Ned Warren fully supported the marriage. Indeed, he'd encouraged Marshall and Bliss to become husband and wife because he hoped the arrangement would make his partner more content, and therefore less likely to complain about Warren's lengthy stays in Boston.[37]

One early item that Marshall, with his wife's help, added to the Met's collection was a Roman jug that dated back to the first century A.D. The item was important because it was signed by Ennion, the most famous and gifted craftsman of the Julio-Claudian era.[38]

Another significant piece the Marshalls obtained for the museum was an Etruscan safety pin that had been made in 500 B.C. and was decorated with tiny carvings of a reclining woman, a youth, and a bird. Other major acquisitions included thirty-two gold plaques that had been created during the Bosporan Kingdom between the fifth century B.C. and the third century A.D.[39]

John Marshall eventually amassed enough money, through his salary, to donate one item to the museum in his own name. That piece was a sandaled ivory foot that had been carved during the Roman Empire and was dated to between 31 B.C. and 14 A.D.[40]

PIONEERING A NEW GENRE OF ANTIQUITIES

By 1910, Warren was able to resume collecting. This turn of events occurred because his lawyers documented that his oldest brother had, indeed, mishandled more than $1 million in family funds. After that revelation, another of Warren's brothers assumed control of the business, so he returned to Europe and to his life with John Marshall.[41]

The fact that Marshall and his wife were, by this point, working well together to secure works for the Met meant that Warren was free to focus on a category of artwork he'd been interested in for many years. As far back as the 1890s, he'd wanted to buy antiquities showcasing homoerotic content, but museum officials had refused to be associated in any way with such items, labeling them "obscene" and, therefore, unacceptable for public viewing.[42]

But when Warren returned to collecting in the second decade of the twentieth century, he decided to try a different tactic. He spent his own money to create a personal collection of homoerotic antiquities that he initially displayed at Lewes House. But his long-term plan was to build a collection of such exceptional quality that, once he'd assembled the items, officials at the Museum of Fine Arts in Boston would want it for their museum.[43]

Some scholars who have studied Warren's life and work have argued that he had a larger goal in mind when he began collecting homoerotic art. One author has written that Warren's intention was to "break down Puritan inhibitions and hypocrisy" with regard to sexual activities between men. A second scholar has stated that Warren's objective was to establish that male-to-male sexual activity was fully accepted in the advanced societies of ancient Greece and Rome, thereby implying that homosexuality should also be accepted in contemporary America.[44]

Whatever the motivation, Warren's effort to acquire homoerotic art received a huge boost in 1911 when he found and purchased a magnificent Roman piece that ultimately would become known as the Warren Cup. Made of silver and dating back to the first century A.D., the item stood about six inches high. The exquisitely detailed relief work on the cup clearly depicted two sets of men engaging in anal intercourse.[45]

In the years that followed, Warren purchased other antiquities decorated with scenes of men participating in homosexual activities. One important item was a two-handled Greek terra-cotta vase dating back to the sixth century B.C. and decorated with a scene of two young men lying together while one masturbated. Warren also acquired several fragments of Roman pottery molds, dating back to the first century A.D., that showed men having oral intercourse with each other.[46]

Precisely when the collection left Lewes House and was accepted— Warren donated the items rather than charging for them—by the Boston museum isn't entirely clear. That uncertainty evolved from Warren's concern that American customs authorities wouldn't allow homoerotic materials to enter the United States, so he obscured their identity. The first of the items were among the ninety-two "miscellaneous objects" that Warren shipped to Boston in 1913, and additional items followed over the next two decades.[47]

While it's not known exactly when the homoerotic antiquities went to Boston, there's no question where museum officials put them: in the basement. The pieces remained in storage, because of their controversial nature, until the 1970s when officials finally decided that sex between men was an acceptable subject for public art exhibitions.[48]

There's also no question that Warren ultimately made both homoerotic art and homosexuality more acceptable in the United States. In the words of the authors of one book about collecting, "Without Ned Warren, we would know much less than we do about homosexuality and classical art."[49]

COLLECTING TO THE END

By the early 1920s, Warren had become the world's leading authority on homoerotic antiquities, while he continued to consult with John and Mary Marshall on acquiring conventional classical artwork for the Met.[50]

From 1910 on, the three collectors were together almost constantly. Indeed, other than at night when the two men shared the master bedroom and Mary Marshall slept in a separate bedroom down the hall, they spent virtually every hour with each other. While at Lewes House, the trio worked out of the same study during daylight hours, spent their evenings reading or listening to music in one of the manor house's parlors, and ate their meals while seated around the same table in the baronial dining room. And when their collecting enterprise called for a trip to Rome, the three of them traveled as a group and then took up residence in their apartment there to conduct business.[51]

By 1915, they also were spending a good deal of time pampering themselves. As often as they could, they traveled to a spa at Bagni di Lucca, a village in the Tuscany region of Italy, where they lived in a sixteenth-century villa. Mary Marshall was drawn to the thermal waters at the spa because they relieved some of the pain she suffered from rheumatism, and John Marshall thought the soothing waters helped treat his liver ailments. For Warren, the appeal was being able to relax in the tiny village with the two people who'd become his life companions as well as his two closest professional colleagues.[52]

That three-person collaboration had enormous benefits, although public recognition went only to the two male members of the group. Renowned classical scholar John Davidson Beazley said at the time, "Warren and Marshall had complete control of the market in classical antiquities. Almost everything that was good, whether a new find or an old, came to them for first refusal. Competition all but ceased." Another antiquities scholar said, in 2003, that the combined works the two men were responsible for bringing to Boston and New York represent "the greatest collection of Greek and Roman art in the world."[53]

Life changed somewhat for the men in 1925 when Mary Marshall died, which meant the two men lost the woman who had spent more than two decades with them. And then, two years later, John Marshall died as well, while he was still working as the Met's agent in Europe. Marshall's took his last breath while Ned Warren sat at his bedside. Servants reported that the dying man's final words were, "Good-bye, Puppy."[54]

One of the couple's closest friends later said, "Ned was ready to die after John's death," telling the people around him that he was "quietly putting his house in order before departure." Warren made that exit in 1928, just one year after Marshall had died.[55]

The *New York Times* published an obituary after Warren's death. That story didn't acknowledge the forty-three-year outlaw marriage that Warren had enjoyed, stating only that the deceased "had been associated with John Marshall of Rome, Italy, in making collections for museums in this country."[56]

Marshall and Warren had given their secretary detailed directions, several years earlier, as to where and how they were to be buried. The location was in the English cemetery in Bagni di Lucca, where their bodies and that of Mary Marshall were to rest under a large marble monument inscribed with the respective birth and death dates of the three of them. Marshall and Warren stipulated that a simple Grecian urn was to be placed on top of the monument as a poignant symbol of their life's work.[57]

Chapter 4

Mary Rozet Smith & Jane Addams

1891–1934

Breaking New Ground in Social Reform and Global Peace

...

In the early 1900s, Jane Addams was the most admired woman in America. She rose to national prominence in the 1890s as the founder of Hull House, a daring social experiment that brought upper-class young women into a poverty-stricken neighborhood so they could help the poor. Building on that success, Addams became widely recognized, early in the new century, as one of the nation's most esteemed social reformers.

When the United States was on the brink of entering World War I, Addams moved from the national stage to the global one, as she led the first meeting of peace activists from around the world. That effort—combined with a string of others that occurred before, during, and after the fighting—propelled Addams into becoming, in 1931, the first American woman to be awarded the Nobel Peace Prize.

Addams wouldn't have been able to enrich the nation and the world to the degree that she did if it hadn't been for Mary Rozet Smith, her life partner for more than four decades. Smith, who was from a wealthy and socially prominent family, provided the financial backing that kept Hull House afloat. She also persuaded many of her well-heeled friends to open their pocketbooks and donate money to the settlement house.

On a more personal level, Smith consistently served as the guardian who kept Addams, who suffered from severe health problems, from physically overexerting herself.

Jane Addams was born into a prosperous family in Cedarville, Illinois, in 1860. Her father owned the largest flour mill in the northern section of the state, and her mother bore and cared for nine children before she died, while in childbirth, when Jane was two years old.[1]

From an early age, Addams felt a driving need to make a difference in the world. Her initial dream was to attend medical school, but her father vetoed that idea and insisted that she follow a more traditional path for a young woman of the time. So she attended the Rockford Female Seminary, located near her home, that offered courses in the humanities and foreign languages.[2]

About the time she completed her studies, Addams experienced a major medical crisis. She'd suffered from tuberculosis as a child, and she'd endured severe back pain throughout her teens. In 1882, she was hospitalized and wore a cast made of steel and whalebone for six months. Her doctors warned Addams that her health would always be precarious and that, therefore, she should avoid stress and overexertion.[3]

In 1888, Addams traveled to Europe with a former seminary classmate, Ellen Starr. The highlight of the trip came in London when the two young women went to Toynbee Hall in one of the city's poor neighborhoods and learned about the settlement house operated by Oxford University graduates. The wealthy young men worked at businesses downtown during the day and offered classes to their largely uneducated neighbors in the evenings and on weekends.[4]

Mary Rozet Smith was born into one of the wealthiest families in Chicago in 1868, her father having amassed a fortune by founding a paper company.[5]

Smith attended one of the city's most exclusive private schools, receiving a general education that prepared her to become a teacher either at her alma mater or another private school. At the same time, the girl's mother taught her how to dress, groom, and behave in the manner expected of a debutante. Mary's parents also exposed her to the world of Renaissance art by having her travel to Europe with them on several occasions.[6]

Toward the end of her teenage years, Smith began to question if she'd be satisfied either with a social life consisting of cotillions and lavish dinner parties or with a married life defined by pleasing a husband and raising children.[7]

Friends and relatives who knew Smith as a young adult described her as "gentle," "shy," "dutiful," and "self-effacing," and characterized her as the kind of person who "preferred to stay out of the limelight" and was "perfectly content to remain in the background."[8]

FOUNDING AN INNOVATIVE INSTITUTION

Jane Addams had, with her visit to Toynbee Hall, found her life's work. She and Ellen Starr returned to the United States and set out to create a settlement house in Chicago, but with one major difference from the one they'd seen in London: theirs would be operated entirely by women.[9]

For the location, they chose a dilapidated mansion that businessman Charles J. Hull had built thirty years earlier before the neighborhood had been taken over by recent immigrants who were crammed into tenement houses. Addams financed the venture with the inheritance she received from her father, who had died while she was at the seminary. Hull House opened its doors in 1889.[10]

Addams and Starr, who at first were the only residents at the settlement house, initially organized only activities for children. A kindergarten class focused on helping six-year-olds learn to count and spell, while a second class concentrated on introducing the joys of drawing to older children. The two women next created activities for adults in the form of weekly receptions— one for Germans and others for Greeks, Italians, and Russians—where food was served and participants were encouraged to chat, sing, and dance.[11]

After these activities attracted large numbers of people to Hull House, the two women began offering academic classes. Addams taught literature, having her students read a particular book and then discuss it, while Starr taught the history of Italian and Russian art.[12]

RECEIVING SUPPORT FROM MARY ROZET SMITH

Addams and Starr quickly realized that if they had any hope of serving the throngs of poor immigrants who were coming to Hull House, they'd need help from other upper-class young women. One of the first nonresident volunteers was Mary Rozet Smith, who came to the settlement house within a month after it opened.[13]

Smith's initial work, in keeping with her training as a teacher, involved immigrant boys. With a goal of getting the young men off the streets, she bought pool tables and chess sets for them to use. Smith also read aloud to the boys. "They listened with enchanted attention," according to one Addams biographer. "Their young imaginations took wing; each boy could feel himself capable of great things. They chose to call their group the Young Heroes Club."[14]

Smith's volunteering quickly expanded. She began teaching a kindergarten class and then was put in charge of the music classes that were added to the schedule of activities. She also lent a hand with the planning, rehearsing, and presenting of dramatic productions that featured recent immigrants in the leading roles.[15]

Within a matter of months, Smith had become a valuable member of the settlement house community, spending virtually every day at Hull House.[16]

CREATING AN OUTLAW MARRIAGE

By 1891, Jane Addams's friendship with Mary Rozet Smith had grown into a romantic relationship that included both emotional and physical dimensions. Addams's nephew later wrote, "Mary Smith became and always remained the highest and clearest note in the music that was Jane Addams's personal life."[17]

Even though Smith had, after two years, become one of the settlement house's most stalwart volunteers, family responsibilities kept her from moving in permanently. Instead, she continued to live with her retired father and invalid mother in their Chicago mansion on Walton Place, while spending her days and many evenings working alongside Addams at Hull House. Smith also frequently slept at the house, with these temporary stays sometimes lasting for as long as two weeks at a stretch.[18]

The fact that Smith's sense of duty forced her to continue living with her elderly parents had its benefits. There were so many activities at the settlement house that Addams frequently worked so hard and so continuously that she became exhausted, which jeopardized her already fragile health. And so, from time to time, Smith talked her partner into spending a few nights at her parents' mansion. These visits served as respites for Addams, as the household servants did everything they could to pamper her. In the words of one Addams biographer, "the Smith home was a refuge."[19]

Regardless of whether Addams and Smith were spending the night at Hull House or at the Smith home, they insisted on sleeping in the same bed. Indeed, when the two women traveled together, they even telegraphed the hotel where they'd be spending the night to make sure their room was furnished with a double bed, rather than two single ones.[20]

By the mid-1890s, Addams was in great demand as a speaker, with reform-minded men and women around the country eager to hear firsthand about the work she was doing in Chicago. Smith accompanied her partner on as many of these trips as she could, partly so the women could spend time alone and partly so Smith could keep Addams from overexerting herself.[21]

When Smith's parents asked her to stay with them rather than travel with

Addams, the dutiful daughter generally complied. On these occasions when the two women were separated, they wrote to each other at least once a day— sometimes twice. Statements in the letters, which have been preserved as part of Addams's personal papers, give a sense of how much the two women meant to each other. In one letter, Addams told Smith, "I bless you, dear, every time I think of you, which is all the time" and "I miss you dreadfully and am yours 'til death." Smith reciprocated with letters to Addams such as one that read, "You have made my life—all its meaning and color come from you."[22]

The correspondence clearly shows that the women thought of themselves as a married couple. "You must know, dear, how I long for you all the time," Addams wrote during one three-week separation. "There is reason in the habit of married folks keeping together." Several Addams biographers have stated point-blank that she and Smith would have become wife and wife if such an option had been available. One biographer wrote, "They came to think of themselves as married to each other," and another said, "Jane and Mary called their forty-year relationship, quite simply, a marriage."[23]

PROVIDING FINANCIAL SUPPORT

The most tangible way that Smith contributed to Addams's work came with her monetary donations to Hull House, which escalated dramatically in 1893.[24]

By that critical point, two significant changes had come about at the settlement house. First, the operation had expanded from a single building into several, including a gymnasium and a residence hall for adult men. Second, the number of young women living and working at Hull House full time had expanded to twelve, which meant expenses for room and board had soared.[25]

Addams initially covered the additional costs through her own inheritance, but, after four years, that money was gone. She also no longer had Ellen Starr to share the burdens, as the other founder of Hull House had left Chicago to study in England.[26]

In desperation, Addams turned to her partner, and, in the words of one scholar, "Mary Rozet Smith was the right woman at the right moment for Jane Addams—financially as well as personally." Smith's early gifts were relatively modest, such as the money to create a children's playground and to buy an organ to support the music program, but they soon grew in size, including paying the entire cost of constructing a new building for children's activities in 1895.[27]

It was during this same period that Smith created a discretionary fund for Addams. That is, Smith made it clear that her partner was free to spend the money any way she chose, including spending it on personal items that brought her pleasure. This monthly gift would continue without interruption for the next forty years.[28]

On several occasions, Addams expressed discomfort at Smith being so generous. "I went to bed quite determined not to accept the check you offered," she wrote in 1895, "but, after a three o'clock vigil, found myself weakly accepting it." Addams saw no other option to taking the money from her partner. In the words of one biographer, "It was Smith's constant overcoming of deficits that literally kept the work going." In addition, there are no statements in any of the couple's correspondence to suggest that Smith had any hesitation about giving the money to support her partner's groundbreaking work.[29]

In the late 1890s, Smith was instrumental in bringing about major changes in the fiscal circumstances at Hull House. Realizing that her own inheritance couldn't sustain the operation forever, she took the lead in transforming the house into a corporation, naming herself as one member of the five-person board of trustees.[30]

Becoming incorporated wasn't a minor detail, as the business-savvy Smith saw this as an essential step if her partner was to succeed at keeping her social experiment afloat. Specifically, Smith knew that many potential donors were reluctant to give money to an enterprise operated entirely by women. But, she speculated, more contributions would arrive if Hull House became incorporated and had men on the board.[31]

After the incorporation process was complete, Smith used her social connections to solicit donations from wealthy Chicagoans who traveled in the same elite circles as her parents did. Indeed, in the words of one scholar, Smith was soon "sweetly dragooning donations from groaning industrialists." Among the millionaires Smith persuaded to provide financial support for the settlement house—including adding more residence halls and other buildings—were farm equipment manufacturer Cyrus H. McCormick Jr., Sears & Roebuck president Julius Rosenwald, and real estate investor Louise deKoven Bowen.[32]

GUARDING AGAINST WORKING TOO HARD

At the same time that Smith was keeping Addams's social reform experiment from failing financially, she also was helping her partner on a much more personal level. That is, Smith took it upon herself to serve as the guardian against Addams overexerting herself by working too hard and, thereby, jeopardizing her physical health.[33]

Smith realized, not long into her outlaw marriage, that her initial strategy of helping Addams relax by arranging for visits to her parents' mansion wasn't an ideal solution to her partner's inclination to overexert herself. The problem was that the respites sometimes lasted only a few days before some crisis pulled Addams back to Hull House, which was located only a few miles away. So Smith came up with the idea of building lengthy vacations into her partner's exhausting schedule.[34]

In 1896, for example, Addams wanted to travel to Russia to visit writer and education reformer Leo Tolstoy. International travel during the late nineteenth century was difficult, however, and so Smith initially opposed Addams making the trip. But after some more thought, Smith offered not only to join Addams on the journey but also to pay all the expenses and make all the travel arrangements. Smith's generous proposal came on the condition that they'd extend the trip and spend a month relaxing in Germany. Addams accepted Smith's offer.[35]

An excerpt from a letter that a Hull House resident wrote to Smith in 1899 shows that other people recognized the role she played in keeping Addams from overexerting herself. "Miss Addams is very tired & has had bowel trouble added to lady-trouble these last few days," the woman wrote, "but of course she did not let either deter her from racing about. I wish you could think of some scheme that would take her for a jaunt." Smith instantly contacted a friend in Baltimore and asked her to invite Addams to speak in that city. The request led to Addams and Smith then spending a two-week vacation in the East.[36]

In the early 1900s, Smith came up with a more long-term plan for building periods of relaxation into her partner's hectic life. By this point, Addams had become involved in a dizzying variety of social issues ranging from regulating child labor to crafting national immigration policy. These activities meant she was constantly attending meetings and hearings in East Coast cities such as Boston, New York, and Washington. So Smith found a house that was for sale in a village near Bar Harbor, Maine, and then suggested to Addams that they buy it as a second home they could call their own. Addams agreed, and in 1904 the two women became joint owners of the home, although Smith paid the lion's share of the cost.[37]

When she'd gone house hunting, Smith had made sure to find a place that was so small it couldn't accommodate more than two people, so Addams couldn't invite guests to the home. Smith also insisted the house they bought had minimal property around it so the maintenance would be low. The cottage fit the bill perfectly, as it only had a few perennials—such as lilacs and peonies. Smith's careful planning worked, as Addams wrote her, soon after they purchased the cottage, "Our house—it quite gives me a thrill to write the words. It is our house isn't it, in a really true ownership." In another letter, this one written after the women had stayed in the cottage numerous times, Addams said to Smith, "I feel as if we have come into a healing domesticity which we have never had before."[38]

Even after they were spending periodic vacations in Maine, Smith continued to pay for her and Addams to go on lengthy international holidays as well—insisting that she make all the arrangements so the travel would proceed at a leisurely pace. During the early 1900s, their destinations included Mexico, the West Indies, and the Middle East.[39]

MOVING ONTO THE GLOBAL STAGE

Jane Addams's emergence as a peace advocate grew out of her life experience. From 1889 onward, Hull House had brought together immigrants who'd recently left their native countries. Despite the dramatic differences in language and culture, Addams had mixed these people together on a daily basis with virtually no conflict. She was convinced that this same success could be replicated on a global scale.[40]

Once the fighting began in Europe in 1914, she made numerous public statements in support of her beliefs regarding international cooperation, and late that year she chaired a peace conference at a settlement house in New York City. In early 1915, Addams organized a larger conference, this one targeted specifically toward women. "I do not assert that women are better than men," she told the three thousand participants, "but we would all admit that there are things about which women are more sensitive than men, and one of these is the treasuring of life."[41]

By this point in Addams's life, people paid attention to what she said because she'd grown into an internationally recognized figure with several major accomplishments to her credit. First on the list was her success with Hull House, which had prompted social reformers across the country to found more than one hundred other settlement houses. In addition, she'd been so effective in her campaign against child labor that the U.S. Congress had passed federal legislation making it illegal for employers to hire workers under the age of sixteen. In recognition of Addams's stature, *Ladies' Home Journal* had repeatedly singled her out as America's most admired woman.[42]

And so, after Addams's statements and activities on behalf of global cooperation became widely known, a Dutch feminist asked her to preside at an international meeting of peace activists in the Netherlands. The proposed event would be unprecedented, not only because the delegates would all be female but also because they would include women from European countries that were, by that time, engaged in armed combat against each other.[43]

Addams didn't reply to the request right away, even though she wanted to accept it, because Mary Rozet Smith opposed the idea for two reasons. First, she was concerned that Addams would be putting herself in harm's way by traveling to Europe during wartime. Second, Smith wanted to guard against her partner jeopardizing her health by adding the responsibilities of leading an international conference to her already substantial burdens.[44]

Smith being worried about her partner's health was fueled by a series of medical crises that Addams had suffered since founding Hull House. She'd contracted typhoid fever in 1896 and had an appendectomy in 1909, with her recovery from both incidents proving much slower and much more complicated than her doctors had expected. In addition, Addams had endured several bouts of bronchitis and pleurisy over the years, as well as one instance of pneumonia—the doctors said that stress and fatigue had contributed to all these illnesses.[45]

Despite Smith's opposition, Addams agreed to preside at the conference. She and forty-six other American women—Smith stayed in Chicago to make sure Hull House continued to function smoothly—sailed to The Hague in April 1915. The travelers encountered considerable difficulty, as British officials blocked their ship for several days. When the Americans finally arrived, they joined eleven hundred other delegates from ten European countries, including the warring Germany and Great Britain.[46]

The most significant proposal that emerged from the conference was for world powers that were still neutral to organize mediation sessions with the warring nations. Immediately after the conference, Addams and a handful of other women traveled to Great Britain, France, Germany, Italy, and Belgium to lobby the leaders of those countries to support their proposal. The United States was still neutral at this point, so Addams also met with President Woodrow Wilson six times between July and December of 1915 in an effort to persuade him to lead the mediation sessions.[47]

Wilson rejected her plea, however, because German submarines had sunk the British passenger ship *Lusitania* off the Irish coast in May 1915, killing more than one hundred Americans. That incident followed by the sinking of several U.S. ships led Wilson to ask Congress to declare war in April 1917. After the United States entered the fighting, a highly disappointed Addams committed her energies to traveling around the country encouraging citizens to conserve food.[48]

OVERCOMING NEW CHALLENGES

Although Smith had initially opposed Addams taking a leading role in the international peace movement, she joined her partner's efforts, after World War I had ended, to provide food relief for war-torn Europe. In the summer of 1919, the two women were the first U.S. civilians to enter Germany, delivering desperately needed food to that beleaguered nation.[49]

As the 1920s unfolded, the couple continued to balance their work at Hull House with their commitment to global issues. Addams helped found the Women's International League of Peace and Freedom, and she chaired the group's annual meetings in Vienna, Dublin, and Prague. Smith attended those events as well, expanding each trip into a vacation and even managing to stretch the one in 1923 into a nine-month journey around the world, with lengthy stops in India, the Philippines, Japan, and China.[50]

While many people her age—she turned sixty in 1920—were retiring, Addams took on new causes. She helped found the American Civil Liberties Union, and she also became a leading advocate for prison reform. In 1925, she delivered a widely reported attack on the controversial issue of capital punishment.[51]

In 1931, Addams made history by becoming the first American woman to receive the Nobel Peace Prize. The citation accompanying the prestigious award first lauded her as "the foremost woman of her nation." It then continued, "In Jane Addams there are assembled all the best womanly attributes which shall help us to establish peace in the world. She clung to her idealism in the difficult period when other demands and interests overshadowed peace."[52]

OUTLIVING THE GUARDIAN

It wasn't until a devastating event occurred in 1934 that the wind finally went out of Addams's sails. Mary Rozet Smith became ill with pneumonia early in the year, and by February she grew tired after even minimal effort. On the fateful final day of her life, Smith had written letters to several long-time acquaintances, telling them that Addams was weak after having suffered a heart attack. Smith went quietly to bed that night, and she never woke up.[53]

Newspaper obituaries reported that Smith had been a stalwart volunteer and financial patron at Hull House. They only hinted at her intimate relationship with Addams, however, by mentioning that the two women often had traveled together.[54]

Addams's friends observed that she never recovered from the loss of the woman who'd been the central figure in her life for four decades. Addams seemed continually ill at ease and even grew impatient with the people she worked with, something no one had ever witnessed when Smith was alive.[55]

After dinner one evening in May 1935, Addams complained of abdominal pains so severe that she could barely stand. She was taken to a hospital where the doctors discovered she was suffering from intestinal cancer that had advanced so far that an operation was useless. She died a few days later.[56]

Newspapers around the country carried obituaries that lauded Jane Addams's groundbreaking contributions both as a social reformer and a peace advocate. Many of the publications, including the *New York Times,* placed their tributes on page one. None of the lengthy articles, however, made any mention whatsoever of Addams's forty-three-year relationship with Mary Rozet Smith.[57]

Chapter 5

Bessie Marbury & Elsie de Wolfe
1892–1933

Founding the Field of Interior Design

...

Elsie de Wolfe was the first person in this country to earn a livelihood by telling other people what furniture to buy, what color to paint their walls, and what other steps to take so their homes would be stylish and attractive. In addition to founding the field of interior design, de Wolfe also revolutionized American home decor by banishing the dark colors and heavy furniture that defined the Victorian Era, replacing them with light color schemes and pieces that were more delicate.

De Wolfe's path to success wasn't an easy one. During the final decade of the nineteenth century, she had struggled in her attempts to become a professional actress. Each time she read another negative review, she became more discouraged. Her same-sex partner, Bessie Marbury, then took it upon herself to provide emotional support and also to make a series of suggestions that ultimately propelled de Wolfe on the course that led to her creating the field of interior designer and transforming American home decor.

...

Elisabeth Marbury was born into one of New York City's most affluent and socially prominent families in 1856. Her father was a successful attorney and real estate speculator, and her mother had a reputation as one of the city's most elegant hostesses.[1]

Bessie—as she was known from an early age—attended the most exclusive private schools in the city. She particularly enjoyed reading the works of William Shakespeare.[2]

During her teenage years, Marbury adamantly refused to become a debutante. "I had danced and played long enough," she wrote in her autobiography. "I had the germ of independence in my system." And so, instead of attending cotillions, she spent her time going to the theater. Her sense of defiance also surfaced in her appearance, as she refused to maintain the slender figure that was expected for a young woman of her high social class.[3]

By the age of twenty, Marbury had made it clear that she had no intention of marrying but planned to remain single and devote her life to writing plays. Going this route was very much at odds with the social dictates of the day, but the Marbury name had such high status that Bessie's unconventional decision did little more than raise a few eyebrows.[4]

Elsie de Wolfe was born in New York City in 1865. Her father was a physician, and her mother took care of the couple's children. During her early years, Elsie attended private school in Manhattan. Her father's medical practice wasn't successful, however, and the costs involved in raising five children became a financial strain on the de Wolfes.[5]

Because of her family's difficulties, de Wolfe was sent to Edinburgh, Scotland, at the age of sixteen to live with her mother's cousin. The girl's next several years were defined by a whirl of social activities, such as attending formal teas and costume balls. De Wolfe enjoyed these events immensely and, in particular, thrived on the attention that came with being the only American girl in her circle of friends.[6]

The young woman also stood apart from her contemporaries because she paid an enormous amount of attention to her appearance. She kept up with the latest trends in the fashion world and repeatedly experimented with new hairstyles, always determined to look her best.

De Wolfe returned to the United States in 1885 and drifted into the amateur drama clubs that were popular at the time. She loved the spotlight and saw the stage as the venue that could give her the celebrity status she increasingly desired.[7]

CREATING AN OUTLAW MARRIAGE

By 1887, many members of New York society were noticing Elsie de Wolfe both on stage and at the late-night parties that followed the performances. The admirer who ultimately would play the most important role in the young woman's life was Bessie Marbury, who later recalled the first time she saw de Wolfe, writing, "There was a buzz of excitement when a slim and graceful young girl passed through the ballroom."[8]

Marbury soon began asking de Wolfe to private luncheons and dinners, with the actress eagerly accepting every invitation. On a practical level, the two women shared not only an interest in the theater—Marbury wrote plays, de Wolfe acted in them—but also a driving desire to become financially independent of any man. On an emotional level, they were falling in love.[9]

The two women created a stereotypical butch/femme couple. Marbury was twelve years older and spoke in a deep and authoritative voice, pulled her dark brown hair into a severe knot on top of her head, and wore clothes whose only virtue was that they covered her massive body—she had a particular fondness for corduroy suits. De Wolfe, by contrast, spoke in a soft and coquettish voice, spent many hours curling her light brown hair, dressed in the latest fashions, and followed a strict exercise regimen to make sure she stayed slender.[10]

For the next several years, the two women continued to live with their respective families while spending many of their days and evenings with each other. They also traveled together on lengthy holidays to Paris and the French countryside, riding bicycles from town to town.[11]

The women didn't spend much time vacationing, though, as they both embarked on substantive career paths. Marbury decided she wasn't a strong enough writer to create successful plays, so she became a theatrical agent instead. In this role, she served as the American representative for European playwrights, overseeing tasks such as having scripts translated, booking U.S. performances, and scheduling the rehearsals. De Wolfe opted to become a professional actress, appearing in plays performed in various East Coast cities.[12]

PIONEERING A NEW FIELD

In 1892, Marbury and de Wolfe moved in together. Their home was on the corner of Seventeenth Street and Irving Place, two blocks below Gramercy Park. The house was the former home of author Washington Irving, and he'd written several of his novels while sitting on the veranda that overlooked the East River.[13]

Marbury's career as a theatrical agent took off. She gained such a strong reputation as a reliable businesswoman that she was hired to represent the entire membership of the French Society of Dramatic Authors as well as British playwrights Oscar Wilde and George Bernard Shaw. Indeed, she soon had so many clients that she hired other agents to work for her and set up offices in Paris, London, Vienna, Milan, and Moscow.[14]

De Wolfe's career as an actress, however, didn't go well. Marbury used her theater connections to help her partner secure her first Broadway role, but the reviews weren't flattering. The only positive comments about her performances had to do with how fashionably she dressed while on stage—she insisted on wearing her own clothes. The weekly New York newspaper *Town Topics* published a fictitious vignette, for example, in which one theatergoer asked, "What did you think of Miss de Wolfe?" and another responded, "I thought she was splendid in the second dress."[15]

Every time de Wolfe read another critical assessment of her acting, she fell into a funk. She had desperately wanted to succeed as an actress, but her efforts clearly weren't working. Marbury tried to raise her partner's spirits by praising her talent, but she soon decided that what de Wolfe really needed was a hobby to distract her.[16]

So Marbury suggested that her partner redecorate their home. When the women had moved into the Seventeenth Street house, they'd found dark woodwork and heavily patterned wallpaper, plus thick velvet drapes covering the windows. De Wolfe had commented at the time that she found the decor depressing, and now, with Marbury's encouragement, she decided to do something about it.[17]

Her first step was to have the woodwork and walls painted in shades of ivory. Then she had sheers hung on the windows, allowing sunlight to pour into the various rooms. She next did away with the dark and bulky furniture, opting instead for light-colored and delicate French antiques, with the cane backs on the dining room chairs adding to the home's airy feel.[18]

Redecorating the house took a number of years, as virtually every choice de Wolfe made was an innovation. Marbury was so proud of her partner's success that she turned their home into a salon on Sunday afternoons so luminaries from the art and theater world could gather for a few hours of literary conversation mixed with smatterings of political talk. Guests were highly complimentary of the elegance and freshness of the home's new decor.[19]

Despite her triumphs at home, de Wolfe continued to struggle on stage. The *New York Times* wrote, in one review, "Miss Elsie de Wolfe's sympathetic grace and charm are not of a kind that makes an instant appeal to an audience, even in the best of parts." After fifteen years as an actress, she gave her last performance in 1904.[20]

At this point, Marbury urged her partner to turn her talent for decorating into a paying enterprise. De Wolfe was hesitant, questioning if people would hire her and pointing out that the vocation her partner was proposing didn't even have a name. When the persistent Marbury announced that the proper term would be "Interior Decorator," de Wolfe had an engraver create business cards for her that contained her name, her address, and her new title.[21]

ACHIEVING INITIAL SUCCESS—WITH A PARTNER'S HELP

It wasn't surprising, considering that de Wolfe was creating an entirely new field, that the cards she sent to friends and acquaintances didn't produce an instant outpouring of commissions. Nor was it surprising, in light of Marbury's continuing support, that the theatrical agent soon secured a major project for her partner.[22]

Marbury was a founding member of the Colony Club, the first large-scale women's club in the United States. In 1902, she and other directors of the organization decided they wanted their own building, so they purchased land at 120 Madison Avenue and hired Stanford White as their architect. As the building neared completion two years later, Marbury persuaded her fellow club members to hire de Wolfe to decorate the club.[23]

De Wolfe was given carte blanche to make every decision about the style of the interior. She then devoted all of her time to the project, first traveling to Europe to purchase dozens of Chippendale chairs and several fireplace mantels embedded with Wedgwood medallions, then returning to New York to begin, in earnest, her effort to define a look that was unlike anything America had ever seen before.[24]

Her final product was a striking departure from the men's clubs of the era with their dark paneled walls, heavy furniture, and leather upholstery. In contrast, the Colony Club's entrance hall was light and airy, with wallpaper in shades of white and spring green. A light green carpet covered the floor, and side chairs upholstered in green and white stripes invited ladies to pause for a few minutes to absorb the cheerful hospitality that de Wolfe's design evoked.[25]

Placing glazed chintz on the club's furniture was one of de Wolfe's most daring moves, as members were initially shocked to see such an inexpensive fabric displayed so prominently in a luxurious urban setting. The decorator defended her decision, pointing out that the fabric was widely used in British country homes as well as London town houses, insisting that chintz was "as much at home in the New York drawing room as in the country cottage."[26]

After an initial period of adjusting to the new look, observers applauded de Wolfe's innovations. In a full-page critique of the Colony Club interior, the *New York Times* pronounced it "delightful" and "a private pleasure ground never before afforded the exclusive fair sex in New York." Other publications gave their seal of approval as well, the *Los Angeles Times* calling de Wolfe's creation "beautiful" and the *Washington Post* crowning it "perfect in every way."[27]

DECORATING THE FINEST HOMES IN AMERICA—
WITH MORE HELP FROM A PARTNER

Marbury's role in securing projects for de Wolfe didn't stop with the women's club, as she also convinced several of her wealthy friends that they should hire her partner. These jobs allowed the decorator to adapt her innovative style to private homes.[28]

Marbury had met Ethel Crocker when the California woman had accompanied her husband, banker William Crocker, on business trips to New York. So when the Crockers built a mansion near San Francisco in 1907, Marbury saw to it that the couple hired her partner to decorate the new home. One of her signature elements that de Wolfe showcased in the project was her use of mirrors. She hung large crystal chandeliers in the drawing room and then made the space appear larger and more elegant by placing ornate French mirrors on all four walls.[29]

De Wolfe's next major commission again came after Marbury nudged a friend to hire her. This project allowed de Wolfe to decorate a mansion in a Chicago suburb constructed at the astronomical cost of $10 million by Lolita and J. Ogden Armour, the meatpacking mogul. The de Wolfe technique most prominent this time was mixing pieces of furniture from different styles and periods. In the garden room, for example, she placed mismatched antique Louis XV chairs around a modern upholstered sofa.[30]

Yet another commission Marbury landed for her partner was decorating a suite of rooms in the Manhattan home of J. Pierpont Morgan that were the personal space of the financier's daughter Anne. This project demonstrated de Wolfe's ability to work on an intimate scale. She divided the girl's large bedroom into a foyer, sitting room, sleeping room, and dressing room. Most important among these spaces, according to de Wolfe, was the one where Anne dressed, which she decorated with mirrors and furnished with items covered in chintz.[31]

SECURING HER STATURE IN THE FIELD—
WITH STILL MORE HELP FROM A PARTNER

By the time de Wolfe had finished the Morgan project, she had much to be proud of. Within half a dozen years after founding an entirely new field, America's first interior decorator had created fresh and stylish looks for a major women's club and for the homes of several of the country's wealthiest families. Despite these successes, though, de Wolfe wasn't happy. The problem was that other people had followed in her footsteps, now making her merely one of several hundred men and women who called themselves interior decorators.[32]

When de Wolfe complained to her partner about the situation, Marbury proposed a strategy to establish the woman she loved as the country's undisputed leader in the field. Specifically, Marbury suggested that de Wolfe commit her extensive knowledge to paper and create the definitive book on decorating the American home.[33]

De Wolfe threw herself into the writing project, publishing *The House in Good Taste* in 1913. In the book, she identified the "holy trinity" of successful home decorating as simplicity, suitability, and proportion. The author also denounced clutter and insisted that garish colors should be replaced with beige, ivory, and light gray. "I believe in plenty of optimism and white paint," she declared. She also said every room in a home should be filled with as much natural light as possible.[34]

Reviews of *The House in Good Taste* were unstinting in their praise. The *New York Times* labeled the prose "lively" and "amusing," while going on to say, "This is no textbook and no dry thesis; it is pleasantly autobiographical, recording the actual and intricate experiences of an established professional decorator." The *Times* left no question that the book's author was the undisputed leader in her field, stating, "Miss de Wolfe's contributions to the art of interior decorating are unsurpassed."[35]

Interior design scholars have credited de Wolfe's book and style with having, in the words of one of them, "tremendous effect on the way that Americans imagined a well-arranged home should look." By stating her principles and illustrating them with concrete examples, she showed homeowners how they could create a residence that was both functional and attractive. Consistent with Marbury's vision, the book succeeded in establishing its author as the country's most influential decorator.[36]

PURSUING NEW INTERESTS

Now that de Wolfe was widely recognized as the foremost figure in the field she'd founded, she decided to add another item to her résumé: the world's most celebrated hostess.[37]

She and Marbury had purchased an eighteenth-century French villa in the town of Versailles, just outside of Paris, in 1905. The couple had then spent their summers at Villa Trianon, expanding the structure by adding a new wing. De Wolfe furnished the palatial home with French antiques and overstuffed easy chairs, the upholstered pieces covered either in vintage tapestry or chintz.[38]

After decorating the villa, de Wolfe began organizing dinner parties and weekend gatherings that grew larger and larger as the years passed. The hostess mixed her guests much as she mixed pieces of furniture—members of European nobility rubbed elbows with wealthy American industrialists and celebrities from the New York stage. De Wolfe was the primary hostess at these events, while Marbury merely attended them, much as an indulgent husband would support his wife's pastimes because he wanted to please her.[39]

For fifteen years, de Wolfe was content spending her summers in France and the rest of the year in New York, working out of her Fifth Avenue showroom to build her firm into the most prestigious one of its kind. But after World War I, her priorities shifted and she spent the majority of her time at Villa Trianon, leaving the day-to-day demands of her firm in the hands of the designers she'd hired to re-create her signature look in the homes the firm decorated.[40]

This shift in de Wolfe's priorities had a major impact on her partner. Marbury's business had continued to grow during the first two decades of the twentieth century, as she became one of America's leading theatrical agents. Never enjoying social activities as much as de Wolfe did, Marbury increasingly remained in New York working while her partner entertained in France.[41]

DIFFERING PRIORITIES THREATENING THE RELATIONSHIP

When de Wolfe's focus on becoming an international hostess propelled her to spend more of each year at Villa Trianon, Marbury became involved in Democratic politics. Her first major work for the party came in 1918 when she joined the effort to elect Al Smith governor of New York.[42]

Marbury's primary role was as a fund-raiser. Just as she'd asked her wealthy friends to hire de Wolfe to decorate their homes a few years earlier, she now urged those same well-heeled men and women to donate money to Smith's campaign. His was an uphill battle, as it marked the first time a Catholic was a viable candidate for the Empire State's highest office.[43]

When the votes were tallied in November 1918, Al Smith won. The Democratic Party leadership's post-election evaluation identified which of its members had played decisive roles in bringing about the victory, and Marbury's name was at the top of the list.[44]

De Wolfe's emergence as an international hostess and Marbury's rise to prominence in American politics had consequences on the couple's relationship. With one partner in France and the other in the United States for lengthy periods, the women's outlaw marriage had changed significantly from the days when they'd lived in the same house day in and day out.[45]

PROCEEDING ALONG TWO SEPARATE PATHS

That the two women were often separated by the Atlantic Ocean didn't mean their relationship had ended. Marbury continued to come to France for the summer, while de Wolfe made several trips to New York each year to oversee her firm's work and to spend time with Marbury in a new home she bought on Sutton Place.[46]

In the early 1920s, de Wolfe popularized a new personal grooming style that ultimately would continue long after her life had ended. Not pleased when her hair started turning gray, she asked her beautician to dye it pale blue. Once de Wolfe began appearing in public with her colored locks, other fashion-forward ladies of a certain age followed her lead, thereby making de Wolfe the first and most celebrated of the world's "blue-haired ladies."[47]

While Marbury didn't create any fashion trends, she continued to head her theatrical agency and devote a great deal of energy to politics. In 1920 when American women won the right to vote, party leaders elected her the first woman to represent the state on the Democratic National Committee. She remained in that high-level position for the next dozen years and also served as an unofficial political adviser to Smith throughout his two terms in office.[48]

SURVIVING A NEW CHALLENGE

Midway through the 1920s, de Wolfe set another goal for herself. Her success as a decorator had made her famous as well as wealthy, but her years as an international hostess had shown her that no amount of money allowed an American to move into the elite social class defined by European nobility. And so, de Wolfe decided she wanted a title.[49]

She pored over the pages of *Burke's Peerage*, the book that lists the names of British nobles, looking for an unmarried man in her general age range. Her choice was Sir Charles Mendl, a press attaché working at the British Embassy in Paris who'd been knighted by the king. At fifty-five years old, Mendl was five years de Wolfe's junior.[50]

Mendl fit the bill as a potential husband on several counts. He dressed impeccably, was well-mannered, and possessed a great deal of charm. What's more, the two negatives de Wolfe uncovered—that he was a womanizer and wasn't very bright—were irrelevant to what she had in mind. Most important, she learned that Mendl had expensive taste but little money, so he might be interested in marrying a woman who could pay his bills.[51]

De Wolfe wasn't positive that her partner of three decades would go along with her plan, so she made sure that Marbury knew, from the start, that her proposed marriage was merely a business arrangement. That is, Mendl would give the title of "Lady" to de Wolfe in exchange for her paying him a monthly allowance. De Wolfe also made it clear that the marriage wouldn't include any physical contact, that she and Mendl wouldn't live together, and that the arrangement wouldn't disrupt her romantic relationship with Marbury.[52]

After absorbing this information, Marbury gave the marriage her blessing—another example of the "husband" indulging his spoiled "wife." De Wolfe and Mendl's wedding then took place in March 1926. After a brief honeymoon, he returned to his Paris apartment, and she—now Lady Mendl—

resumed her life at Villa Trianon. The couple saw each other only on weekends when Mendl participated in his wife's social events, while de Wolfe and
Marbury continued their outlaw marriage.[53]

WEATHERING A SERIES OF SETBACKS

In the late 1920s, de Wolfe suffered the first of several challenges when the
Great Depression drastically reduced the number of people who could afford to decorate their homes. She recovered by expanding her business into
hotel decorating. Leaving her husband in France, she spent months at a time
in New York, first reworking the interior of the Savoy-Plaza Hotel on Fifth
Avenue and then doing the same for the Hotel Pierre, St. Regis Hotel, and
Essex House.[54]

Part of the reason de Wolfe took on the hotel projects was that her lengthy
stays in Manhattan allowed her to spend time with Marbury, who was happy
to provide the decorator with a place to stay—and to continue their intimate
relationship.[55]

The next setback was one that even the indefatigable de Wolfe couldn't do
anything about. For in January 1933, Marbury suffered a heart attack. This crisis wasn't a complete surprise, as Marbury's obesity had led to various health
problems in previous years. This time, however, the results were more serious,
leading to the seventy-six-year-old woman's death. Of the many newspapers
that published obituaries, only the *New York Times* mentioned de Wolfe, stating that she and Marbury had jointly owned a home in France.[56]

Yet another regrettable event that wasn't within de Wolfe's control came in
1940 when the German army marched into France, forcing her to relocate to
New York, this time with her husband in tow, until the end of World War II.[57]

LIVING OUT THE FINAL YEARS

When de Wolfe returned to France in 1946, she found her home in shambles.
She devoted the next three years to restoring the villa to what *Architectural
Digest* would later call "its fabled glory," while at the same time resuming her
legendary entertaining.[58]

She also agreed to undertake a few decorating projects for select friends.
Most notable among them were England's Duke and Duchess of Windsor.
De Wolfe's friendship with Wallis Simpson had begun in the early 1930s and
continued during the American divorcée's courtship by the Prince of Wales,
later Edward VIII. After the king abdicated in 1936 and the couple married,
de Wolfe decorated their mansion in Paris and their chateau near Cannes.[59]

Meanwhile, de Wolfe's marriage of convenience to Sir Charles Mendl
was still working after more than two decades. He had dutifully obeyed the
boundaries she'd set for him—if he wanted to enter her bedroom, for exam-

ple, he had to ask the butler in advance to get her approval. Proof that the rules had been followed came when Mendl told friends, during the 1940s, "For all I know, the old girl's still a virgin." Mendl, now in his mid-seventies, continued to have affairs. De Wolfe didn't object to the liaisons, encouraging her husband to bring the attractive young women to Villa Trianon so she could admire them, too.[60]

In 1950, however, the eighty-four-year-old de Wolfe was confined to a wheelchair because spinal problems made it impossible for her to walk. Mendl knew the end was near when his wife ordered stationery from Cartier that she told him to use when responding to the many letters of condolence she knew he'd receive after her death. That day came in July.[61]

In her will, de Wolfe left the bulk of her estate to a foundation providing scholarships to design students, while she gave Mendl only a modest annual allowance.[62]

America's leading newspapers published obituaries reporting de Wolfe's death, along with tributes praising her extraordinary achievements. The *Los Angeles Times*, for example, stated, "She was our best-known decorator, and homes throughout the country will forever stand as beautiful monuments to her good taste." Only the *New York Times* made any mention of the woman who'd been in an outlaw marriage with de Wolfe for forty-one years. The *Times* said, "For many years, Lady Mendl was associated with the late Elisabeth Marbury."[63]

Chapter 6

J. C. Leyendecker & Charles Beach

1901–1951

Taking the Art of Illustration to a New Level

...

During the early decades of the twentieth century, J. C. Leyendecker was the nation's most popular and most successful illustrator. Hundreds of his hand-painted images appeared on the covers of such leading magazines as *Collier's, Vanity Fair,* and the *Saturday Evening Post.* Adding to Leyendecker's fame were the myriad high-profile advertisements he created for a long list of companies—the most significant of them were for Arrow shirt collars.

Leyendecker didn't make his achievements entirely on his own, as his same-sex partner of fifty years, Charles Beach, played an enormous role in his success. Beach began supporting Leyendecker by serving as the strikingly handsome model for many of the illustrator's images. As time passed, Beach gradually made more and more of the decisions that resulted in the artist's work expanding in new directions. Indeed, Beach's creative and farsighted ideas ultimately succeeded in transforming a talented illustrator with limited aspirations into a wealthy and widely celebrated artist who succeeded both in the magazine and advertising worlds.

Joseph Christian Leyendecker was born in 1874 in the village of Montabour in southern Germany. His father made his livelihood as a coachman, and his mother took care of the couple's three children.[1]

When Joe was eight years old, the Leyendeckers emigrated to the United States in search of a more prosperous life. They settled in Chicago where the head of the household took a job with a brewing company.[2]

Leyendecker's interest in art surfaced soon after the family arrived in America. "I was eight at the time and was already covering schoolbooks with rudely colored examples of my work," he later recalled. "At home I kept myself busy with more pretentious paintings which, for want of canvas, were done on oilcloth of the common kitchen variety."[3]

When Leyendecker turned sixteen, he became an apprentice with an engraving firm that produced line drawings for Bibles and religious pamphlets. He proved highly adept at the work and began creating images that were much more intricate than those of his fellow illustrators. Eager to progress, he enrolled in evening classes at the Art Institute of Chicago.[4]

Charles Beach was born in Ontario, Canada, in 1886. Few details about his early childhood have been documented beyond the fact that he received very little formal education.[5]

One fact that's known about the boy's teenage years is that he developed into an extraordinarily handsome young man. Beach left Canada at the age of sixteen and moved to New York City, hoping to parlay his good looks into a career in the theater.[6]

Beach suffered something of a setback when a series of producers rejected him for starring roles he auditioned for, each of them telling him he had no talent. The young man's efforts weren't in vain, however, as he was cast in minor roles in a number of plays, solely because he looked good on stage. Beach also began applying for jobs as a model.[7]

ENTERING THE WORLD OF ART
Early in 1896, J. C. Leyendecker received the first public recognition for his creative work when he won a contest to design a cover for *Century* magazine. His entry, in keeping with the Art Nouveau style popular at the time, featured a woman in a loose-fitting white gown, her eyes closed and her long hair flowing into a field of red poppies. In addition to the image being published on the magazine cover, it was also issued and sold as an art print.[8]

Leyendecker's share of the profits from selling copies of the image were sizeable enough that he was able to quit his job at the engraving firm and move to Paris, the center of the international art world, in the fall of 1896. Twenty-two-year-old Joe took his younger brother, Frank, five years his junior and also interested in art, with him to Europe. Both men enrolled at the prestigious art school Académie Julian.[9]

Joe showed immediate promise and received special attention from the faculty. Less than a year after he arrived in Paris, a French publishing house commissioned him to paint a promotional poster, which meant the image he created, which featured a woman lounging on a sofa, was emblazoned on the walls of buildings along the Champs d'Elysées. Several of Leyendecker's paintings of Paris street scenes also appeared in a one-man show in the city.[10]

When the exhibition closed, the Leyendecker brothers returned to the United States, both of them having completed the full curriculum of coursework at the art school. The men then opened a studio in downtown Chicago.[11]

RELOCATING TO NEW YORK CITY

Leyendecker soon became frustrated with his and his brother's failure to secure commissions. He decided the problem was their Chicago location, as all major projects were going to artists located in New York City, the center of American publishing.[12]

And so, in 1900, Leyendecker relocated to Manhattan and rented a studio on East 32nd Street. This time, he took along not only his brother but also his sister, Mary, who agreed to cook for her brothers and clean the town house near Washington Square that Joe rented for them. After the three Leyendecker siblings settled in, their parents moved into the town house as well.[13]

Once in New York, Joe and Frank Leyendecker both received a steady stream of commissions for oil illustrations that were published either in magazines or books. They often worked as a team, with Joe coming up with the concept for an image and then the two of them doing the sketching and painting. Frank frequently lost interest in projects, however, and Joe then had to finish them on his own.[14]

Despite Frank's shortcomings in the partnership, in 1901 he did something that changed Joe's life forever: he hired Charles Beach.[15]

CREATING AN OUTLAW MARRIAGE

Joe Leyendecker happened to be away from the studio on the day that Frank, in need of a young male model for a particular commission, interviewed and then offered the job to the seventeen-year-old Beach.[16]

It was Beach's physical attributes that caused Frank to hire him. Famed illustrator Norman Rockwell, a great admirer of J.C. Leyendecker's work, would later describe Beach as "tall, powerfully built, and extraordinarily handsome—looked like an athlete from one of the Ivy League colleges." Rockwell also said that Beach "was always beautifully dressed. His manners were polished and impeccable." One of Leyendecker's biographers added more specifics to the description of Beach, calling him "confident and charming" and going on to say, "He stood about six feet two inches tall and had an Adonislike figure with a narrow waist and a flat stomach."[17]

Beach was a dramatic contrast to Joe Leyendecker, both in appearance and in how he carried himself. The illustrator was five feet six inches tall and skinny, with nondescript facial features and what one biographer called "an unnaturally sallow complexion and a weak jaw." He also was described as being socially awkward and so painfully shy that he stuttered when any person of authority asked him to speak.[18]

From the moment Joe Leyendecker laid eyes on Charles Beach, he was smitten. Frank Leyendecker also found Beach appealing—both of the brothers, by this point in their lives, recognized that they were sexually attracted to men—but he didn't stand in the way of Joe becoming Beach's lover. J. C. Leyendecker biographers speculate that Beach was attracted to the illustrator, who was twelve years his senior, partially because the younger man admired the older one's artistic talent.[19]

When the model began posing for the Leyendeckers on a regular basis, he rented a small apartment on West 33rd Street, within a few blocks of the brothers' studio. Joe's official residence continued to be the town house that he rented for his siblings and parents, but he spent most of his nights in Beach's apartment.[20]

FOCUSING ON MALE SUBJECTS
Beach's influence on J. C. Leyendecker's illustrations was both immediate and dramatic. Before 1901, the artist had concentrated on painting either women or street scenes. But as soon as Beach entered his life, Leyendecker's most frequent subject became men—most of them handsome and with well-developed physiques similar to his partner's.[21]

For example, when Leyendecker received a commission to create a cover for the September 1902 issue of *Collier's*, he submitted the image of a brawny blacksmith who was shirtless as he worked at an anvil. This illustration was followed by others for the same magazine that also placed good-looking men front and center, including a track star with his muscles bulging as he leaped over a hurdle.[22]

A few months after Beach and Leyendecker met, the model gave up acting and devoted all of his time to modeling and otherwise helping his partner. Norman Rockwell recalled that Beach initially merely washed the paintbrushes after Leyendecker used them but then started taking care of business details, thereby freeing the illustrator to concentrate on his creative work. Meanwhile, Joe passed some of the more routine tasks on to his brother, Frank.[23]

Before long, Beach was hiring and paying the models, buying the art supplies and renting the costumes and props that Joe and Frank needed, while also taking care of more and more of the financial details. Beach began negotiating the specific dollar amounts that magazines paid for each commission. Rockwell said, "Beach transacted all Joe's business for him, did everything but paint his pictures."[24]

CREATING HOLIDAY MAGAZINE COVERS

Beach's role in his partner's professional life rose to a whole new level in 1903 after he read an editorial in the *Saturday Evening Post* that urged readers to celebrate not only Christmas and Easter but also other national holidays such as Thanksgiving, the Fourth of July, and Memorial Day. With Beach's prompting, Leyendecker then went to the magazine's art editor and suggested that he begin creating covers specifically for the various holidays. From that point onward for the next several decades, Leyendecker provided the cover images for the weekly issue of the *Post* closest to each holiday.[25]

Numerous of those covers showcased men. One Thanksgiving image was of a handsome athlete in a tight-fitting jersey preparing to kick a football. Other examples included a Fourth of July cover featuring a young patriot, with chiseled facial features and his shirt opened to show off his bare chest, playing a snare drum, and a Memorial Day illustration highlighting an earnest young man with long eyelashes escorting an elderly veteran toward a grave site.[26]

Creating the holiday covers was an enormous boost to Leyendecker's career. "The public came to expect Leyendecker images for the holiday issues, and the magazine thrived," one of the artist's biographers has observed. "So popular were Joe's holiday covers that *Post* subscriptions increased with each one; by 1913, circulation had risen to two million copies a week, making it the most popular magazine in the world."[27]

Beach used the magazine's soaring circulation figures as a negotiating tool. When Leyendecker had handled his own finances, the easily intimidated artist had accepted whatever the *Post* offered him for a piece of cover art. Once Beach entered the picture, however, he set the hefty fee of $2,000 per illustration—a higher figure than any previous magazine illustrator had been paid—and also persuaded the art editor to commit the magazine to purchasing a minimum of ten Leyendecker cover images each year.[28]

In his next step, Beach used the fee he'd negotiated with the *Post* as leverage to force other magazines to raise their payments to this same amount. With a plethora of commissions coming from such magazines as *Collier's, Life, Literary Digest, McClure's,* and *Vanity Fair,* Beach pushed Leyendecker's annual income to more than $50,000.[29]

MOVING INTO THE WORLD OF ADVERTISING

Of comparable importance to Beach's contributions to his partner's work with magazine covers was his success at persuading Leyendecker to create images for advertisements. This proposal was a controversial one, as Frank Leyendecker adamantly opposed it, insisting that he and his brother should avoid such blatantly commercial work.[30]

Joe sided with Beach rather than his brother, however, and soon began splitting his time between painting magazine covers and painting images designed to sell products. Advertising to a mass audience was still a relatively new enterprise in the early 1900s, and Leyendecker became a pioneer in the field. "As early as just after the turn of the century, Leyendecker was already changing the course of advertising," one scholar has observed. "Leyendecker was able to discern trends and advertisers' needs for satiating customers' demands. The times were evolving quickly from Victorian into modern."[31]

Physically attractive men appeared in Leyendecker's ads even more often than they appeared on his magazine covers. This frequency came about because many of the companies that hired him depended on his ads to sell men's clothing, which meant displaying items of apparel on handsome male models who showed the clothes to their best advantage. The first of the companies, B. Kuppenheimer menswear, was soon followed by Hart, Schaffner & Marx. Then came Interwoven socks, Cooper underwear (which later became the Jockey brand), and the full line of men's clothing sold by A. B. Kirschbaum and Carson Pirie Scott department stores. "His paintings for fashion advertisements," the *New York Times* later reported, "soon were known throughout the country."[32]

DEFINING THE IDEAL AMERICAN MAN

Ultimately, the best known of Leyendecker's advertising clients was Arrow brand detachable shirt collars, with Charles Beach consistently being featured as the model in the ads that began appearing in 1905.[33]

"Over the next twenty-five years," according to one Leyendecker biographer, "the 'Arrow Collar Man' became the symbol of fashionable American manhood. Leyendecker, through the Arrow ads, defined the ideal of the American male as a dignified, clear-eyed man of taste, manners, and quality." One advertising scholar has written, "The term Arrow Man became a popular expression referring to a handsome, desirable, stylish man. Tall and well built, with broad shoulders, a strong jaw, chiseled features, and muscular hands, he was a visual representation of the New American Man and the male equivalent of the Gibson Girl who represented the New American Woman."[34]

The quintessential image in the Arrow campaign had Beach wearing a white shirt and cream-colored trousers as he stood casually on the deck of a ship, his sleeves rolled up to the elbow and his light green necktie blowing in the spring breeze. The handsome model with his soft smile shaped by gently curving lips exuded the confidence of a young man who didn't have a care in the world. His light brown hair was perfect, as were his bone structure, his light brown eyes, and the creamy texture of his skin. Beach's broad shoulders and a muscular torso tapered down to a slender waist.[35]

Another popular ad featured Beach sitting astride an elaborately carved table stacked with leather-bound books; the perspective this time focused the viewer's eye on the model's impressive chest, as the front of his pleated shirt fit snugly against his well-toned pectoral muscles. A third ad had Beach positioned on a flowered sofa and holding a book; his head was turned to the side to show off his matinee-idol profile, complete with long eyelashes and straight-as-an-arrow nose.[36]

CREATING THE NATION'S FIRST MALE SEX SYMBOL

These flattering images that appeared in the country's leading magazines hundreds of times during the first three decades of the twentieth century transformed the Arrow Collar Man into what scholars have labeled the nation's first male sex symbol.[37]

"Today, it is difficult to imagine the sensation the advertisements caused," one author has written. "In one month in the early 1920s, the Arrow Collar Man received 17,000 fan letters, gifts, and marriage proposals—a deluge surpassing even actor Rudolph Valentino's mail at the star's apex. The term 'Arrow Collar Man' became a common epithet for any handsome, nattily dressed gent, and the Arrow Man was the subject of admiring poems, songs, and even a Broadway play. In 1918 Arrow Collar sales rose to over $32 million."[38]

The images made Charles Beach such a widely recognized celebrity that strangers who saw him walking on the street or sitting in a restaurant frequently stopped to ask him if he was the man they thought he was. Despite the fame that became a routine element in Beach's life, his millions of admirers had no inkling that this handsome symbol of American manhood was a gay man whose heart belonged to the artist who painted the images of him.[39]

At the same time, Beach took great pleasure both in his celebrity status and in the wealth that he and Leyendecker now enjoyed. The model routinely carried a walking still as he strolled down the streets of Manhattan. In the winter, he wore an elegant wool overcoat that was accented with a Persian lamb collar and more fur at the cuffs and hem.[40]

COMMITTING TO EACH OTHER

From soon after they met in 1901 and for the next fifty years, J. C. Leyendecker and Charles Beach were a same-sex couple fully devoted to each other's well-being. Likewise, they shared a commitment to keeping their outlaw marriage out of the public eye, fearing that the stigma attached to homosexuality would jeopardize their livelihoods.[41]

For the first decade and a half they were together, Leyendecker and Beach maintained separate residences, keeping up the charade of living apart in deference to the Old World values of Leyendecker's parents. Joe told people he lived in the Washington Square town house with his family, and Charles said he lived in his efficiency apartment near the Leyendecker studio.[42]

In reality, though, the two men spent almost every minute of the day and night together. Their after-work schedule typically began with a steak dinner at Longley's, a popular restaurant in the Manhattan theater district. Later in the evening, the two men had drinks and conversation at one or more of New York City's bars and lounges where they socialized with the actors Beach had come to know during his days in the theater. When it came time for bed, the couple spent the night together in Beach's apartment.[43]

This living arrangement continued after Leyendecker's mother died in 1905 and the family rented a house in New Rochelle, a suburb sixteen miles from midtown Manhattan. Another change came in 1910 when the Leyendecker brothers moved to a larger and more luxurious studio at 40th Street and Sixth Avenue. The new studio included a side bedroom where Beach slept—with his partner next to him.[44]

In 1914, the Leyendecker family moved into a fourteen-room house in New Rochelle that Joe designed and had built on a new street that he named Mount Tom Road, an Americanized version of the name of the German village where he'd been born. Although Charles Beach played a major role in the construction of the house by serving as clerk of the works, he continued to list his residence as the Manhattan studio.[45]

LIVING TOGETHER—OFFICIALLY

It wasn't until after Leyendecker's father died in 1916 that he and Beach finally began living full time under the same roof. About this same time, Beach set out to help his partner secure even more advertising commissions. Beach's strategy is well summarized in the phrase "mixing business with pleasure."[46]

That is, Beach exploited his celebrity status as the Arrow Collar Man by organizing lavish social events where his and his partner's friends from the theater world rubbed elbows with the top executives of the nation's leading companies, along with such wealthy and socially prominent glitterati as Walter Chrysler and Reggie Vanderbilt. Thanks to the contacts J. C. Leyendecker made at the parties, he was soon creating ads not only for men's clothing but for an impressively wide range of products—from Karo syrup and Pierce-Arrow automobiles to Kellogg's corn flakes and Amoco oil, and from Chesterfield cigarettes to a whole array of household products manufactured by Procter & Gamble.[47]

Despite the hefty commissions that made Joe the most successful and wealthiest illustrator in the country, neither Frank nor Mary Leyendecker agreed with Beach's strategy, believing it was unsavory to use social contacts to advance business ventures. The brother and sister grew so resentful of Beach, who always had Joe's support, that in 1923 a huge confrontation erupted, culminating in Mary Leyendecker slapping Charles Beach and then spitting in his face. After that incident, Joe's two siblings moved out of the house and set up separate residences of their own, while Frank also left the firm.[48]

Frank Leyendecker's life soon spiraled downward. Depressed by his inability to secure commissions on his own and his failure to sustain a long-term relationship with a partner, he drank heavily and took an excessive amount of drugs. Within a year after the confrontation with Beach, Frank Leyendecker died of a drug overdose, at the age of forty-five.[49]

LIVING LARGE

Meanwhile, the Leyendecker/Beach home in New Rochelle expanded into *the* place to be seen for business executives as well as A-list celebrities from the New York theater world and the Hollywood film community—including Clara Bow, Al Jolson, and John and Ethel Barrymore.[50]

Indeed, the legendary parties that Beach organized not only helped his partner secure new clients but also, according to the authors of one Leyendecker biography, changed the American culture. "The popular gossip maven Walter Winchell, in particular, frequented the parties," the scholars wrote. "The coverage set fashion fads, established drinking and smoking trends, even dictated which automobiles were acceptable, and forever changed the shape of journalism by exposing private lives with salacious stories."[51]

The newspapers never reported, however, that the Leyendecker/Beach relationship was a romantic one, as the men didn't want their sexuality to become public. The journalists kept this detail out of their stories because they feared that if they wrote anything the couple didn't like, they would no longer be invited to the parties.[52]

Several biographers who have chronicled the grand lifestyle of J. C. Leyendecker and Charles Beach during the 1920s have compared them to the characters in the iconic novel *The Great Gatsby* that F. Scott Fitzgerald wrote to capture the hedonism of the decade. "Both Joe Leyendecker and Jay Gatsby rose from impoverished Midwestern beginnings to live lives of great wealth, sophistication, and lavish spending," the author of one book about the illustrator wrote. "Charles and Joe enjoyed entertaining and had what were considered to be 'the best' parties. Fitzgerald's written descriptions of Gatsby's parties echo Leyendecker's visual interpretations of his guests: they included 'businessmen, theatre people, even a prince.'"[53]

Leyendecker and Beach continued to "live large" throughout the 1920s, hosting their extravagant parties while enjoying the spoils of a thriving business. A chauffeur drove them back and forth to Manhattan in a Lincoln limousine, they expanded their already spacious home by adding two large wings, and they had major work done to the nine acres of grounds surrounding the house, including adding a Japanese garden complete with gazebo, footbridge, and waterfall. The partners also furnished their home with museum-quality French antiques and tapestries.[54]

ENCOUNTERING DIFFICULT TIMES

Like most Americans, Leyendecker and Beach were negatively affected by the 1929 stock market crash. The big problem was that most of the companies that had hired the illustrator to create images for them no longer had money to spend on advertising. So the couple stopped hosting the grand social events that had, during the Roaring Twenties, defined their lives. Fortunately, thanks to the contracts Beach had negotiated, Leyendecker continued painting covers for the country's leading magazines. Indeed, by the end of the 1930s, he was able to boast that his artwork had appeared on the cover of the *Saturday Evening Post* more than three hundred times.[55]

The 1940s were a more difficult time in Leyendecker's professional life. Changes in the public taste meant the demand for his particular style of images dwindled, and a new editor at the *Post* awarded the magazine's lucrative contracts to other artists. In 1945, Beach helped his partner secure a contract to paint the covers for a Sunday newspaper supplement titled the *American Weekly,* but the newsprint that the artwork was printed on didn't show off the illustrator's work to the degree that the slick magazines of earlier decades had.[56]

Health problems also began to plague Leyendecker by this point, as he suffered from heart disease. Beach eventually became so concerned about his partner overexerting himself that he refused to allow anyone to come to the house except a courier who arrived once a week to pick up the latest image for the *American Weekly.*[57]

COMING TO THE END

In the summer of 1951, the man who had once been the country's leading illustrator sat in the garden of his palatial home, enjoying a glass of rum and orange juice with his partner of half a century. When the glass slipped from Leyendecker's hand and shattered on the slate terrace, Beach raced to his side. A few minutes later, the artist died of heart failure, his head cradled in his lover's arms.[58]

After burying Leyendecker in the family grave site at Woodlawn Cemetery in New York City, Beach carried out his partner's request and destroyed all their correspondence in an effort to conceal the fact that they had a romantic relationship. J.C. Leyendecker's will split his estate between Charles Beach and Mary Leyendecker, who'd continued to rely on her brother's financial support after the family dispute twenty-five years earlier.[59]

Charles Beach lived in the Mount Tom Road house until he died, just a year after his partner had, in the summer of 1952.[60]

Despite Leyendecker and Beach having lived in an outlaw marriage for half a century, neither their romantic relationship nor Beach's contributions to his partner's success was publicly acknowledged during their lifetimes. The Leyendecker obituary published in the *New York Times* referred to Beach as the celebrated illustrator's "associate," while the local New Rochelle newspaper called Beach the artist's "secretary."[61]

Chapter 7

Alice B. Toklas & Gertrude Stein

1907–1946

Expanding the Dimensions of American Literature

...

The name Gertrude Stein is widely recognized today. She is remembered, in literary circles as well as in the general population, as an avant-garde author and also as a mentor to such iconic novelists as Ernest Hemingway and F. Scott Fitzgerald.

Largely forgotten, however, is the fact that as Stein approached the age of forty and had been toiling away at her writing for two decades, she'd failed miserably in her efforts to interest anyone in publishing her work.

It was at this point that the author's same-sex partner, Alice B. Toklas, decided it was high time for the world to learn about Stein's literary genius.

Gertrude Stein was born on the outskirts of Pittsburgh in 1874. Her father made a fortune in manufacturing, while her mother cared for the couple's five children. The family moved to Europe soon after Gertrude was born, returning to the United States four years later and settling in Oakland, California.[1]

Both of Stein's parents died when their youngest daughter was still in her teens, and Gertrude's inheritance made her financially independent for the rest of her life.[2]

In 1893, Stein enrolled at Radcliffe College near Boston, soon gaining a reputation as being unconventional because she wore a sailor's cap everywhere she went. At the same time, though, she was well liked because of her spirited personality.[3]

After graduation, Stein entered Johns Hopkins Medical School in Baltimore. It wasn't long until she veered away from becoming a doctor, however, as she began devoting her time and energy to exploring the connection between the written word and the human brain.[4]

In 1901, Stein fell in love with a student at Bryn Mawr College. When the young woman ended the relationship, Stein plummeted into a period of depression. Partly to put the affair behind her, she relocated to Paris in 1904, moving into an apartment where her brother Leo was already living.[5]

Alice Babette Toklas was born into an upper-class San Francisco family in 1877. Her father owned a dry goods store, and her mother was a full-time homemaker.[6]

Because Alice was highly precocious, her parents sent her to the most academically challenging private schools in the city. When she was eight, they also took her on a trip to Europe in an effort to broaden her education.[7]

Toklas enrolled in the music conservatory at the University of Washington after high school and embraced college life with great enthusiasm. She surrounded herself with a circle of artistic friends who helped her gain an appreciation for painting and sculpture. By this point, she'd also adopted a bohemian personal style, dressing in Chinese silk robes and frequenting San Francisco's various ethnic restaurants.[8]

Life changed dramatically for the teenager when her mother was diagnosed with cancer. Toklas then dropped out of school and began keeping house for her father and younger brother, while also caring for her ailing mother until her death in 1897.[9]

A part of Toklas was content devoting her days to cooking, cleaning, and doing the laundry, but another part grew restless. As her thirtieth birthday approached, she became increasingly eager to see and experience more of the world.[10]

WRITING PROSE THAT WAS DETACHED AND MELANCHOLY

Leo Stein's major activity in Paris was collecting modern art. The first painting to grace the walls of the Stein apartment, located near the Luxembourg Gardens, was by Paul Cézanne. That work was soon joined by the paintings of Edgar Degas, Henri Matisse, Pablo Picasso, and Henri de Toulouse-Lautrec.[11]

By 1906, anyone living in Paris who wanted to see the best in modern art was obliged to visit the Stein apartment, as no public museum yet recognized this emerging genre of creative work. The Steins established Saturday evenings as the set time each week when people could come see the paintings and join in literary discussions.[12]

Gertrude Stein conferred with her brother on many of the art purchases, but her major activity was writing. The specific question that intrigued her was how the process of creating prose was linked to consciousness. This interest propelled her into becoming perhaps the single most experimental American writer of the twentieth century.[13]

Experts who have studied the literary work created by Stein during this period have characterized it as being about people the author observed from afar, as well as being melancholy in tone. "It is obsessed with failure," one scholar has written. "Its heroines—servants, downtrodden people—are all doomed."[14]

CREATING AN OUTLAW MARRIAGE

Soon after arriving in Paris, Stein hired a young American woman to type her words after she wrote them out in long hand. Stein also coerced her employee into becoming a guinea pig for her theories on character. The author probed the depths of the girl's personality by asking her intimate questions and by reading her mail.[15]

The correspondence that the girl received from one friend in particular piqued Stein's interest, as the letters revealed that the writer was sexually attracted to women. Alice B. Toklas's words also described her artistic interests and her desire to move to Europe. And so, by the time Toklas came to Paris in 1907, Stein already knew a great deal about the woman.[16]

Stein was so familiar with Toklas through the letters, in fact, that she purposely presented herself, when they met, as more forceful than she naturally was, believing this was the character trait that Toklas would find appealing. Stein's calculated behavior succeeded, as Toklas was so strongly drawn to her that they soon became lovers.[17]

From the outset, Stein filled the role of domineering husband, while Toklas became the nurturing wife. "Pet me tenderly and save me from alarm," Stein wrote her partner at the time. "I hear you praise me and I say thanks for yesterday and to-day." The author also made it clear that, as in any marriage of the early twentieth century, the husband would be the power figure in the relationship. "A wife hangs on her husband," she wrote. Toklas was fully in concert with this arrangement, telling Stein, "I am your bride."[18]

With regard to Stein's writing, Toklas assumed a proactive role. The author wrote her words and then refused to edit them, relying on her initial creative impulse. So Toklas took it upon herself not merely to type the words but also to, as she put it, "tidy them up." Specifically, Toklas corrected the spelling and grammar, added and deleted words to make the prose read more smoothly, and reworked sentences so they became, in her estimation, more effective.[19]

Although Stein and Toklas became a couple in 1907, they didn't start living together until three years later when Leo Stein moved out of the apartment. This change in circumstance came about partly because the two women wanted to share the same home and partly because the brother and sister had a falling out when Leo Stein called his sister's writing "an abomination."[20]

ALICE B. TOKLAS BECOMING HER PARTNER'S MUSE

Literary experts who have studied Gertrude Stein's writing have observed that Toklas entering the author's life marked a major change both in the content and the tone of her prose. Stein's work now focused primarily on the lives of people who were close to her, while the melancholy pall that had defined her earlier work had largely disappeared, replaced with a sense of joy and playfulness.[21]

Stein's new approach was to create verbal collages consisting of scraps and morsels from her everyday life that she wove into sentences. She combined bits of conversation with descriptions of the physical settings surrounding her. And because she and her partner were now together virtually all the time, Toklas became an enormous presence in what Stein wrote.[22]

One of the most prominent themes in the author's work was the pleasure that life with Toklas brought her. "I have so much to make me happy," she wrote on one occasion, and on another she said, "We have been very happy." Many of the passages expressing this sentiment contained examples of Stein's unusual word choices as well as her fondness for repetition and unique phrasing. "I know all that I am to happiness, it is to be happy and I am happy. I am so completely happy that I mention it."[23]

Stein's prose was also dotted with statements of her love for Toklas. One example—difficult to follow because of its sparse punctuation—read, "I love cherish idolise adore and worship you. You are so sweet so tender so perfect." Some of the references to Stein's feelings for Toklas contained descriptions of physical intimacy between the two women, such as:

> Kiss my lips. She did.
> Kiss my lips again she did.
> Kiss my lips over and over and over again she did.[24]

ALICE B. TOKLAS SERVING AS HER PARTNER'S LITERARY AGENT

In 1913, Toklas decided her partner's words merited a larger audience. Up to that point, Stein's only work that had appeared in print was the self-published *Three Lives,* which consisted of portraits of a trio of immigrant women. The reviews of that book had been unenthusiastic—the *Nation* magazine said it "utterly lacked construction and form."[25]

The first step in Toklas's role as literary agent involved one of the guests who attended the weekly salon that she and Stein hosted in their apartment after Leo Stein moved out. Toklas lavished attention on Carl Van Vechten, whom she knew was a good friend of a New York publisher. Van Vechten and Toklas both enjoyed gossiping, and she used this common interest to grow so close to him that she could ask for his help in publishing a manuscript consisting of Stein's definitions of everyday objects. Van Vechten then persuaded his friend to release the book in 1914.[26]

Reviews of *Tender Buttons* were resoundingly negative. The *Chicago Tribune* called the book "a nightmare," and the *Los Angeles Times* opted to make its statement about the problems with the author's work by reproducing her definition of a dog: "A little monkey goes like a donkey that means to say that means to say that more sighs last goes. Leave with it. A little monkey goes like a donkey."[27]

After the harsh reviews, Toklas knew she had to develop an entirely new plan for getting more of her partner's work into print. A strategy came to her as she was typing one of the poems Stein wrote for her next book. The line "A rose is a rose is a rose" caught Toklas's fancy because she saw it as a masterfully poetic rephrasing of the more mundane saying "Things are what they are." Toklas transformed Stein's clever witticism into her partner's motto, which she hoped would capture the public imagination. The wife-turned-agent had the words embossed on Stein's stationery and also highlighted them in letters she wrote to potential publishers for the new book.[28]

Toklas's plan had mixed results. On the one hand, a Boston publisher was so impressed by Stein's clever "A rose is a rose is a rose" motto that he agreed to print the book. On the other hand, the reviews were every bit as negative as those of her previous work, with the *Baltimore Sun* dismissing the new book as "blather of the worst sort."[29]

After having gotten two of her partner's books into print but with Stein still not being recognized as a literary genius, Toklas founded her own publishing enterprise. In her new role, she hired a company to print copies of Stein's works and then personally promoted and distributed the books to individual libraries and bookstores. Through this method, Toklas saw that five more of her partner's books were published.[30]

The reviews of Stein's work remained stubbornly negative. The *New Or-*

leans Times-Picayune pronounced her writing "ineffectual," and a *Philadelphia Public Ledger* critic sniped, "A page or two of hers at first makes me a little cross-eyed, and then puts me quite conclusively to sleep."[31]

PARTNERS COLLABORATING ON A BEST SELLER

At this point, Stein had dedicated three decades of her life to writing, but her published works had failed to lift her to the position of prominence in the literary world that she felt she deserved. Toklas had consistently supported her partner's efforts, editing everything Stein wrote plus serving as her muse and literary agent. In 1933, Toklas concluded that the only way Stein would reach her proper stature was by writing a popular book.[32]

Toklas argued that her partner could easily put together a memoir—using a conventional prose style—that highlighted her associations with such famous artists as Picasso and Matisse and such popular writers as Hemingway and Fitzgerald. Stein rejected the idea, saying that such a project would mean abandoning her commitment to experimental prose.[33]

When Toklas persisted, however, Stein came up with an innovative literary device she found acceptable. The author said she'd produce a book that looked at her many famous acquaintances not through her own eyes, but through those of Toklas.[34]

It was a brilliant idea. Toklas had always provided the definitive version of any anecdote from the couple, as her memory was better than her partner's. Indeed, Toklas later confided to a friend that many of the stories that ended up in the manuscript had originated with her. One example was the book condemning Hemingway for mimicking Stein's style but not understanding it—Toklas didn't like Hemingway because he admitted being sexually attracted to Stein.[35]

Stories in *The Autobiography of Alice B. Toklas* were written as though the gossip-loving Toklas had dictated them, complete with her deadpan humor and acerbic tone. Stein captured her partner's style of speaking so precisely, in fact, that friends who knew both women were sure that Toklas had written the entire book, though she denied doing so.[36]

Regardless of how much was Stein and how much was Toklas, the pages exploded with names the public was eager to read about. For example, Picasso was quoted as saying that Stein had been, at one point early in his career, his only friend, and the artist's portrait of her was called the first cubist painting ever created. Many of the gossipy tidbits had an edge. One damning passage portrayed poet Ezra Pound as having limited intellectual timber, the exact words reading, "Gertrude Stein liked him but did not find him amusing. She said he was a village explainer, excellent if you were a village, but if you were not, not." Another insult was directed as Matisse's wife, Amélie, who was described as having a "mouth like a horse."[37]

Toklas didn't have to spend time looking for a publisher for the manuscript, as a top literary agent quickly secured a contract with the prestigious Harcourt, Brace and Company.[38]

Autobiography's reviews were resolutely positive. The *Los Angeles Times* described it as "astounding," *Time* dubbed it an "eminently readable memoir," and the *Washington Post* called it "an altogether delightful book, rich as a plum-pudding with good-humored, amusing and sensible tidbits."[39]

RETURNING TO THE UNITED STATES IN TRIUMPH

Autobiography's rave reviews prompted Stein's agent to organize a series of lectures in the United States to promote the book. The tour was an unmitigated triumph, with sold-out crowds greeting the author everywhere she went. Stein was such a cause célèbre by the time she reached the nation's capital that she was the guest of honor at a White House tea hosted by First Lady Eleanor Roosevelt.[40]

Newspapers and magazines consistently cast the author in a favorable light. The *Nation* stated simply, "We admire and like her," while the *Boston American* explained its fondness by saying, "Stein has the gift of making everyone who hears her feel that she is an old and dear friend. Her voice is friendly. Her eyes have a cheerful sparkle. And there is that smile. It cannot be resisted."[41]

One especially noteworthy moment during the tour came in Oakland, California. Stein wanted to see the house she'd lived in as a girl, but it was no longer standing. She then tried to visit the school she'd attended, but that building too had been destroyed. Finally, she asked about the synagogue where her family had worshiped, but again the structure was gone. Stein then coined what ultimately would rank as one of her most frequently quoted witticisms: "There is no there there." She originally used the phrase to lament that the buildings she'd grown up with had disappeared, but she later used it to describe any person or concept that lacks substance.[42]

Stein and Toklas also had, by the end of their six-month trip, made history. Never before had a same-sex couple been so uniformly embraced by the American press and public. Toklas accompanied Stein everywhere the author went—including to the White House—with no one questioning that she belonged at her partner's side, just as any wife would stand next to her famous husband. Newspapers and magazines often mentioned that the two women had lived together in Paris for thirty years, giving no sense that such an arrangement was anything other than entirely appropriate.[43]

INFLUENCING LITERARY GIANTS

Among the themes that emerged from the hundreds of flattering articles written during Stein's lecture tour was the impact her writing was having on American literature. Typical was a statement in the *Chicago Tribune* that read, "Gertrude Stein has influenced many of the most brilliant young writers of the generation."[44]

One of the first men to emulate her work was Sherwood Anderson. He traced Stein's impact on him back to his reading of *Three Lives* and *Tender Buttons,* saying the books had been his inspiration for writing his best-selling *Winesburg, Ohio.* "What she is up to in her word kitchen in Paris," Anderson wrote in a tribute to Stein, "is of more importance to writers of English than the work of many of our more easily understood and more widely accepted word artists."[45]

Ernest Hemingway was also eager to tell the world, despite the unflattering comments that Toklas had written about him in *Autobiography,* that Stein had been invaluable in his evolution as a novelist. Hemingway credited Stein with teaching him, in particular, how to use rhythm and repetition to their maximum effect. That instruction proved invaluable, he said, when he wrote *The Sun Also Rises* and *A Farewell to Arms,* which led to him receiving the Nobel Prize for Literature.[46]

A third author who lauded Stein as his writing mentor was F. Scott Fitzgerald. They'd met in 1925, Fitzgerald said, and she consistently encouraged him while also urging him to stretch himself in new ways. Fitzgerald took Stein's advice to heart and began working on *Tender Is the Night.* When the novel was published in 1934, he sent Stein a copy with the inscription "Is this the book you asked for?" She promptly replied that it was.[47]

Thornton Wilder was yet another literary giant who praised Stein for the help she gave him. Wilder was a young professor when she made her U.S. tour, and, after hearing her lecture, he introduced himself. Wilder told Stein at the time that he felt the two of them shared a sense of breaking away from nineteenth-century novelists and moving literature into the modern era. After Stein returned to France, she began corresponding with him, many of the letters containing detailed discussions about writing. Wilder later said that Stein "was *the* great influence on my life," crediting her with teaching him how "to write drily and objectively." The most significant work he thanked her for influencing was *Our Town,* the drama that earned him a Pulitzer Prize.[48]

ENJOYING THE GOOD LIFE

By the late 1930s, Stein and Toklas were spending much of their time at their country house in the south of France. Toklas typically rose at 6 a.m. to gather berries for breakfast and pick roses to decorate the house so everything was in order by the time Stein awoke at 10. The rest of each day was spent in the couple's garden where Toklas tended the vegetables while Stein wrote—and looked on approvingly.[49]

This idyllic life became somewhat less so when the rumblings of war began and then German forces occupied France in 1940. Friends who feared that the two Jewish women would be sent to a concentration camp encouraged them to cross the border into Switzerland. Stein and Toklas wouldn't budge, however, continuing to live quietly in their tiny French village throughout World War II.[50]

While the couple managed to survive the global conflict, they weren't able to escape health problems. Stein first noticed in late 1945 that she was feeling tired after even minimal activity. By the spring, her physician recommended surgery. She rejected the idea and was soon diagnosed as suffering from cancer. She died in July 1946, at the age of seventy-two.[51]

Major American newspapers gave the passing of the literary icon prominent coverage, many of them placing her obituary on page one. Every paper mentioned that Toklas had been at Stein's bedside when she took her final breath, but the publications varied widely in precisely how they identified the woman who'd shared the famous author's life for four decades. The *Los Angeles Times* opted for "friend and confidante," while the *Washington Post* went with "companion of many years" and the *San Francisco Chronicle* used the term "Girl Friday."[52]

A PARTNER BECOMING AN AUTHOR

Toklas's priority after Stein's death was making sure the reading public had access to her famous partner's numerous works that remained in manuscript form. It was no longer a Herculean task to find publishers for the now deceased writer's work, and so, Toklas succeeded in having numerous additional titles released.[53]

By the early 1950s, Toklas found herself in a new role vis-à-vis the literary world when a number of publishers suggested that she write a memoir, saying readers would be interested in learning more about the woman who'd lived in the shadow of her larger-than-life partner.[54]

For her approach, Toklas chose to write a book that contained some of her favorite recipes interspersed with anecdotes from the couple's outlaw marriage. When Toklas suggested such a book to an editor at Harper's publishing house, he immediately offered her a hefty advance.[55]

As the deadline for submitting the seventy thousand words grew near, however, Toklas found it difficult to put so many words to paper. She then asked friends to help her with the project by sending her their favorite recipes that she'd mix in with her own to meet the editor's length requirement. Ultimately, one of those borrowed recipes turned the final product into a storied publishing phenomenon.[56]

The contribution came from painter Brion Gysin, and Toklas accepted it without testing or reading the recipe that he accompanied with the warning, "Two pieces are quite sufficient." Most of the items called for—including sugar, butter, and cinnamon—were innocuous, but one ingredient was something few cooks found in their cupboards: *cannabis.* And so, the directions for what became known as "Alice B. Toklas brownies" were sent out into the hands of thousands of eager readers, many of them developing an interest in cooking for the first time.[57]

Reviews of *The Alice B. Toklas Cook Book,* published in 1954, were highly positive. The *New Yorker* praised it as "a book of character, fine food, and tasty human observation," and *Time* reported that "what gives the book its special charm is the stream of Alice's prattle." Among the anecdotes that made the book come alive was the author's recollection of the day a friend gave her a crate of six white pigeons. Toklas wrote that she knew she had to kill, pluck, and clean the half dozen birds before Gertrude Stein returned home, as her partner "didn't like to see work being done." Toklas went on to say that she didn't enjoy ending the lives of the birds, "though as I laid out the sweet young corpses, there was no denying one could become accustomed to murdering."[58]

Alice B. Toklas died in 1967 at the age of eighty-nine. America's leading newspapers took note of her passing, most of them running brief obituaries identifying her as Stein's "friend" or "companion." A few papers, however, opted to publish longer stories. The *Washington Post* included details about the cookbook she wrote as well as the special brownies that carried her name. Toklas was buried in Père Lachaise cemetery in Paris, next to her more famous partner.[59]

Chapter 8

Janet Flanner & Solita Solano

1919–1975

Pioneering a New Style of Journalism

...

From 1925 through 1975, Janet Flanner served as the Paris correspondent for the *New Yorker*. During her remarkable half century as the author of the "Letter from Paris" column, she played a leading role in developing the unique style and voice that came to define the widely respected magazine. Her journalistic prose was widely praised as crisp, intelligent, and sophisticated. Flanner also authored several widely praised books—the first of them winning a National Book Award.

Flanner wouldn't have succeeded without the help she received from her same-sex partner. It was Solita Solano who first suggested that she and Flanner leave the United States and move to Europe, mainly to jump-start the fledgling journalist's career. Solano also worked closely with Flanner both in crafting her early columns and in writing her books.

...

Solita Solano was born into a middle-class family in Troy, New York, in 1888. She was christened Sarah Wilkinson, but that name wasn't exotic enough for her, so she gave herself the new one while in her mid-teens.[1]

By that point, the adventurous girl also had eloped with a civil engineer, Oliver Filley, who was headed for a job in the Orient. The couple lived in China, Japan, and the Philippines for four years before Solano had the marriage annulled, accusing her husband of beating her.[2]

In 1910, Solano made her way back to the United States and embarked on a career in journalism. She entered the field as a rookie reporter for the *Boston Traveler*, and, after succeeding in that job, she was promoted first to feature writer and then to drama critic and editor. She gained a reputation for being frank and fearless, as well as highly competent both as a writer and an editor.[3]

The ambitious young woman next moved up to the *New York Tribune*, being hired in 1918 as the prestigious paper's drama editor. She had no problem holding her own in the largest journalism market in the country, bringing to her job an intensity that was equal to that of any man she came up against.[4]

Janet Flanner was born in Indianapolis in 1892. Her family was securely positioned in the middle class, with her father earning his living as a mortician and her mother devoting her energy to caring for her husband and their three daughters.[5]

By the age of eight, Janet had decided she wanted to pursue a career as a writer. She excelled in her composition and literature courses while attending high school, publishing a short story when she was fifteen.[6]

Flanner enrolled at the University of Chicago but soon rebelled at the regimen of academic life. "I became engaged in a struggle with the university and its regulations," she later wrote, "in which the university was the victor." She dropped out of college after two years.[7]

In 1917, Flanner landed a job with the *Indianapolis Star*. She was hired to review local art exhibits, but she soon began critiquing movies and local theater productions as well. The most frequently recurring theme in her reviews was that Indianapolis residents were woefully limited in their aesthetic sensibilities. In one piece, for example, she characterized the city's general population as being "more concerned with the price of beans than with art."[8]

Flanner enjoyed writing for the paper, but she felt stifled "by the manners and mores of Indianapolis." After working for the *Star* for a year, Flanner escaped from the Midwest by marrying Lane Rehm, a friend from her days at the University of Chicago. Flanner confided to friends that she married Rehm because he was an investment banker in New York City, the location she believed offered the best opportunities for an aspiring journalist.[9]

After their marriage in 1918, Rehm and Flanner, who kept her maiden name, moved to Greenwich Village. The two years Flanner lived in New York were a mixture of failures and successes. Both her marriage and her career fell into the negative column. As she later admitted, "I was not very good to my husband." Her only job, as a reporter for the *New York Sun,* ended after a week because her editor said her news stories were too opinionated. In the positive column, Flanner met many creative people who broadened her perspective on the world.[10]

CREATING AN OUTLAW MARRIAGE

The most significant of Flanner's new friends was Solita Solano. Flanner had recognized her sexual attraction to women soon after arriving in New York, and she soon fell in love with Solano. They met in early 1919 and immediately began spending as much time together as possible. Flanner wanted to move in with Solano, but the situation was complicated by two factors—she was still married, and she didn't want her family to know she was a lesbian.[11]

It was Solano who came up with a solution: the two women should leave the United States and live abroad. Solano insisted that Flanner's failure as a journalist was due to New York being saturated with talented reporters. Solano also argued that being several thousand miles away from the Flanner family would allow the two women to live together as a couple.[12]

In the summer of 1921, Solano put in place the kind of situation she'd been hoping to find, as *National Geographic* magazine offered to send her on a freelance assignment to Greece. Flanner expressed concern that she'd be a burden on Solano because she had no money to pay her share of the travel expenses, but Solano ignored her partner's protests and bought two tickets on a ship bound for Piraeus.[13]

Solano made the most of the next several months, writing stories about Greece and Turkey that the editor at *National Geographic* lauded as "brilliant." In particular, the editor praised the descriptive passages that Solano wove into her pieces. Solano and Flanner traveled to Italy before moving on to Austria and Germany, with Solano writing more articles for *Geographic*.[14]

MAKING A HOME IN PARIS

In the fall of 1922, the two women rented a room in a Paris hotel that ultimately became their home for the next seventeen years.

"The Hotel Napoleon Bonaparte was perfect for our purposes," Solano later wrote. "It cost a dollar a day and was near the Seine, the Louvre, and the auto buses." Although the couple had to walk up five flights of stairs to reach their room and had to share a bathroom with the other dozen residents in the hotel, those inconveniences were more than offset by the Bonaparte being in an area of the city where many other expatriate Americans lived, near the historic St. Germain-des-Prés church. "We were a literary lot," Flanner said. "Each of us aspired to become a famous writer as soon as possible."[15]

Because Flanner couldn't find a job for the couple's first few years in Paris, she had the time to develop friendships with the other young people who frequented neighborhood cafés. The most celebrated of those friends was Ernest Hemingway, who agreed to read and critique some of Flanner's writing. Many years later, she wrote what the famous novelist had said about a piece she'd written on bullfighting: "Listen, Jan, I just want you to know that if a journalistic prize is ever given for the worst sports writer of the western world, I'm going to see you get it, pal, for you deserve it. You're perfectly terrible."[16]

In light of negative comments such as Hemingway's combined with her own assessment of her articles of the period as "dreadful hack things," Flanner turned her attention toward writing a novel. She complained that she found this kind of writing difficult, but Solano insisted that her partner's work was excellent. "The first publisher that sees it will snap it up," Solano wrote Flanner's sister. "I know of no one who writes more lovely prose than Janet."[17]

BECOMING A MAGAZINE WRITER

In 1925, Flanner received a letter from a woman she'd known during her New York days. Jane Grant had been a reporter for the *New York Times* back then, but she'd since left the paper to help her husband, Harold Ross, start a new magazine. Flanner had kept in touch with Grant by sending her gossip-filled letters about life in France, and Grant was writing to ask Flanner to become the Paris correspondent for Ross's publication, the *New Yorker*.[18]

Flanner jumped at the offer, as writing the biweekly letter meant she'd finally have an ongoing job in journalism. She'd also be earning a steady income, which meant she'd no longer be a financial burden on Solano, who'd been paying both women's living expenses for four years by writing freelance pieces.[19]

In fact, Solano had wanted, for some time, to immerse herself in writing fiction but had felt compelled, because someone had to pay the bills, to continue accepting assignments to write news and travel stories for several American magazines and newspapers. Now she'd be able to concentrate on her fiction writing while Flanner became the breadwinner.[20]

Before the two women could move into their new roles, however, Flanner had to figure out how to produce the kind of pieces that Harold Ross had in mind. There were indications that satisfying the editor wouldn't be easy, as he'd already fired three Paris correspondents in the five months since he'd launched the magazine.[21]

Flanner knew, based on what Jane Grant told her, that Ross wanted the letters from France to consist mostly of "anecdotal and incidental stuff on places familiar to Americans," while at the same time communicating a high level of sophistication and urbanity. Flanner knew she could deliver on these counts, as she was comfortable writing about the art museums and operas that were part of her and Solano's life in Paris. Flanner also was confident she could infuse her letters with humor and satire, another of Ross's expectations, because her reviews in the *Indianapolis Star* had contained plenty of these elements.[22]

But other of Ross's requirements worried Flanner. First of all, he wanted the letters to contain not merely the correspondent's personal observations and opinions but also "facts, facts and more facts"—the author would have to be both a critic and a news reporter. In addition, Ross wanted the letters to contain descriptive passages so rich in detail that they'd bring vivid images instantly to the minds of *New Yorker* readers.[23]

Flanner had no objection to incorporating these elements into her writing, but she didn't know how to do it. Her reviews in the *Star* had consisted of criticism with only a minimal number of facts and virtually no description. So Flanner turned to the much more experienced Solano, who for fifteen years had been making her livelihood by writing a combination of news articles based on facts and travel pieces overflowing with description.[24]

WRITING AS A TEAM

Flanner and Solano's first piece appeared in the *New Yorker* in October 1925. Ross gave his thumbs-up to the letter's style and substance by printing it exactly as he'd received it and also by signing it "Genêt." The fact that he'd given Flanner a nom de plume meant that he'd accepted her into his stable of authors. Ross didn't print the real name of any of his regular writers, wanting readers to become accustomed to the entire *New Yorker* staff speaking in a single voice consistent with the combination of sophistication and irony that he wanted every piece to communicate.[25]

Ross never told Flanner exactly why he chose to identify her as Genêt. She speculated, however, that "to his eyes and ears, it seemed like a Frenchified form of Janet."[26]

In some early *New Yorker* pieces that Solano and Flanner wrote, the factual information came in the form of updates on Paris prices. "Bread has advanced to one franc eighty the kilo," one letter reported, while another told American readers that, now that spring had arrived, "violets are three francs the bunch on the boulevards." Another category of facts the women incorporated into their writing had to do with the price of artwork. "Art dealer Marcel Duchamp's sale of works by Francis Picabia is being widely discussed here," one letter reported. "He received about 89,000 francs for his entire collection of 80 Picabias, the famous 'Mind the Paint' bringing only 320 francs; a good hat costs more."[27]

The women also relied, from time to time, on public documents as their sources. One Paris letter reported, "The annual statement of the National Bureau of Tourism has just been made public. Some 220,000 Americans visited France within the last year, and left in their wake $226,160,000. The society optimistically computes that two travelers in every hundred were millionaires, and, even more optimistically, that twenty-eight in every hundred were teachers."[28]

With regard to descriptive passages, the couple crafted numerous statements about the latest trends in fashion. "Tailored suits are still chic," one letter read, "and evening frocks are carrying even more flowers, which are now pinned on the back, just above the last rib." They also described performances they attended. One letter about poet Maurice Rostand read, "When he recites his poetry, he slips out on the stage, almost surreptitiously, and stands quiet at one side before a grey velvet curtain, clasping the drapery with his wan, pale hands. It's quite something to look at as well as to hear, and one succumbs."[29]

In addition to helping Flanner develop the two new writing techniques she needed to master, Solano also assisted her partner in striking the appropriate tone. That is, because her pieces were in the form of letters, Ross wanted them to be written in a conversational style, as if the author were chatting casually with her readers. So Solano came up with a plan: after Solano and Flanner finished a draft of a letter, Solano read it out loud. The women then jointly revised the portions of the letter that sounded stilted or overly formal when they'd heard them spoken.[30]

Solano played a major role in helping to write the Paris column in 1925 and 1926 until Flanner became more confident with the new techniques her partner had taught her. When Flanner worked on her first profile for the magazine in January 1927, however, she again turned to Solano, with the two women conducting joint interviews with the subject, dancer Isadora Duncan. By the time Flanner took on her second profile nine months later, she interviewed designer Paul Poiret on her own, although Solano still helped her write the piece before they sent it off to New York.[31]

RISING IN THE WORLD OF JOURNALISM

By the late 1920s, Flanner and Solano were enjoying precisely the kind of life they'd envisioned when they'd moved to Paris. "There's a kind of gilt on the cage of life over here that is entrancing, delightful," Flanner said of living in

Europe. "There's no sense of captivity." Flanner and Lane Rehm officially divorced in 1926, and she and Solano expanded their living space in the Hotel Bonaparte to a suite of several rooms in 1928.[32]

On a professional basis, Solano published three novels by the end of the decade, although reviewers spoke harshly of them and none of the trio sold well. Flanner's income from writing the Paris letter and an occasional profile, however, was more than sufficient to pay the couple's routine expenses and to allow them to vacation in the south of France periodically.[33]

By the early 1930s, the *New Yorker* had become not only a financial success but also a highly regarded journalistic institution. Flanner had emerged as one of the magazine's most admired writers and was increasingly recognized as an arbiter of the finer things in life—from art, music, and theater to smart cafés and the latest trends in fashion. The epicenter of all these aspects of the cultured life, Flanner consistently wrote, was the city she now called home. "Paris is the capital of Europe," she said in one letter, "for a kind of obstinate civilization and a cerebral style."[34]

As time passed, the editors at the magazine sent Flanner to cover breaking news elsewhere in Europe. In 1936, she went to Berlin to report on the Olympic Games and to London to chronicle the historic abdication of Great Britain's Edward VIII.[35]

Flanner also became widely known as the profile writer who introduced American readers to such influential artists as Russian composer Igor Stravinsky and Spanish painter Pablo Picasso. Her other subjects included perfumer Francois Coty, legendary hostess Elsa Maxwell, and European royalty such as England's Queen Mary—Flanner reported that the British monarch had a passion, while inside Buckingham Palace, for the very un-royal habit of whistling.[36]

Flanner's most controversial profile was of Adolf Hitler. The 1936 piece illuminated the human side of the Nazi leader in great detail, including that he abstained from drinking alcohol, smoking cigarettes, and eating meat. This personal approach didn't sit well with a writer for *New Republic* magazine, who accused Flanner of being a Fascist because she included positive details about Hitler in her profile. Editors at *Time, Collier's,* and *McCall's* had a very different take on the piece, being so impressed by it that they asked Flanner to write similar articles for their magazines, although she turned down the offers.[37]

On a personal level, Solano and Flanner remained committed to each other, but they weren't monogamous. Flanner was the one who wanted their outlaw marriage to be an open one because, in the words of one biographer, she "had a roving eye." She particularly enjoyed spending time in Parisian bars and nightclubs where women dancing and being affectionate with each other was much more widely accepted than in New York—or Indianapolis.[38]

LIFE BECOMING MORE COMPLICATED

The coming of World War II forced Solano and Flanner to leave France in 1939 and relocate to the United States, where they chose to live separately. Flanner then worked out of the *New Yorker*'s Manhattan office, her most significant pieces telling about life in France under German occupation.[39]

In 1940, Flanner fell in love with an Italian-born woman who was ten years her junior. Natalia Danesi Murray was working in New York as a broadcaster for NBC when she and Flanner met and, within a matter of months, moved in together. Despite Flanner's new relationship, she continued to correspond with Solano, hiding the letters from Murray.[40]

Flanner soon left both women behind when she was named an official war correspondent for the *New Yorker*. Dressed in an American military uniform, she flew first to London and then traveled throughout Europe to provide eyewitness accounts of the fighting.[41]

Articles that Flanner wrote in the aftermath of the war contributed to her growing stature as a journalist of the first order. She covered the trial of Nazi war criminals in Nuremberg, Germany, and also wrote a blockbuster investigative series that exposed how the Nazis had stolen millions of dollars worth of artwork from the private collections of European Jews.[42]

Partly because of these high-profile pieces, she had earned a reputation, by the 1950s, as one of America's most respected reporters. A highly laudatory profile of Flanner in the *New York Times* stated, "Hers is exemplary journalism in every sense of the word."[43]

BECOMING A TEAM ONCE AGAIN

In 1963, Flanner faced a new professional challenge when an editor at Atheneum publishing house in New York asked her to put together a book largely consisting of the best of the magazine pieces she'd written over the previous four decades.[44]

Flanner initially rejected the offer, saying she didn't have time to take on such a labor-intensive project. When Solano heard about the book offer, however, she urged Flanner to reconsider.[45]

Solano then volunteered to read through all of Flanner's *New Yorker* pieces and select which ones should be preserved between hard covers. Solano had, by this point, returned to France and was working as a freelance editor. Flanner took Solano up on her offer.[46]

It's likely that Solano had ulterior motives, as she knew that Flanner's relationship with Natalia Danesi Murray was troubled. The problem was that Murray spent the bulk of her time in the United States to be near her grown son and his family. Flanner repeatedly complained that she wanted to spend more time with Murray, who responded that she had other priorities in her life.[47]

When Solano and Flanner began working together on the book, they typically met in the room in the Hotel Ritz in Paris where Flanner now lived. Solano would take the train into the city from the French village, an hour away, where she had a small house. Solano and Flanner's time together wasn't all work and no play, as they often had dinner together and whiled away the evening over wine and conversation. On many of these occasions, Solano stayed the night, with the two women resuming their physical relationship.[48]

Flanner's book, titled *Paris Journal,* was released in 1965 to rave reviews. The *Washington Post* gushed, "No better modern history of France has been written than this book. Miss Flanner is that paragon of foreign correspondents—the one with a first class brain, plus the best set of senses in the business," and the *New York Herald Tribune* weighed in by calling Flanner "the foremost expatriate writer in Paris."[49]

Flanner's acclaim rose to an even loftier level in 1966 when *Paris Journal* received the National Book Award in the category of arts and letters. Judges in the competition praised her writing as "enlightened and humane, her account of France recalling French political thinker and historian Alexis de Tocqueville's earlier study of our own country."[50]

After the flood of positive reviews and the prestigious award, executives at Atheneum asked Flanner to choose more examples of her magazine work to create a second collection. She signed the book contract only after the publisher agreed to hire Solano to read her articles and choose which ones would be included. So Solano thereby played the same role she had with the first book, except this time she didn't volunteer her time but was paid for it.[51]

When volume two of *Paris Journal* was released in 1971, that event spawned another flurry of admiring comments; *Saturday Review* said, "Janet Flanner's tapestry, her brilliantly colored and intricately patterned portrait of Paris enchants, educates and inspires." Similar praise followed the publication of a third volume of pieces, titled *Paris Was Yesterday,* which Solano again helped Flanner put together; the *Washington Post* wrote, "Flanner's letters combine social, political, literary, art and theatrical history that is laced with style, wit, humor, erudition and insight." And still more applause came in the wake of a fourth volume, titled *London Was Yesterday;* the *Chicago Tribune* lauded Flanner as "a master at picking out the details that indicate something broader about a subject."[52]

BEING SEPARATED BY DEATH

By the time that last collection of pieces had been published in early 1975, Solano's failing health reduced her role in the selection process because traveling by train had become too physically taxing for her. Flanner continued to write Solano, however, filling her letters with statements such as, "Rarely does a day go by that I don't think of you." Solano died in late 1975, at the age of eighty-six. A four-paragraph obituary in the *New York Times* stated, "For 20 years Miss Solano lived with Janet Flanner."[53]

Flanner's final "Letter from Paris" was published in the summer of 1975. The author then moved back to the United States and lived with Natalia Danesi Murray, who was now directing the New York office of an Italian publishing house.[54]

American news organizations told their readers about Flanner's death in 1978, of a heart attack at the age of eighty-six, not only through a plethora of lengthy obituaries but also with any number of tributes. *Newsweek* called her "the most lively and perceptive chronicler of France that the U.S. news media has ever known," and the *New York Times* wrote, "With a keen eye for the significant in politics, art, the theater and the changing conditions of life, Miss Flanner condensed her observations every two weeks into 2,500 words of chatty but polished prose."[55]

Despite having plenty of space to praise Janet Flanner's achievements, none of these titans of American journalism nor the others that reported her passing—including the *Boston Globe, Chicago Tribune, Los Angeles Times, Philadelphia Inquirer,* and *Washington Post*—so much as mentioned the name of the woman who'd contributed immeasurably to the celebrated journalist's life and work: Solita Solano.[56]

Chapter 9
Greta Garbo & Mercedes de Acosta
1931–1960

Making Hollywood the Celebrity Capital of the World

...

Greta Garbo was the epitome of the Hollywood movie star. The stunningly beautiful actress was so talented, so glamorous, and so captivating on screen that fans clamored to see her films and to devour every morsel of information about her personal life that the press could feed them. In short, Garbo is an apt representative of that charismatic group of men and women who transformed Hollywood into not only the movie capital of the world but also the home to the most talked-about celebrities on the planet.

Garbo was assisted in several key ways by her same-sex partner, Mercedes de Acosta. On a personal level, the highly cultured de Acosta taught the star how to speak, how to dress, and how to live in the style expected of cinematic royalty. On a professional level, de Acosta advised Garbo on which film roles to accept and which to reject, while also lending a creative hand in shaping how the characters she played ultimately came across on screen.

...

Mercedes Hernandez de Acosta was born into a wealthy and socially prominent New York City family in 1893. Her father, who was born in Cuba, earned
a high salary as a top executive for a steamship company, and her mother,
who was descended from Spanish nobility, devoted much of her time to the
Catholic church.[1]

Mercedes attended private schools on the East Coast and in France, showing a particular talent for writing. During her teenage years, she mixed with
the sons and daughters of the wealthiest members of New York society by attending cotillions and formal dinners.[2]

De Acosta recognized, by her early twenties, that she was attracted to
members of her own sex and then had a series of affairs. Among the beautiful young woman's early lovers were world-renowned dancer Isadora Duncan
and Broadway star Eva Le Gallienne.[3]

In 1920, de Acosta surprised her closest friends by marrying a wealthy
portrait painter named Abram Poole. She later wrote that she took that step to
please her mother, who'd repeatedly told her daughter, "I would die in peace
if I knew you were happily married."[4]

After the wedding, de Acosta continued to have affairs with various
women. When Poole learned about his wife's repeated infidelity, he divorced
her.[5]

The 1920s also was the period in de Acosta's life when she launched her
writing career. She initially dabbled with poetry, but she eventually settled on
becoming a playwright. During the decade, she had three of her plays staged,
two on Broadway and one in Paris.[6]

Consistently negative reviews—the *New York Tribune* said de Acosta's dialogue was "so flowery that it resembles a seed catalogue"—led to all three productions closing after only a handful of performances.[7]

By 1930, de Acosta was so frustrated by her experiences with the theater
that she shifted to creating movie scripts. She then persuaded officials at RKO
Studios to bring her to Hollywood to work as a screenwriter.[8]

Greta Garbo was born Greta Gustafsson in Stockholm, Sweden, in 1905. Her
father worked as a street cleaner, and her mother as a housekeeper. The family lived in a cold-water apartment in one of Stockholm's poorest neighborhoods.[9]

When Greta was fourteen, her father died and she dropped out of school
to help support her mother and siblings. Her first job was selling hats in a department store, and, within a few months, the pretty young girl was also appearing as an unpaid model in ads for the store.[10]

In 1922, Greta had the good fortune to sell a hat to a Swedish film director. Taking note of her "good looks and bouncy figure," he cast the seventeen-year-old in a minor role in one of his movies. She then quit her sales job and won a scholarship to study at Sweden's Royal Dramatic Theater Academy.[11]

Greta studied acting for less than a year before one of the country's top film directors came to the school in search of new talent and chose her to play a major role in one of his movies. The director found his young protégé's name too ordinary, however, and changed it to Greta Garbo.[12]

The actress's next break came in 1925 when Louis B. Mayer of Hollywood film studio Metro-Goldwyn-Mayer saw her on screen while he was traveling in Europe. The movie mogul was so dazzled by Garbo that he brought her to the United States and placed her under contract.[13]

COMING TO HOLLYWOOD

When Garbo arrived in Hollywood, the gaggle of reporters who interviewed her dutifully wrote down the first words of awkward English that came out of her mouth when asked about her plans: "I wait for what the studio decides for me to do." The newsmen also made critical comments about her appearance, pointing out that one of her nylon stockings had a run in it and that her shoes needed new heels.[14]

Mayer signed Garbo to a two-year contract at a weekly salary of $400. Various studio employees were then summoned to work their magic. A fitness expert helped her shed twenty pounds, a beautician straightened her frizzy hair, and a secretary took her to a dentist to have her teeth straightened. No one was assigned to help Garbo with her English, seeing as how the era's silent pictures didn't require her to speak.[15]

Garbo's first role was in *The Torrent,* a melodrama about a Spanish peasant who sleeps her way to opera stardom. With a simple plot and a translator to help her understand the director, Garbo did well. When the film was released, the trade paper *Variety* crowned the new actress "the find of the year."[16]

The young star, however, was miserable. Shortly after arriving in Hollywood, she wrote a friend in Stockholm that she regretted having made the move. She complained, in particular, about being lonely. "Oh, my enchanting little Sweden," she wrote longingly, "how happy I shall be to get home to you again!"[17]

In 1927, Garbo starred in two more films and hired a financial adviser. She soon had a new contract for $3,000 a week and was investing her earnings in real estate.[18]

HATING HOLLYWOOD

Despite Garbo's continuing professional success, she still wasn't happy. One of her new complaints, by 1930, was that every character she played was shallow and predictable. "Always the vamp I am—always the woman with no heart," she told a friend.[19]

Another annoyance was the studio's insistence that Garbo do more than act. When MGM proposed, for example, that she endorse Palmolive soap and allow her face to appear on the product's wrapper, she flatly refused, asking, "Are not the good movies be enough?"[20]

Studio officials, for their part, thought Garbo's insistence on privacy was extreme, as she wouldn't talk to reporters, wouldn't sign autographs, and wouldn't attend any public events—not even the premieres of her own films.[21]

Biographers who've studied Garbo's career have made the point that she became the first major movie star who vehemently avoided publicity. They've also observed that shunning the spotlight ultimately added both to her celebrity status and to the mystique that became part of her public persona. "The press coverage of Garbo became obsessive," one scholar has written, "and so did public curiosity."[22]

CREATING AN OUTLAW MARRIAGE

In the summer of 1931, Garbo crossed paths with the woman who became the love of her life and also helped enormously in her evolution into a Hollywood icon.[23]

The actress met Mercedes de Acosta at the home of a mutual friend. Garbo was instantly smitten, and she arranged to spend time alone with de Acosta two days later. On that occasion, they talked at length and danced together to the song "Daisy, You're Driving Me Crazy."[24]

For their third meeting, which came just a few days after the second, Garbo invited the screenwriter to her home. Years later, de Acosta quoted Garbo as saying at the time, "I never ask anyone to my home, but today, as a great exception, I am inviting you."[25]

After the women talked for several hours, they made their way to a nearby beach where they made love. "As the sun rose," de Acosta later wrote, "we walked and picked rambler roses as we went along." Garbo recalled that momentous evening, many years later, by identifying precisely what had attracted her to the woman who then became the central figure in her life. "Mercedes possessed vivacity, charm and a great knowledge of love," the actress said. "She excited me in everything she did."[26]

While these initial meetings were unfolding, Garbo went to the studio each day to film her next movie, *Susan Lenox*. As soon as the shooting ended, she asked her new partner to spend six uninterrupted weeks with her on Silver Lake in the Sierra Nevada Mountains, where the two women had a small island entirely to themselves.[27]

In her memoir, de Acosta described the vacation as perfect in every way. "In all this time, there was not a second of disharmony between Greta and me," she wrote. "We had brilliant sunshine every day." The women spent their nights sleeping in a small cottage and their days canoeing, swimming in the nude, and taking photos of each other—including Garbo posing with her breasts bared.[28]

After that trip, Garbo moved into a house half a block from de Acosta's, and the couple began alternating which residence they spent the night sleeping in. They started each day with a ten-mile hike through the Hollywood Hills, and during other leisure hours they played tennis and went horseback riding. "Sometimes we also took picnic lunches," de Acosta later wrote, "and spent the whole day on the beach far up toward Malibu."[29]

ACQUIRING A SOCIAL COACH

Spending so much time with de Acosta did more for Garbo than give her someone to love. The daughter of dirt-poor Swedish laborers learned a great deal from a woman whose family had, when de Acosta was a girl, routinely socialized with such bluebloods as the Astors and the Vanderbilts. As one Garbo biographer put it, "Greta recognized immediately that her new lover was the perfect social coach for a newly rich Hollywood star. Mercedes was a walking workshop in good manners, upper-class proprieties, and a knowing style."[30]

First on the list of changes was how the star spoke. Because de Acosta had been educated in elite private schools, she spoke impeccable English. And so, now that she was with Garbo every day, the star lifted herself to a new level of diction. Director George Cukor later credited the highly cultured Latina with teaching Garbo what he called "the beautiful English" she was speaking by the mid-1930s.[31]

Next on the list of changes was how the star dressed. The Swedish beauty had previously told a reporter, "I care nothing about clothes," but her new partner said this attitude worked against her success. De Acosta coached Garbo to create a signature look by becoming one of the earliest Hollywood actresses to wear trousers in public. The impact of de Acosta's fashion advice was visible in the first film Garbo made after the women began their outlaw marriage. Among the outfits the star wore in *Mata Hari* was a backless lamé gown with metallic leggings—an outfit that de Acosta had designed.[32]

Yet another area of the star's personal style that her partner shaped was the kind of house she lived in. By the time the women met, MGM was paying Garbo well, and therefore she could afford to live in luxury. And yet, her house was so dark and so sparsely furnished that de Acosta described it as "gloomy and unlived in." And so, Garbo's style-conscious partner persuaded the actress to move to a house that was bright and had a lush garden and terrace—perfect for the couple to sunbathe in the nude.[33]

Once Garbo had relocated to the home that was more appropriate to her stature as a major movie star, de Acosta set about decorating it. The actress left all the details in her partner's hands, not seeing any of de Acosta's choices until they were in place. When that moment came, Garbo approved of every change her lover had made, which included having the rooms painted in tasteful, understated colors such as pale rose and light gray.[34]

CHOOSING FILMS OF SUBSTANCE

When the women became a couple, Garbo was so disenchanted with Hollywood that she was seriously considering the possibility of shifting to a stage career in Sweden.[35]

De Acosta opposed the idea, insisting that her partner's unhappiness wasn't with the movie business but with the roles she'd been forced to play. So when Garbo's contract expired in 1932, de Acosta had her sign a new one that gave her the right to reject parts she didn't like. De Acosta also persuaded Garbo to demand that she be paid $250,000 per film.[36]

The first movie MGM offered the star under her new contract was *Grand Hotel*. It was a risky project because the film broke from the standard formula of being built around a single story line. Instead, it wove together several independent plots, each involving a guest living at the storied Berlin residence. Garbo's proposed role would be dicey, too, as she would play—at the youthful age of twenty-six—a Russian ballerina at the end of her career.[37]

When Garbo read the script for the first time, she didn't like it. But when her partner read it, she was ecstatic. The ballerina was a great role, de Acosta insisted, because she wasn't a temptress, the character type Garbo previously had been pigeonholed into. After pressuring from her partner, the actress agreed to appear in the movie.[38]

Grand Hotel was a triumph. It was enormously successful both financially and critically, with reviewers raving, in particular, about how poignantly Garbo had delivered the line that ultimately became the most famous one she'd ever speak: "I want to be alone." There's no question that her performance was the strongest one in the film and that it played a major part in the movie winning the Academy Award for best picture of the year.[39]

Garbo's strong-willed partner was an even more significant force in the next film the actress starred in, as she was the person who proposed to the studio that it make a historical drama based on the life of a European queen from the seventeenth century. The film would be ideal for Garbo, de

Acosta argued, because of two similarities between the actress and Queen Christina—they both were Swedish and they both had independent natures. She also pointed out that the film would do well in the European market because of the national heritage that the star and the leading character shared.[40]

De Acosta's influence on *Queen Christina* didn't end with MGM agreeing to make the movie, as she gave the director several lines of dialogue she said should be spoken by certain characters. Among her suggestions that made it onto celluloid was having the queen's closest adviser beg her to produce an heir by saying, "You can't die an old maid," and then having Garbo respond, "I have no intention of doing that. I shall die a *bachelor*."[41]

Although it's not clear exactly which pieces of dialogue in Garbo's later films came from her partner's creative mind, there's no question that there were many. During the 1930s, de Acosta worked under contract as a screenwriter for MGM, which meant she helped craft any number of the lines that came out of Garbo's perfectly shaped mouth.[42]

REDEFINING THE RELATIONSHIP

Despite the enormous influence de Acosta had on Garbo, the vast majority of movie fans didn't know that the screenwriter even existed, while most Hollywood insiders thought the two women were merely friends. When Garbo was asked about her romantic life during the rare interview she granted, she responded in a firm voice, "I cannot say. That is a personal thing. We like to keep some things to ourselves."[43]

In fact, though, the women were spending every night together. When Garbo traveled, de Acosta generally came along, with their destinations including New York City and Sweden in 1932, Yosemite National Park in 1933, and Sweden again in 1935. They went on so many trips together, in fact, that the *Los Angeles Times* ran a story—on page one—describing de Acosta as the star's "close friend" and "traveling companion."[44]

By the middle of the decade, Garbo's insistence on keeping her same-sex love a secret led to friction between the women. On one occasion when the star was planning a trip and said she wanted to travel alone this time, de Acosta accused her of acting out of fear that a reporter might accuse the women, if they were seen together too often, of being lovers. In an unguarded moment, Garbo impulsively snapped back, "You're right!"[45]

After that unpleasant exchange, Garbo refused to see de Acosta for several days. Only when the actress was ready did she resume their intimate relationship. Several similar periods of separation followed later in the decade.[46]

Garbo's concern about rumors regarding her sexual orientation was fueled by the fact that de Acosta was one of the country's few high-profile women who refused to hide her lesbianism. During the mid-1920s, she and former lover Eva Le Gallienne had been openly affectionate with each other while in public. In the words of one biographer, "Mercedes was a woman who stood up courageously for her beliefs and values."[47]

SUCCEEDING AS A STAR

Beginning with Garbo's first American film in 1926 and continuing through 1939, movie reviewers consistently praised her acting. The *New York Times* said she "merits nothing but the highest praise," the *Los Angeles Times* pronounced her screen performances "triumphant—no one is able to take first honors from this star," and the *New York Herald Tribune* gushed, "Never before has a woman so alluring, with a seductive grace that is far more potent than mere beauty, appeared on the screen."[48]

Garbo's fellow filmmakers also lauded her acting. She was nominated for Academy Awards on four occasions. In 1930, she received two nods, one for *Romance* and the other for *Anna Christie;* observers believe her double nomination worked against her by splitting her votes. In 1936, Garbo was nominated for *Camille* and in 1939 for *Ninotchka,* although she failed to take home the Oscar each time.[49]

Although Garbo and de Acosta's outlaw marriage continued throughout these years, the Latina beauty had a second lover for several years. De Acosta met the German-born actress Marlene Dietrich in 1932, and their love affair began almost immediately. The women took care to keep their frequent liaisons out of the public eye, as de Acosta didn't want to jeopardize her relationship with Garbo. After several years passed, Dietrich found de Acosta's intensity to be exhausting and allowed the affair to fade. By 1938, Garbo was again the only woman in de Acosta's life.[50]

A FILM CAREER COMING TO AN END

In 1941, Garbo agreed to star in the film *Two-Faced Woman.* She had accepted the role during one of the interludes when she'd distanced herself from de Acosta. Once the women were communicating again, it was too late for the star to back out of the picture, despite the improbable plot: Garbo played a priggish ski instructor who poses as her sexy twin sister so she can seduce and win back her errant husband.[51]

The film suffered from a pair of serious problems. First was the drubbing by reviewers, with the *Los Angeles Times* calling the movie "pallid" and the *Washington Post* dismissing it as "trivial." Second was World War II, which destroyed the European market for American films—a huge segment of the audience that had supported the Swedish beauty's previous work.[52]

Garbo wasn't willing to expend the energy that would have been required to counteract these negative forces. Nor was she up to the challenges that ageism posed for a thirty-six-year-old actress trying to maintain a movie career. So she made the statement that Mercedes de Acosta had talked her out of making a decade earlier, "I will never act in another film."[53]

By this point, de Acosta was also frustrated with the movie industry, as her screenwriting career hadn't gone well. The nadir came when MGM production chief Irving Thalberg told her to write a subplot for a historical drama the studio was making about Rasputin. Specifically, Thalberg wanted to depict the Russian religious mystic as having seduced Princess Irene Yusupov. De Acosta refused to write the scenes, saying they would distort history because Rasputin and the princess had never even met. Thalberg then fired her.[54]

PUTTING HOLLYWOOD BEHIND THEM

In 1942, de Acosta and Garbo decided to relocate to New York City. The writer took a job as associate editor for a small magazine titled *Tomorrow,* a position that allowed her to write several articles related to her Spanish heritage. Garbo ceased working and moved into a large apartment in the Hotel Ritz Tower. De Acosta then rented—because the actress insisted they maintain separate residences—a much smaller unit in the same building.[55]

By the time they went east, Garbo was unhappy with de Acosta not only for being too open about her sexuality but also for telling other people details about the actress's private life. "She's done me such harm, such mischief," Garbo confided to a friend. "You can't shut her up." For a woman who prized her privacy to the degree that Garbo did, de Acosta's willingness to share personal information was proving to be a fatal flaw.[56]

Garbo's displeasure with her partner resulted in several more periods of separation during the 1940s. The women sometimes went for several weeks without having contact with each other except through letters that de Acosta sent.[57]

Despite the disagreements, Garbo and de Acosta kept getting back together. One particularly pleasant reunion came in 1947 when they took a romantic trip to Paris. They stayed in a hotel near the Eiffel Tower, went for long walks in the Tuileries Gardens, and enjoyed leisurely dinners in several small cafés where Garbo wasn't recognized.[58]

Garbo was, by this point, involved in a second relationship that ultimately became the longest one she ever had with a man. She met George Schlee in 1945 through his wife, the famous designer Valentina. The three of them initially socialized together, but soon Garbo and the businessman became a twosome. For almost two decades, they spent their summers together at Schlee's villa on the French Riviera. The unconventional relationship, which apparently didn't include a sexual dimension, continued until Schlee died in 1964.[59]

DRIFTING APART

By the 1950s, the life circumstances for Greta Garbo and Mercedes de Acosta differed dramatically. Simply put, the actress was doing very well, but her partner was doing very poorly.

Garbo was a wealthy woman because of the real estate investments she'd made during her Hollywood years. In 1953, she purchased a luxury apartment on Manhattan's fashionable Upper East Side and decorated it with museum-quality antiques. A year later, members of the Motion Picture Academy honored the star with a special Oscar to recognize "her unforgettable screen performances," even though Garbo refused to attend the awards ceremony.[60]

De Acosta, by contrast, struggled financially because she was no longer able to work due to recurring problems with her vision. Those difficulties began when she accidentally poured cleaning fluid, thinking it was eyewash, into her right eye. She was living in a tiny rental apartment some twenty blocks from Garbo's lavish one.[61]

The women's relationship careened from highs to lows, depending on what the famous partner wanted. In 1952, Garbo suggested that she and de Acosta should, after two decades of maintaining separate residences, set up housekeeping together. The actress never acted on that offer, however, and two years later she told a friend that she and de Acosta had "drifted apart" because her partner "needs to possess and envelop me, with marriage or the equivalent." It was also in 1954 that Garbo told de Acosta that she was cutting off all contact between the two of them—including letters. But then, in 1958, Garbo tearfully pleaded with de Acosta to resume the intimacy of their early years, saying, "I have no one else to look after me."[62]

REVEALING TOO MUCH

Desperate for money, de Acosta secured a contract to publish her autobiography, which she titled *Here Lies the Heart*. When the book was released in 1960, the reviews were excellent, with the *New York Times* calling it a "readable memoir of a quite extraordinary personality."[63]

Garbo, however, was livid. For thirty years, the actress had done everything in her power to keep her personal life out of the public eye, and now de Acosta had, in her book, published details about their holiday on Silver Lake in 1931. Indeed, de Acosta had even reproduced one of the topless photos of the actress that de Acosta had taken. And although the book made no specific statement about Garbo's sexual orientation, there were plenty of implications.[64]

Shortly after the memoir was published, the author crossed paths with Garbo while they both were shopping at a health food store. When their eyes met, the actress said nothing, causing de Acosta to ask, "Aren't we on speaking terms today?" Garbo turned and left the store, without uttering a word. The next January, de Acosta phoned Garbo to wish her a happy new year, but the actress hung up. That was the last communication the women ever had.[65]

Medical problems, including brain surgery, continued to plague de Acosta, although royalties from her memoir lessened her financial difficulties somewhat. "As we grow older, life becomes increasingly sad and difficult," she wrote a friend in 1964. "I never realized this when I was young, but now I do."[66]

Mercedes de Acosta died in 1968, at the age of seventy-five. Her *New York Times* obituary included the terse statement, "She was a close friend of Greta Garbo," but included no details about their life together or de Acosta's contributions to the actress's success.[67]

SPENDING THE FINAL YEARS VERY MUCH ALONE

Greta Garbo lived her final two decades largely in seclusion. She stayed inside her apartment most of the time, with her only recurring guest being the niece who ultimately inherited her estate.[68]

Garbo remained in good health for many years, dying in 1990 at the age of eighty-four. Her *New York Times* obituary, which appeared on the front page, stated that the paper was honoring her request for privacy by not reporting the cause of her death. None of the obituaries or numerous tributes that appeared in the nation's major publications made any mention of Mercedes de Acosta.[69]

Chapter 10

Aaron Copland & Victor Kraft

1932–1976

Inventing a Distinctly American Style of Music

...

Aaron Copland is widely acknowledged to be one of the most celebrated composers in this country's musical history. The winner of a Pulitzer Prize, an Academy Award, and a Presidential Medal of Freedom, Copland is credited with inventing a uniquely American style of music—simple yet memorable and inspirational—through such enduring works as *Fanfare for the Common Man* and *Appalachian Spring*. When he died in 1990, *USA Today* wrote:

> Aaron Copland gave American music its identity. While previous U.S. composers sounded like their European elders, Copland broke free and created a sound of his own that suggested a land of endless expanse and limitless possibilities.[1]

Music critics and historians who have looked closely at Copland's career, however, have pointed out that his initial works were unremarkable and forgettable . . . until he met a free-spirited young violinist named Victor Kraft.

Aaron Copland was born in Brooklyn, New York, in 1900. His parents had immigrated from Russia in the 1870s to take advantage of the opportunities available in the United States. Aaron's father operated a neighborhood variety store, and his mother kept the books for the business while raising Aaron and his four siblings.[2]

The boy began taking piano lessons at the age of seven and started writing his own music a year after that. During his teens, he advanced to private instruction in composing, and, when he was twenty-one, he moved to Paris and studied under the widely respected teacher Nadia Boulanger.[3]

Unlike many expatriate Americans living in the French capital, Copland didn't choose a bohemian lifestyle. One biographer described him, during those days, as being "reserved" and "a model of propriety." Copland recognized his attraction to men, but he didn't become sexually involved with anyone while living abroad.[4]

After studying in Paris for three years, Copland returned to New York City and began, in earnest, to compose music.

Victor Kraft was born Victor Hugo Etler in rural New York state in 1915. The son of Russian immigrants, Victor attended public schools in New York City.[5]

When he was an adolescent, the boy was identified as a violin prodigy. He gave solo concerts in various venues, and, at the age of ten, he was identified in a *New York Times* article as one of the city's most gifted young musicians. He was awarded a scholarship that allowed him to study at the prestigious Juilliard School in Manhattan.[6]

By the age of sixteen, Victor had graduated from high school and had set his sights on becoming a professional violinist. He'd also, by this point, adopted his mother's maiden name, Kraftsov, and shortened it to Kraft.[7]

CREATING MEDIOCRE MUSIC

Aaron Copland's career received a significant boost in 1924. Nadia Boulanger believed so strongly in her former student's potential that she persuaded the conductors of the symphony orchestras both in Boston and in New York to perform Copland's creations.[8]

The concert-going public, however, didn't embrace his work. "Audience reaction to Copland's early music," according to one biographer, "ranged from courteous applause to jeering sneers to catcalls and hisses." Critics were equally harsh, with the *New York Herald Tribune* condemning the composer for being "unimaginative."[9]

These negative reactions continued into the early 1930s. The *New York Times* dismissed the composer's music as "derivative," and *Modern Music* magazine denigrated his work by calling it "ineffective and dull."[10]

STRUGGLING FOR A ROMANTIC LIFE

Copland was also failing to succeed in his personal life. Part of the difficulty was that the only men he found appealing were significantly younger than he was. In the words of one of the composer's biographers, "Most of his lovers were in their late teens or early twenties when he took up with them."[11]

Adding to his difficulties was that the fledgling composer wasn't physically attractive. One biographer described Copland as "a Jewish Ichabod Crane—tall, gangly, careless about his clothes, with a face dominated by a large, curved beak, protruding teeth, and a receding chin." He stood six feet tall and weighed 150 pounds. "When he was a young man," another biographer wrote, "his spectacles, dark suits, and thinning brown hair made him look older than his years."[12]

Copland's first love was Israel Citkowitz, who was sixteen when he and the twenty-six-year-old composer met in 1926. Citkowitz was trying to succeed as a musician, and Copland offered the handsome lad professional advice. Knowing how much Nadia Boulanger had helped him, Copland advised Citkowitz to study with his former teacher, which the boy did. When the older man expressed his love for the younger one, however, Citkowitz made it clear that he had no romantic feelings for Copland.[13]

Next came Paul Bowles, who met Copland in 1929—Bowles was nineteen, Copland was twenty-nine. The composer was immediately infatuated with the youthful musician, who was described as "exceedingly elegant and well-groomed." Copland initially gave the youth daily lessons himself and later persuaded Boulanger to accept him as a student. As had been the case with Citkowitz, though, Bowles didn't have romantic feelings for his mentor. By 1931, Copland had given up any hope of Bowles becoming his lover.[14]

CREATING AN OUTLAW MARRIAGE

In the fall of 1932, Copland went on a trip that changed both his music and his life. The journey came in response to an invitation from Carlos Chávez, a Mexican composer he'd met a few years earlier.[15]

Victor Kraft entered Copland's life in the summer of 1932, after the composer had accepted Chávez's invitation but before he left New York. Once he met Kraft, Copland alerted his Mexican host that he'd be traveling with a guest. "I am bringing with me a young violinist who is a pupil," Copland wrote. "I'm sure you will like him."[16]

Kraft fit the profile of the kind of youth who appealed to Copland—the composer was thirty-two, the violinist was seventeen. One biographer described Kraft as "strikingly handsome, with wavy brown hair, piercing blue-gray eyes, a statuesque physique, and a deep, mellifluous voice." At five feet eleven inches tall and weighing 165 pounds, Kraft was about the same height as Copland but had a much more muscular body.[17]

The big difference between Kraft and the young men who previously had caught Copland's eye was that this one returned the composer's affections. Mutual friends observed that one trait, in particular, that the two lovers shared was a complete lack of guile.[18]

When he'd accepted Chávez's invitation, Copland had made it clear that he planned to work the entire two months he'd be in Mexico City. After he and Kraft arrived, however, the younger man persuaded the older one to take a break from his composing and have a real holiday—the first one of his adult life.[19]

At Kraft's suggestion, the two men spent many of their daytime hours on the beach near the capital city, sunning themselves and frolicking in the water. The playful, fun-loving teenager also enjoyed being photographed, and the smitten older man was more than willing to stand behind the camera as his winsome companion positioned himself in various nude poses.[20]

They also took day trips to Cuernavaca and Xochimilco. Whether whiling away the day in the sun or visiting a small town, they always returned to Mexico City in time for an evening of drinking and dancing in various clubs, often not getting home until 5 in the morning. Between their various activities, the two men found plenty of time for sex, either in the bed at the apartment where they were staying or on the beach.[21]

The only unpleasant moments during the trip came when Copland performed his work during a concert that Chávez had arranged. The Mexican audience didn't like the music any better than American ones had. "Some of the listeners began to hiss with characteristic Latin vigor," Copland later wrote.[22]

Other than during the concert, the composer's time in Mexico was the most enjoyable of his life. Indeed, the trip was so pleasurable that Kraft repeatedly talked Copland into extending it until a full five months had passed, including a visit to Acapulco so they could swim in the Pacific Ocean.[23]

FINDING INSPIRATION BY HAVING FUN

Copland's various biographers agree that the 1932 holiday with Kraft was the turning point in the composer's career. Once he was back in New York, he returned to his strict regimen of writing every day, but now his music reflected the simple, uncomplicated style of living that Kraft had exposed him to during their time in Mexico.[24]

The first tangible product of the change came with *El Salón México,* an orchestral piece by Copland that was inspired by a colorful nightspot of the same name where he and Kraft had spent many carefree hours. "My thoughts kept returning to that dance hall," Copland later wrote. "It wasn't so much the music or the dancers that attracted me as the spirit of the place. Being there had given me a live contact with the Mexican 'people'—that electric sense one gets sometimes in far-off places, of suddenly knowing the essence of a people—their humanity, their shyness, their dignity and unique charm."[25]

Copland acknowledged that Kraft had led him into this new phase of his composing career by dedicating *El Salón México* to his young lover. Various associates and friends of Copland also spoke highly of Kraft and his influence on the music his partner began creating. Verna Fine, the wife of composer Irving Fine, said, "Victor was charming and handsome and helpful," and Rosamond Bernier, a friend of Copland's from his days in Paris, added, "I was very fond of Victor Kraft. He was intuitive and affectionate, helping Aaron get in touch with the joys of living a simple life."[26]

The benefits of Copland writing accessible works came through loud and clear in reviews of *El Salón México.* It was the first piece he'd written that received universal praise. The *Washington Post* called it "a treat" to listen to, the *New York Times* labeled it "a fine piece of music," and the *Los Angeles Times* wrote, "Copland has created a clever work easily understood and enjoyed."[27]

TAKING THE MUSIC IN A NEW DIRECTION

Encouraged by the reviews, Copland stopped writing complex works and concentrated, instead, on creating simple music that appealed to a general audience.

Among his major projects during the next several years were an opera titled *The Second Hurricane* and a ballet titled *Billy the Kid.* Critics had nothing but positive comments for both works. *Time* magazine wrote, for example, "Copland's music for the ballet 'Billy the Kid,' much of it based on cowboy songs, is close-knit and incisive, wasting not a note."[28]

It was also during the second half of the 1930s that the composer was invited to write a musical score for a major Hollywood motion picture. That project was the film version of John Steinbeck's classic novel *Of Mice and Men.* Copland won accolades for this new area of creative effort, with his score being nominated for an Academy Award.[29]

Copland's friends and family members initially didn't take his relationship with Victor Kraft seriously, seeing the fifteen-year age difference as too dramatic for the men to overcome. The skepticism faded, however, when

Kraft became a central figure in Copland's personal and professional life. They lived together in a small loft apartment in Manhattan, frequently asking other composers and artists to join them for informal get-togethers. "Victor shopped and cooked for these gatherings," Copland later recalled. "And he also was a very charming host. He made everyone feel welcome and perfectly at ease. He was much better at that than I was."[30]

Another role Kraft played in Copland's life was making sure the composer took periodic breaks from his writing. Copland often became obsessed with his work, which meant he was in danger of losing touch with the light-hearted and easy-going aspects of life that were now essential parts of his creative process. At Kraft's suggestion, though, from time to time he became refreshed by leaving Manhattan to spend a few weeks in other locations, such as the cabin on Lake Bemidji in northern Minnesota where the men vacationed in 1936.[31]

Kraft made a dramatic change in his professional life during this period by giving up the violin and pursuing work as a news photographer. His decision wasn't driven by a lack of talent but by a lack of confidence in himself. Copland supported the career change by buying Kraft a high-quality camera and putting him in touch with several friends who were photographers. These men served as guides for Kraft as he entered his new vocation, helping him master the techniques of the craft and then secure freelance assignments.[32]

ACHIEVING GREATNESS

Copland experienced a string of major successes beginning in 1942 when the conductor of the Cincinnati Symphony Orchestra asked him to write a short piece for brass and percussion. The conductor's specific request was that the work be so "stirring and significant" that it would boost the country's sagging morale brought on by the hardships of World War II.[33]

Copland then created *Fanfare for the Common Man,* which premiered in March 1943, and today ranks as the renowned composer's most famous work. "It is intended to bring a lump to the throat," the *New Yorker* magazine gushed, "and it does exactly that, even on the thirtieth hearing." Other observers instantly applauded the piece as well, with the *New York Times* calling it "impressive" and the *Washington Post* crowning it "outstanding."[34]

For the six decades that have passed since Copland created it, this two-minute work has enjoyed an unparalleled degree of popularity as what experts have labeled "America's anthem." In the 1970s, the Rolling Stones rock group chose *Fanfare for the Common Man* as its opening theme, and in the 1990s the piece was used as background music in recruitment ads for the U.S. Navy and was featured prominently in the Oscar-winning film *Saving Private Ryan.* More recently, it was played as the wake-up music for the crew of the space shuttle crew orbiting the Earth in 2008 and was Barack Obama's choice to open his inaugural celebration at the Lincoln Memorial in 2009.[35]

CONTINUING THE OUTLAW MARRIAGE

Victor Kraft's role in Aaron Copland's life proceeded in the 1940s much as it had during the previous decade. That is, the two men continued to share their apartment in Manhattan, with Kraft earning his livelihood as a photographer while making sure his partner's life wasn't all work and no play. The younger man also frequently talked the older one into campy activities such as standing hip to hip with several friends and kicking their legs high into the air, in unison, to create an all-male chorus line à la the Rockettes at Radio City Music Hall.[36]

Kraft continued to cajole Copland into taking breaks from his work by going on vacation, with the younger man doing everything he could to extend the trips for as long as possible. One such holiday took them back to Mexico where they spent several weeks in a remote village. "We live on the top of a hill opposite a 17th century church," Copland wrote a friend. "It's all incredibly quiet and picturesque." Another lengthy trip took them first to Cuba and then on to several South American countries.[37]

Copland also decided, during this period, that he could benefit from having a second home away from the hustle and bustle of Manhattan to work on his music. Kraft then took on the task of finding such a place, ultimately choosing a small cottage in rural New Jersey that had only enough room for the two men—no visitors allowed. "When we went there, I told very few people where I was going," Copland later recalled, "with the idea of having some uninterrupted composing time."[38]

RISING TO ICONIC STATURE

By the end of the couple's first stay at the cottage in 1944, Copland had written *Appalachian Spring,* a ballet that includes country fiddlers and an elaborate finale based on a Shaker hymn titled "Simple Gifts." Martha Graham was the principal dancer when her company performed the work in the spring of 1945, receiving rave reviews. The *New York Herald Tribune* wrote, "Mr. Copland's score is a marvel of lyricism, of freshness and strength."[39]

That summer, Copland was propelled to a new stature among the country's composers when *Appalachian Spring* was awarded the Pulitzer Prize for music.[40]

It was also during the 1940s that Copland made his most noteworthy contributions to motion pictures. His musical score for the film adaptation of Thornton Wilder's play *Our Town* was nominated for an Academy Award in

1940, as was his score for the film *The North Star* three years later. His biggest triumph came in 1949 when his work on the film *The Heiress,* the film adaptation of Henry James's novel *Washington Square,* garnered him the Academy Award for the year's best musical score.[41]

Victor Kraft accompanied his partner to California early in the decade when he traveled there, often for months at a time, to work on the various films. This situation changed in 1945, however, when Kraft ended his stint as a freelancer and accepted a position as a full-time photographer for *Harper's Bazaar* magazine, which was based in New York.[42]

SHIFTING TO A NEW KIND OF RELATIONSHIP

Copland and Kraft's outlaw marriage changed drastically in the 1950s. Primary among the forces that brought about the shift was that Copland continued to be attracted to very young men, and Kraft—having entered his early thirties—was too old to fit the profile.[43]

Although Copland was in his fifties, his fame meant that he had no problem finding lovers who were twenty or thirty years his junior. Among those men were Erik Johns, a professional dancer, and John Brodbin Kennedy, an aspiring composer. Copland's affairs with both men lasted for several months.[44]

Kraft initially responded to Copland's infidelity by trying to make him jealous, so the younger partner began sleeping with composer Leonard Bernstein. When the affair didn't have the effect Kraft had hoped for, he married a woman, writer Pearl Kazin, in 1951. That marriage lasted only a matter of months.[45]

Copland and Kraft then settled into a relationship in which the older partner continued to have affairs with very young men. Copland had sex with Kraft as well, while both men remained committed to each other on an emotional level. They also continued to live together, although the younger partner was frequently traveling on assignments for his job with the magazine.[46]

Determined to remain a central part of the composer's life, Kraft voluntarily took on various tasks. He wrote letters for Copland, kept his car in working order, and took photos at public events where the now famous composer made appearances. When Copland decided he wanted to move out of Manhattan permanently, Kraft found him a large and airy clapboard house near Peekskill, New York, an hour from the city.[47]

Copland agreed to be interviewed by numerous journalists who wrote profiles and feature stories about him, but he opted not to speak publicly about his homosexuality. When questioned about his private life, his stock response was that his primary commitment was to composing. "I'm married to my music," he told more than one reporter, "in the tradition of Ludwig van Beethoven and Johannes Brahms."[48]

REMAINING LOYAL THROUGH DIFFICULT TIMES

By the late 1950s, Kraft was showing signs of emotional instability. He quit working, picked fights with Copland's young lovers, and often threw tantrums that included fits of crying. The younger partner also physically threatened the older one—including an incident when he came close to striking Copland with a wrench.[49]

Kraft refused to seek professional counseling, even though his partner offered to pay for it. In 1960, Kraft sought to stabilize his life by marrying a woman named Rheba Robinson. He and his wife then moved into a home only a few miles from Copland's and soon announced they were having a baby. The fact that the child, named Jeremy Aaron, was born with slight brain damage apparently pushed the father over the edge.[50]

The once handsome man let his hair grow long and scraggly, and he no longer paid attention to how he dressed. Kraft drifted into the counterculture, routinely smoking marijuana and occasionally using LSD. At one point, he begged Copland to move into a windmill with him. Another time, Kraft kidnapped his seven-year-old son and took the boy out of the country for several months.[51]

Despite this erratic behavior, Copland refused to cut Kraft out of his life. When a friend told the composer he should end all contact with the unstable man, Copland wouldn't hear of it, saying, "Many years ago, he introduced me to a way of life that inspired my best music. How could I possibly abandon him now?"[52]

While not turning his back on Kraft, Copland opted not to invite him to high-profile events, fearing that the unpredictable man might publicly humiliate himself. The composer chose, for example, to go alone to the White House in 1964 where Lyndon B. Johnson awarded him the Presidential Medal of Freedom, the highest honor that can be awarded to a civilian, and to New York two years later when he received a Grammy for his recording of opera highlights performed by the New York Philharmonic Orchestra.[53]

Activities in the privacy of his home were a different matter. Copland made sure that he and Kraft spent holidays together, and they also continued to have a sexual relationship. In addition, they traveled together from time to time, including taking a trip to Israel in 1968, soon after Kraft and his second wife had separated, and another to England in 1970.[54]

DEATH ENDS AN OUTLAW MARRIAGE

Some of the authors who have chronicled the events in Aaron Copland's life have speculated that he blamed himself for Victor Kraft's emotional problems. These biographers suggest that because the composer had, over the years, repeatedly had affairs with very young men, he feared that he may have caused his partner to become overwhelmed by feelings of rejection and betrayal.[55]

Those biographers also have written that Kraft's behavior was one of the reasons why Copland wasn't able to create music during his later years. One author described how the composer would sit down at the piano in his Peekskill house and try to write a new work, but invariably was interrupted by Kraft entering the room and either chattering incessantly or screaming hysterically.[56]

Along with his emotional difficulties, Kraft also had a long history of heart problems. In 1976 while vacationing in Maine, he suffered cardiac arrest and died almost immediately, at the age of sixty.[57]

When Copland learned that his partner of more than forty years had died, he was deeply saddened. One friend told the composer he was better off without Kraft, but Copland vehemently disagreed, insisting that he entered a state of clinical depression the moment he learned that the love of his life was gone.[58]

Copland was the godfather to Kraft's son, and the composer was committed to taking care of Jeremy Aaron Kraft in every way he could. He paid for the boy to attend private school and later helped the young man complete training as an auto mechanic.[59]

GOING SOLO IN THE FINAL YEARS

By the time Victor Kraft died, Aaron Copland was widely acknowledged to be the unofficial "dean" of American classical music. Among the long list of prestigious awards he received were Kennedy Center Honors from President Jimmy Carter in 1979 and a Medal of the Arts from President Ronald Reagan in 1986.[60]

Although his stature as an American icon meant that he could have continued having sexual relationships with much younger men, Copland ceased that indulgence after Kraft died. He made this decision, biographers believe, because of his feelings of guilt that his earlier affairs had contributed to the emotional demons that had troubled Kraft during the final decades of his life.[61]

Copland outlived Kraft by many years, dying at the age of ninety from respiratory failure. His passing in 1990 was marked by obituaries that appeared on the front pages of the country's leading newspapers. The one in the *New York Times* lauded Copland for having "touched a chord in the American psyche reached by no other classical musician this country has produced." That high-profile tribute made no mention, however, of Victor Kraft or his role in Copland's life, describing the legendary composer as "a lifelong bachelor."[62]

Chapter 11

Frank Merlo & Tennessee Williams

1948–1963

Lifting American Theater to New Heights

...

The list of theatrical masterpieces that Tennessee Williams wrote during his four decades as a playwright is both long and impressive. Biographers who have looked closely at his life, however, point out that Williams's career almost ended after he completed only two important works. Those scholars say that physical and emotional exhaustion thrust Williams, at the age of thirty-six, into an extended period of drug use and promiscuity that threatened to bring his creative output to a premature end.

Then came Frank Merlo. The rock-solid World War II veteran stabilized the playwright's life so his creative juices could begin flowing again. Indeed, generations of theatergoers owe a deep debt of gratitude to Merlo for helping Williams regain an equilibrium that allowed him to write many of his finest plays—including the Pulitzer Prize–winning *Cat on a Hot Tin Roof.* Williams's same-sex partner also contributed more directly to several of the playwright's most important works.

...

Thomas Lanier Williams was born in Columbus, Mississippi, in 1911. His father was a traveling shoe salesman, and his mother was a stay-at-home wife who took care of the couple's three children.[1]

In 1918, Tom's father was promoted to a management position in a shoe company and moved the family to St. Louis. Tom soon grew distant from his father because the physically frail boy's favorite pastime was reading, rather than sports, which prompted the head of the family to refer to his son by the denigrating nickname "Miss Nancy."[2]

Other forces shaping Tom's early years included his father's addiction to alcohol, his mother's melancholy moods because she missed the South, and his sister's gradual drift into an inner world of darkness and unreality that led to frequent fits of hysteria.[3]

When it came time for college, Tom enrolled at the University of Missouri, majoring in journalism. He was only a mediocre student, however, because he spent the lion's share of his time writing for his own pleasure.[4]

It was also during this period that Tom changed his name. His mother's parents had paid his college tuition, and he also spent summers at the couple's home in Memphis, Tennessee. And so, partly as a tribute to them, Tom had his first name legally changed to Tennessee.[5]

The bigger event in the Williams family during this period involved the young man's sister, Rose. Her mental state had deteriorated to the point that her doctor feared she might harm herself or others, prompting her parents to have a lobotomy performed on her. That is, a nerve in her brain was cut, eliminating the potential for violence but also permanently limiting her emotional and intellectual development to that of a child. Tennessee wasn't told of his sister's operation in advance, and he never forgave his parents for having it done.[6]

Williams left college after two years because of poor grades and family financial setbacks. He worked for his father in the shoe business for three years and then returned to the classroom, this time at the University of Iowa. He also became interested in the theater, switching his major to drama and earning his degree in 1938.[7]

Frank Philip Merlo was born in Elizabeth, New Jersey, in 1922. He came from a poor family—the Merlo home didn't have indoor plumbing—that was defined by a strong work ethic and a commitment to retaining its Sicilian heritage.[8]

After graduating from high school, Frank entered the Navy and served as a pharmacist mate during World War II, receiving commendations for being highly dedicated to his work. With his honorable discharge in hand, he returned to New Jersey so he'd be close to his family. He earned his livelihood as a truck driver and moved into his own apartment.[9]

Friends and relatives characterized Merlo, during his twenties, as a highly responsible and mild-mannered young man who was well liked by everyone who knew him. His major leisure activity was going to the theater, traveling into New York City as often as he could to see Broadway's latest offerings.[10]

ACHIEVING INITIAL SUCCESS

After Tennessee Williams graduated from college, he moved to New Orleans, attracted to the city's reputation for retaining an air of Old South gentility. He threw himself into writing plays, while waiting tables to pay the rent.[11]

Another reason why Williams liked the Big Easy was that the city provided him with ample opportunity to act on the same-sex desires he'd been feeling for several years. He invited the first man into his bed in 1939, and plenty more then followed.[12]

In that same year, Williams entered a competition sponsored by an organization committed to encouraging new theatrical talent. Williams didn't win the contest, but the judges found his plays strong enough to forward them to a theatrical agent.[13]

By 1941, Audrey Wood was representing Williams and had persuaded him to move to New York City so he could see the latest Broadway productions. He lived in a YMCA and worked as an usher in a theater. Everything changed in 1944 when Wood found producers who were willing to finance a Broadway staging of Williams's play titled *The Glass Menagerie*.[14]

The drama is narrated by the character Tom, whose overbearing mother pushes her son to invite a coworker home for dinner. The mother hopes the guest will become a suitor for her daughter, who walks with a limp and is incapable of coping with the outside world. But the guest soon flees, claiming he's already engaged. Tom also leaves to make his own way in the world.

Reviewers loved *The Glass Menagerie*. The *Chicago Tribune* reported that everyone who saw the play was "caught in the spell" of the masterful work, and the *Washington Post* was so impressed that it dubbed Williams "the new young hope of the American theater." A week after *Menagerie* opened, the New York Drama Critics' Circle named it the best new play of the year.[15]

Williams was showered with more praise three years later after the Broadway opening of *A Streetcar Named Desire*. This play centers on Blanche DuBois, an aging southern belle who comes to New Orleans to visit her sister and brutish brother-in-law, Stanley Kowalski. Blanche portrays herself as a chaste schoolteacher, but Stanley uncovers her sordid past as a seducer of teenage boys. By the end of the taut drama, Blanche suffers a nervous breakdown and is led away to an asylum.

The *New York Herald Tribune* described the play as one of "heroic dimensions," and the *New Yorker* pronounced it nothing short of "brilliant." Members of the New York Drama Critics' Circle honored *Streetcar* as 1947's best play, and, early the next year, the drama received the most prestigious award possible for a theatrical work, the Pulitzer Prize.[16]

SPIRALING DOWNWARD

A few days after *Streetcar* opened, Williams boarded a ship bound for Europe so he could rest and relax. He traveled alone and told no one how long he'd be gone.[17]

Biographers have observed that writing and staging *Streetcar* had taken a huge toll on the playwright, both physically and emotionally. Several of those scholars also have said that Williams believed, at this point in his life, that his writing career had ended. In the words of one of them, "Tennessee Williams brought from himself a play he was convinced was to be his last—that he would never have the energy to write another one."[18]

By the time Williams reached Paris, he was complaining, in letters to friends, about how exhausted he was because of "the accumulated fatigue" of the previous months. He was soon hospitalized, his symptoms indicating—in his words, "signs of a grave illness." Sure that he was near death, Williams entered what ultimately became the longest period in his adult life that he did no writing whatsoever.[19]

This lack of productivity wouldn't have been a problem in and of itself, except that he filled his days in France first with drinking whiskey—he had his first glass as soon as he woke up in the morning—and consuming large quantities of pills. He soon admitted to his agent that these substances were dominating his life.[20]

At the same time that Williams sought comfort through alcohol and other drugs, he also looked for it in the arms of strangers. Being robbed by a man he'd brought to his hotel room for sex failed to dissuade him from having more such encounters when he moved on to Italy. He wrote a friend that all a man needed to enjoy European travel was "one suit, two shirts, and a pocket full of prophylactics."[21]

An incident that summer revealed Williams's sorry state. *The Glass Menagerie* was to open in London in July, and a major celebration was planned to mark the premiere. Audrey Wood had come from the United States, as had Williams's mother and brother. Publicity for the soiree promised that Williams would be present for the opening and the lavish reception to follow. On the night of the gala, however, the playwright didn't show up. It was several days later that Williams's mother finally received a telegram saying that her son had fallen unconscious after taking a sedative.[22]

The playwright's absence from that celebration served as a wake-up call, as he left Europe and returned to New York a few days later.[23]

CREATING AN OUTLAW MARRIAGE

Promiscuity wasn't a new experience for Williams when it became part of his downward spiral in 1947 and 1948. Indeed, it was through a one-night stand the summer before he left for Europe that he'd met the man who ultimately became the love of his life.[24]

At five feet five inches tall, Frank Merlo was an inch shorter than the playwright. Merlo's muscular body and ruggedly handsome facial features, however, made him much more attractive than Williams. Merlo's face was somewhat elongated, giving him what Williams described as a "horsey look" that led to the playwright's pet name for him, "Little Horse."[25]

Williams and Merlo had sex on the dunes in Provincetown, Massachusetts, one night in July 1947 and then went their separate ways. Their paths crossed again soon after Williams returned to New York, after his European travels, when they were both eating at a delicatessen on Lexington Avenue. They recognized each other from their tryst a year earlier, and Merlo congratulated the playwright on *Streetcar,* saying he'd seen and enjoyed the play.[26]

Within weeks after that second meeting, Merlo moved into Williams's apartment. The playwright soon spoke, in his personal journal, about his love for the man who quickly took center stage in his life. "I love Frankie—deeply, tenderly, unconditionally. I love him with every bit of my heart," Williams said in one entry, and in another he wrote, "My heart is full of love for Little Horse and only for Little Horse."[27]

BRINGING ORDER TO A CHAOTIC LIFE

After Merlo moved in, he became much more than Williams's lover, as he took on any number of practical tasks that made the playwright's life easier. Merlo cooked his partner's meals, drove him where he needed to go, and wrote letters for him. The younger man also made sure the apartment stayed clean and orderly.[28]

More important than taking on these chores, though, was Merlo's success at weaning Williams off his dependence on alcohol, pills, and casual sex—both men drank alcohol but in moderation. With these distractions gone, the theatrical genius again concentrated on his writing. In short, Frank Merlo single-handedly stabilized Tennessee Williams's life and career.[29]

People who cared about the playwright consistently praised Merlo. Paul Bigelow, one of Williams's friends from the theater world, said, "We were all very pleased when Frank moved in with Tenn. Frank was a warm, decent man with a strong native intelligence and a sense of honor. Frank wanted to care for Tenn and bring order to his chaotic life. And with great love, this is what Frank did." Writer Christopher Isherwood, who'd known Williams for fifteen years, echoed those same sentiments, saying, "Frank looked after Tenn in a way that was uncanny. And he wasn't just some kind of faithful servitor. He was a lovable man with a strong will." Cheryl Crawford, who produced several of Williams's plays, added, "Frank was the only one who really understood Tennessee, really knew how to deal with him and help him."[30]

At the same time that Merlo took care of the man he loved, he wasn't a saint. He drank a lot of beer, smoked four packs of cigarettes a day, and joined Williams in spending several nights a week in the gay bars that had proliferated in Manhattan by the late 1940s.[31]

CREATING ARTISTIC MASTERPIECES—WITH A PARTNER'S HELP

Merlo didn't have any formal training or experience in the theater. Nevertheless, he ultimately had significant impact on several of Williams's most important plays.

The work that most dramatically reflects Merlo's central place in the playwright's life is *The Rose Tattoo*. "It was permeated," Williams later wrote, "with my happy young love for Frankie." Several elements of the work can be traced directly to Little Horse. Williams's partner was of Sicilian heritage; the play celebrates the Sicilian lust for life. The play's male lead is a truck driver; Merlo was driving a truck when he and Williams met. The work is Williams's only major one with a resolutely happy ending; he wrote the play while he and Merlo were in the infatuation stage of their outlaw marriage.[32]

During 1950 when Williams wrote *Tattoo,* he and Merlo made two trips to Sicily so the playwright could get a better sense of the culture. Williams was so taken by the language, in fact, that he seriously considered having his characters speak Sicilian during much of the play—Merlo talked him out of it, arguing that using the foreign language would annoy American audiences.[33]

The Rose Tattoo revolves around a high-spirited widow who retreats from the world after her husband dies. Serafina reawakens to life's joys when she meets the happy-go-lucky Alvaro. She initially resists his advances out of respect for her dead husband, but the likeable suitor wins her over when she discovers that he, like her dead husband, has a rose tattoo on his chest.

Critics praised the work when it opened on Broadway in 1951. The *Chicago Tribune* called it "fresh, provocative and stimulating," and the *New York Times* added the adjectives "original, imaginative and tender," before going on to gush, "It is the loveliest idyll written for the stage in some time." At the annual Tony Awards ceremony, *Tattoo* was honored as the best new play of the season.[34]

Williams acknowledged that Merlo and his life were the inspiration for the play by dedicating it to him.[35]

BUILDING A PARTNER'S CONFIDENCE

Merlo's role in his partner's next big hit, *Cat on a Hot Tin Roof,* involved the writing process. Williams struggled with the work because its themes were so similar to *Streetcar*'s that he was sure the critics would compare the two. And so, he convinced himself, if the new play didn't rise to the exceptional quality of *Streetcar,* the reviewers would instantly pronounce it a failure. Williams's anxiety and emotional instability soared.[36]

So Little Horse became his partner's comforter and confidence builder, offering sympathy and tenderness when Williams became distraught, which happened almost daily throughout 1954. What's more, Williams became so dependent on Merlo that the playwright turned to his partner for critiques of his work, finishing the draft of a scene and then reading it out loud and asking for instant feedback. José Quintero, who directed several of Williams's plays, said, "Frank was one of the few people that told Tenn the truth without being afraid."[37]

Cat on a Hot Tin Roof revolves around a secret that Brick, a former football star, is keeping from his highly sexual wife and domineering father. The wife is frustrated because her husband has grown distant since his best friend, Skipper, committed suicide. It gradually emerges that Brick and Skipper had been lovers, making the play one of the earliest Broadway productions that dealt with homosexuality.

When *Cat* opened in 1955, the critics had nothing but praise, despite Williams's earlier worries. The *Chicago Tribune* called the drama "perceptive," the *New York Times* crowned it "stunning," and the *Washington Post* said it was "superior to both A Streetcar Named Desire and The Glass Menagerie."[38]

A month after the opening, *Cat* won Williams his third New York Drama Critics' Award, and, soon after that, it gave him his second Pulitzer Prize.[39]

The theater world knew nothing of Merlo's behind-the-scenes role in *Cat*'s creation, but Williams was well aware of how crucial his lover's support had been throughout the painful writing process. Williams showed his gratitude by giving Little Horse, as he'd done with *Tattoo,* 10 percent of the play's profits.[40]

Merlo again supported Williams when the playwright began work on his next major success, *The Night of the Iguana.* As when he was writing *Cat,* Williams struggled with a crisis in confidence. "He felt that his star was in

decline by this time," said Frank Corsaro, who had directed a one-act version of *Iguana* and then waited for Williams to finish the second and third
acts. "Frank was the best part of Tennessee's life. He was a street kid who had
grown up and become a real, literate gentleman." Merlo put his partner on a
strict schedule, demanding that he write for four hours each day. "Frank took
no nonsense from Tennessee," Corsaro said.[41]

The Night of the Iguana focuses on an Episcopal priest who brings a group
of American tourists to a remote Mexican hotel. During a stormy night, the
alcoholic man of the cloth confronts his demons—including frantic sexuality and religious guilt. He also learns important lessons from the earthy hotel proprietor.

When *Iguana* opened in late 1961, the *New York Daily News* called it "a
beautiful play," and the *Washington Post* said "any aficionado of drama will
be thrilled" by Williams's latest work. Dwarfing the individual critiques,
though, was *Time* magazine's decision to mark the play's triumph as "a box-
office sellout" by placing a photo of Williams on its cover. The story inside
anointed Williams "America's greatest playwright."[42]

Neither the *Time* article nor other stories that included glimpses into Williams's personal life mentioned his sexuality. This omission wasn't because
the playwright denied being gay—he never did—but because news organizations preferred not to talk about the subject.[43]

A month after *Iguana* premiered, members of the New York Drama Critics' Circle voted it the best new play of the year—the fourth work by Williams
to win that honor.[44]

FACING CHALLENGES IN THE RELATIONSHIP

There's no question that Frank Merlo stabilized Tennessee Williams's life and
career after his indolent period in the late 1940s, just as there's no question
that the younger partner helped the older one with several of the theatrical
projects he created during the 1950s and early 1960s. Neither of these facts,
however, should mask the reality that the two men struggled with several
issues that continually threatened their outlaw marriage.

The list begins with the fact that Merlo insisted, when they became a
couple in 1948, that Williams be sexually faithful to him. The playwright's
correspondence and entries in his personal journal, however, show that he
sometimes strayed. In a letter Williams wrote to a friend in 1951, for example,
he described a solo trip to Europe by saying, "I had my best time and most ex-
citing lay in London." Likewise, in a 1954 journal entry while he was alone in
Spain, Williams wrote, "Sex has been disappointing. My appeal, even to the
hustlers, seems to have suffered a decline this summer."[45]

A second issue had to do with Merlo's occupation—or, more precisely, his lack of one. When Little Horse moved in with Williams, he voluntarily stopped driving trucks and took on the duties of being the playwright's cook, chauffeur, and secretary. Williams saw this situation as a problem, as he felt guilty that his needs were keeping his partner from having an independent career. Merlo didn't share this concern and, in fact, made light of his role. In 1949, for instance, Williams and Merlo flew to Hollywood so the playwright could begin working with the head of Warner Brothers studio, Jack Warner, on the film version of *The Glass Menagerie*. Williams forgot to introduce his partner to Warner, and so, after a few minutes, the movie magnate turned to Merlo and asked, "And what do you do, young man?" Without missing a beat, Little Horse smiled and responded, "My job is to sleep with Mr. Williams."[46]

A third issue facing the Williams/Merlo partnership was the playwright's return to using alcohol and other drugs. Merlo had weaned his partner off these substances in the late 1940s, but Williams gradually began consuming them again. For several years, he succeeded in keeping his drug use a secret, but that period ended in June 1960 when he told a *Newsweek* reporter that he took barbiturates. When Merlo read the published story, he was livid, telling Williams that he felt betrayed.[47]

After that confrontation, the relationship became increasingly strained. In the words of one biographer, "Williams spent more time with other men at bars and on the beach. There seemed to be a quiet *diminuendo* to what had once been the lively, tender duet of Tennessee Williams and Frank Merlo."[48]

A PARTNER DYING BEFORE HIS TIME

As early as 1960, people around Little Horse began noticing that he had a hacking cough that wouldn't go away. He also lost weight and complained that he became exhausted after even minor physical exertion.[49]

Williams was vacationing in London in 1962 when he received a telegram from his agent telling him that Merlo had been sitting at an outdoor café when he suddenly leaned forward and a stream of blood poured from his mouth. The playwright left England immediately and was by his partner's side the next afternoon. Soon after that, Merlo was diagnosed as having inoperable lung cancer—an illness connected to his heavy smoking.[50]

The playwright paid the medical bills and made Little Horse's life as pleasant as possible, staying with him in Key West, Florida, because Merlo had always loved that city. But not even the wealthiest playwright in the country could stop the gradual deterioration in his partner's health that continued for the next year. Of the last weeks, Williams later said, "Frankie never lost a fraction of his pride in the face of the most awful death a person can have."[51]

It was in September 1963 that the final scene in the couple's life together played out. Merlo was in his hospital bed when he removed his oxygen mask and, with a sudden burst of energy, climbed into a chair. The older man urged the younger one to conserve his strength, saying he'd been looking better lately—which they both knew was a lie. The lovers then sat in silence, and when Williams offered to leave so his partner could sleep, Merlo asked him to stay, saying softly, "I'm used to you."[52]

Merlo died later that night, at the age of forty-one.

SPIRALING DOWNWARD ONCE AGAIN

After Merlo's death, Williams entered a period reminiscent of the difficult time in 1947 and 1948. "As long as Frank was well, I was happy," the playwright later recalled. "He had a gift for creating a life for us, and, when he ceased to be alive, I couldn't create a life for myself. So I went into a seven-year depression."[53]

Williams drank two fifths of alcohol—one of bourbon, one of vodka—each day, while also using drugs. The *New York Times* later quoted him as saying, "I had suffered a great loss in my life, and I sought oblivion. While I continued to write every morning, through the use of 'speed' injections and amphetamines taken muscularly, I was not in a very real world and unconsciously I might have been seeking death."[54]

As had been the case during his period of spiraling downward in the late 1940s, Williams also turned to sex as a way of numbing his pain. The playwright initially invited a young poet into his bed and later replaced him with a paid companion from the theater.[55]

America's foremost playwright continued to churn out new works during this period, but none of them held a candle to his earlier masterpieces.[56]

In 1969, Williams's brother checked the playwright into a drug rehabilitation center. The patient had severe physical reactions to the withdrawal that the facility required, suffering three major seizures and two heart attacks within the first two days of treatment.[57]

Once he was released from the center and for the next thirteen years, Williams devoted his energy to the craft of writing, even though the results were never satisfying. A pair of much more positive events occurred in 1979 when he, along with Aaron Copland, was awarded Kennedy Center Honors and a year later when Jimmy Carter gave him the Medal of Freedom.[58]

Tennessee Williams's life came to an abrupt end in 1983 when he accidentally choked to death, at the age of seventy-one, while taking a prescription drug.[59]

The country's major newspapers published obituaries as well as tributes to him. The *Boston Globe* called Williams "a towering figure of the American theater," and the *Washington Post* wrote, "He was the greatest American playwright. Period." The *New York Times* began its praise by calling Williams the "most important and influential playwright" in the history of the American stage, and then stated that seven of his plays had become "a permanent part of the international theatrical repertory." Only two of those works had been written before Little Horse had stabilized Williams's life and career, while the other five had been written during the years the two men had been a couple.[60]

Several of the newspapers made brief references to the playwright's life partner. The most telling of those statements came in the *Los Angeles Times* when it said of Williams: "His longtime companion of 15 years, Frank Merlo, died of cancer in 1963. After that, the playwright said, 'Everything sort of fell apart.'"[61]

Chapter 12

James Baldwin & Lucien Happersberger
1949–1987

Attacking Racism through Literature

...

During the 1950s and 1960s, James Baldwin took his place among the giants of American literature. His eloquent prose reflected on his experiences as a black, gay man living in a predominantly white, straight nation. Two of his books—*Go Tell It on the Mountain* and *Giovanni's Room*—received consistently positive reviews from critics, while two others—*Another Country* and *The Fire Next Time*—became national best sellers. Baldwin was lauded not only as one of the finest writers the country had ever produced but also as an effective advocate for racial equality.

Although the public is familiar with Baldwin, few people recognize the name Lucien Happersberger, even though he played a critical role in the writer's life and career. It was only when Baldwin fell in love with Happersberger that the aspiring author was finally—after ten years of effort—able to complete his first novel. Baldwin biographers have noted, in fact, that all of his best writing occurred during the periods when Happersberger provided him with the emotional security he desperately sought throughout his life.

James Baldwin was born in 1924 to an unmarried domestic who cleaned houses in the Harlem section of New York City. He never knew his biological father, but, when he was three years old, his mother married a Baptist minister. The stepfather then abused the boy, physically as well as emotionally.[1]

Jimmy was a frail child who had a voracious appetite for reading. By his early teens, he knew he wanted to be a novelist, and his intellect and writing talent were so clear that he was offered two college scholarships. Soon after he graduated from high school, however, his stepfather died and he was thrust, as the oldest child in the family, into the role of supporting his mother and his eight half brothers and half sisters. He worked as a dishwasher and elevator boy.[2]

It was during this period that Baldwin met the man who became his lifelong mentor and confidant, Beauford Delaney. In 1940 when the boy came to know Delaney, who was more than two decades older than he was, he saw for the first time that an African American man could function as a self-supporting artist. In the words of one Baldwin biographer, "It was as if Jimmy had found his long-lost father."[3]

At the age of twenty and with Delaney as his role model, Baldwin began to pursue a writing career. His first step was to stop supporting his family, and the second was to focus on his creative work. He soon published a book review and an essay that won him a literary fellowship. He used the money to pay his way to Paris, believing his creative juices would flow more freely in what was widely viewed as the world's most cultured city.[4]

By this point, Baldwin recognized his homosexuality and went to bed with various men he met while working as a waiter. This became a time of mental turmoil for Baldwin, who was haunted by feelings of extreme loneliness. "In Paris," one biographer later wrote, "Jimmy threw himself into an expatriate life dominated by a frantic search for the kind of companionship that would answer his cravings to be loved."[5]

Adding to Baldwin's despair was the frustration that came with having his heart set on completing a novel, but not being satisfied with anything he wrote.[6]

Lucien Happersberger was born in Lausanne, Switzerland, in 1932. All that's been documented about his early years is that his family was from the middle class and that he showed, during his adolescence, a talent for painting.[7]

When Lucien turned sixteen, he left his family and moved to Paris in hopes of earning a living as an artist. He then joined the legions of young men who tried to sell their paintings by displaying them on the streets of the French capital.[8]

Baldwin biographers describe Happersberger as a young man who was "quick-thinking and witty" and who possessed a "devil-may-care hedonism."[9]

CREATING AN OUTLAW MARRIAGE

From the moment Baldwin set eyes on Happersberger in a seedy Parisian bar in 1949, he was smitten. At least part of the appeal was physical, as the Swiss lad—six feet two inches tall, slender, and good looking—was much more attractive than Baldwin, who stood five feet six inches tall and was as skinny as a scarecrow, his dominant physical features being his protruding eyes and heavy eyelids that had earned him the disparaging boyhood nickname of "Frog Eyes."[10]

Another part of the appeal was that both young men—Baldwin was twenty-five, Happersberger was seventeen—enjoyed having a good time. The couple's first evening together set the standard, as they enjoyed several drinks at various bars before spending the night in Baldwin's bed. Their connection clearly wasn't intellectual, as neither of them knew enough of the other's native language to converse in full sentences.[11]

After that first night, they immediately became a couple. Their mutual interests—other than alcohol and sex—extended to laughing a lot and using their ingenuity to survive on very little money. "We used to meet late in the day at a café," Baldwin later recalled, "and pool the few francs we'd managed to raise that day and then we'd eat. We shared everything." Happersberger's assessment of what made their outlaw marriage work is captured in his statement, made many years later, "We accepted each other exactly as we were. That's rare."[12]

FINDING EMOTIONAL STABILITY

Shortly after the two men became a couple, Happersberger expressed concern that Baldwin's jittery nervousness meant he was on the verge of a mental breakdown. So the younger man took his new lover to Switzerland, where the pace was slower and the air was healthier than in Paris. They landed in the tiny village of Loèche-les-Bains, where the Happersberger family had a small chalet. "There was nothing else for Jimmy to do in that village," Happersberger later said, "but to work on his novel."[13]

The partners then went about pursuing their individual creative interests—Happersberger painting and Baldwin writing. For the latter, the words flew onto paper more quickly and more gracefully than ever before. He immediately began making progress on the novel he'd been struggling to complete for more than a decade. He read draft passages to his young lover as he finished them, and, as Happersberger's English improved, the Swiss youth occasionally made a comment that was helpful.[14]

When either man needed a break, they either made love or listened to music. "One activity we both very much enjoyed," Happersberger recalled decades later, "was listening to Bessie Smith and Fats Waller. That jazz music also carried Jimmy back to his childhood, where he needed to be in order to write about the subject he had in mind."[15]

Finally, in February 1952, the couple walked to the nearest post office, the completed manuscript in Baldwin's hands. He sent his novel to Knopf publishing house in New York, hoping it would attract the attention of an editor there. Meanwhile, he continued to feel secure and confident, writing to friends that Happersberger was "the love of my life."[16]

FACING COMPLICATIONS IN THE RELATIONSHIP

For Baldwin, those three years in the Swiss village were both enormously productive professionally and highly satisfying emotionally. There were soon signs, however, that the outlaw marriage would have to overcome some serious challenges.[17]

The problem was a dramatic difference in what the two men were looking for in a relationship. Baldwin wanted a faithful partner who would live with him in a stable domestic arrangement that was comparable to a conventional marriage. "Jimmy was very romantic," Happersberger told an interviewer in 1990. "He had a dream of settling down." Happersberger, by contrast, loved Baldwin but wanted the freedom to pursue sexual activities with other people—women as well as men. One Baldwin biographer wrote, "Lucien loved men, but he loved women as well."[18]

Happersberger had told Baldwin, from the beginning, that he wasn't willing to be monogamous. And yet Baldwin deluded himself into thinking he and his teenage partner's mutual love for each other bound them together in an idealized relationship that had no room for infidelity and that would last forever.[19]

The contrast between Baldwin's dream and the realities of the situation came crashing down on him when Happersberger began inviting a former girlfriend to spend weekends at the chalet. Baldwin then found himself sleeping alone in one bedroom while Happersberger and the woman, whose name was Suzy, slept in the bedroom next door.[20]

More reality entered the picture when Happersberger announced, in the summer of 1952, that Suzy was pregnant with his child. Baldwin's initial reaction was anger, but that feeling was soon tempered by his memories of how unhappy his own early years had been because his biological father hadn't been part of his life. And so, he urged his lover to marry Suzy and help her raise the child, which Happersberger did. When the couple's son was born, they named him Luc James, after Baldwin, and asked the writer to be the boy's godfather.[21]

These disruptive developments in Baldwin's relationship with Happersberger coincided with good news from the United States. An editor at Knopf liked the manuscript Baldwin had sent, and he was interested in working with the author on a few revisions before publishing it. Baldwin then left Europe and returned to America.[22]

Baldwin had written the semi-autobiographical *Go Tell It on the Mountain* from the perspective of a poor African American boy growing up in 1930s Harlem and struggling to gain the love of a distant stepfather. Much of the novel focuses on religion, portraying the church as a source not only of inspiration and community but also of repression and hypocrisy.[23]

When the book was released in 1953, reviewers were impressed. *Time* magazine described the work as "compelling," and the *New Yorker* called it "a first novel of quite exceptional promise."[24]

EXPERIENCING A SECOND PERIOD OF STABILITY AND PRODUCTIVITY

By 1954, Baldwin was feeling a mixture of emotions. On the one hand, he was pleased that critics had lauded *Go Tell It on the Mountain*. On the other hand, he desperately longed for the emotional stability he'd enjoyed while living with Happersberger. Because of the latter feelings, the author was "lonely and unhappy," according to one biographer, and experiencing a period of "deep depression," according to another.[25]

Adding to Baldwin's gloom were developments in the life of Beauford Delaney. The author and his mentor remained in frequent contact, and Baldwin talked at length with the older man about his despair at not being with the love of his life. Baldwin became concerned, however, because Delaney drank heavily and sometimes seemed to lose touch with reality.[26]

Baldwin tried to start a new novel, but his feelings of loneliness kept him from writing anything he liked. An old friend from school who was now at a publishing house approached him about putting together a collection of essays. Baldwin initially resisted taking on the project, preferring to work on his novel. When he couldn't make progress on the fictional work, though, he agreed to focus on the essays, which were published under the title *Notes of a Native Son*.[27]

It's unclear whether Baldwin or Happersberger was the catalyst for the two men reconnecting in late 1954. Regardless of which man had the idea of the artist moving to the United States, Baldwin was at the airport to meet

Happersberger—who arrived without either his wife or his son—when he landed in New York City.[28]

The couple moved into a small apartment in Greenwich Village, Baldwin telling friends they planned to re-create the blissful life they'd enjoyed in Loèche-les-Bains. In the words of one biographer, "He was obsessed with the idea of having a happy, settled domestic life with Lucien." The New York location proved to have benefits for Happersberger, who found plenty of interesting scenes in the city to paint, although he sold very few of his finished works.[29]

Living with the man he loved once again propelled Baldwin into a productive period. His project this time was titled *Giovanni's Room,* and he made major strides forward with the novel in early 1955. Baldwin acknowledged the central role that his partner played in his completing the book by dedicating it "To Lucien."[30]

Giovanni's Room differs from *Go Tell It on the Mountain* not only because the protagonist is bisexual rather than straight, but also because he is white rather than African American. That main character, David, falls in love with an Italian man, Giovanni, but both of the characters suffer enormously because of David's inability to accept his sexuality.[31]

Before the publisher had even released *Giovanni's Room,* the problems between Baldwin and Happersberger had resurfaced. "There were many fights," one friend of the couple recalled. "Nothing really had changed. Jimmy wanted a lover to end all lovers; Lucien wanted a friend. When several women came into Lucien's life, Jimmy was hurt." The two men again separated. Baldwin returned to Paris, while Happersberger stayed in New York.[32]

The novelist found some comfort in the fact that the reviews of *Giovanni's Room* were highly positive. The *San Francisco Chronicle* praised the author "for portraying the homosexual struggle with dignity and compassion," and *Harper's* magazine wrote that "the intensity with which Baldwin endows ideas is very nearly miraculous."[33]

Giovanni's Room was one of the most explicit novels about same-sex love written up to that time, and Baldwin didn't deny that he was gay if someone asked him. And yet, the American news media were so uncomfortable talking about homosexuality that neither the reviews of the book nor the feature stories about Baldwin discussed the author's lifestyle or mentioned his relationship with Happersberger.[34]

ACCEPTING AN UNCONVENTIONAL RELATIONSHIP

After the failure of Baldwin's second attempt to live with the man he loved, he again spiraled into depression. One friend later recalled, "Lucien remained somewhere at the center of Jimmy's being, and he still hoped for a future with him."[35]

One night the writer became so distraught over having lost Happersberger that he attempted suicide. Fortunately, a friend arrived at Baldwin's apartment shortly after he'd swallowed several dozen sleeping pills. Realizing what the writer had done, the friend forced him to empty his stomach by repeatedly vomiting.[36]

With regard to his writing, Baldwin again found it impossible to create the quality fiction he'd produced in his first two novels. So he resorted to producing short stories and essays instead. These works were published as *Nobody Knows My Name*. In the introduction, Baldwin characterized the years since he'd published his last novel—which coincided with the period since he'd lived with Happersberger—as "sad and aimless."[37]

The first indication that this period was nearing its end came in late 1960 when Baldwin received a letter from Happersberger offering to reconnect. The artist proposed that the two men live together in New York, but this time he wanted to place two conditions on the arrangement. Specifically, Happersberger insisted that, from the start, Baldwin had to agree that, first, they'd reside under the same roof only for a few months and, second, they wouldn't be monogamous.[38]

Baldwin accepted the terms and rented an apartment, finding one that was large enough that the two men could live together but, at the same time, have separate spaces where they could work and sleep independently when they wanted to.[39]

Within a matter of weeks after Baldwin and Happersberger reunited, the author finished the manuscript for *Another Country*. Various friends of Baldwin's had come to recognize, by this point, the stabilizing influence that having Happersberger in his life had on the writer. In the words of one of them, "Lucien had an intuitive understanding of Jimmy's needs and feelings."[40]

Precisely when Baldwin and Happersberger stopped living together this time is unclear, partly because of the unconventional nature of the arrangement. That is, because Happersberger had said from the outset that he wouldn't be sexually faithful to Baldwin, he often spent several nights in a row away from the apartment. The two men definitely were living apart by the time *Another Country* was published in 1962.[41]

The novel has a complex plot structured around the lives of eight racially and sexually diverse men and women living in Greenwich Village. The many conflicts among the characters symbolize what Baldwin saw as the crises that dominated America in the 1960s. One of the most controversial aspects of the work is that it portrays gayness as having redemptive power—perhaps even being the basis on which a bold new world could be built.[42]

Another Country received mixed reviews, although the positive ones outnumbered the negative. The *New York Times* considered it "a sad story, brilliantly and fiercely told," and the *Atlantic Monthly* praised it as a "powerful and disturbing novel by one of the most talented of our young writers." *Time,* by contrast, concluded that *Another Country* was "a failure" that "does not live up to advance hopes."[43]

Regardless of what the critics had to say, readers bought copies of *Another Country* at a feverish pace. The novel quickly jumped to the top of the national best-seller list and stayed there for several months. "Many younger people," one Baldwin biographer wrote, "seemed to identify with the way of life the book described." The fact that the book was condemned as "obscene" in New Orleans, and therefore banned from being sold in that city, also boosted its popularity among many prospective readers.[44]

COMING TO A PARTNER'S RESCUE

Baldwin had been thinking, since the late 1950s, about writing a book that would contribute to the evolving civil rights movement. After *Another Country* became a best seller, he was determined to move forward on this project, as he now was confident that what he wrote had the potential to attract a large audience and, consequently, have major impact.[45]

Unfortunately, though, *Another Country*'s commercial success brought Baldwin so much attention that he couldn't concentrate on his writing. With relatives asking for financial support, magazine editors requesting articles, and other authors begging him for advice, the demands were so overwhelming that Baldwin could barely function.[46]

Then Lucien Happersberger came to the rescue. Seeing that Baldwin needed to distance himself from the various distractions if he was to focus on the project he really cared about, Happersberger took the author back to the Swiss chalet where he'd finished his first novel.[47]

As had been the case each of the other times Baldwin and Happersberger had lived together, the author made rapid progress on the project at hand. In the words of one biographer, "For four decades, Happersberger had played a role in each significant act of Baldwin's life."[48]

In *The Fire Next Time,* Baldwin argued that American history is primarily the story of whites being relentlessly inhuman to blacks. Baldwin didn't offer easy answers as to what would right the nation's wrongs, but he made it clear that America couldn't thrive until it began treating blacks as equals. "The price of the liberation of the white people," he wrote, "is the liberation of the blacks—the total liberation, in the cities, in the towns, before the law, and in the mind."[49]

When *The Fire Next Time* was released, it immediately soared to number one on the best-seller list, attracting even more readers than *Another Country* had. Baldwin's latest offering also spawned a plethora of positive reviews, along with a few strongly negative ones. In the positive camp, *The Nation* called the book a "tract of the times," and the *Atlantic Monthly* praised it as "eloquent in its passion and scorching in its candor." In the negative camp, the conservative *National Review* said Baldwin was misguided because "more racial progress has been made in the past generation than in all the past history."[50]

SHIFTING FROM LITERATURE TO ACTIVISM

The Fire Next Time's publication in January 1963 turned Baldwin into a high-profile racial activist virtually overnight. He began speaking at civil rights rallies and demonstrations throughout the country, and news reporters often turned to him for his comments on the latest development in the struggle for black equality.[51]

A sense of Baldwin's new stature came in early May when, during a rally in Los Angeles, he criticized President John F. Kennedy for not doing enough to advance the cause of African Americans. After he made that statement, the president's brother, Attorney General Robert F. Kennedy, invited Baldwin to his Manhattan apartment for a private meeting—an event that landed Baldwin's name on the front page of the *New York Times* three days in a row. Even after that session in which the attorney general tried to mollify Baldwin, however, the author continued to demand more action from the White House.[52]

Time magazine reinforced Baldwin's lofty status later that spring by placing his photo on its cover and describing his beliefs inside. "American history, as Baldwin sees it," according to the piece, "is an unending story of the white man's refusal to see the black man as a human being." *Time* praised Baldwin as an articulate voice for his race, saying, "In the U.S. today there is not another writer who expresses with such poignancy and abrasiveness the dark realities of the racial ferment in North and South."[53]

Baldwin agreed with the nonviolent approach that the Reverend Martin Luther King Jr. championed, and the two men often appeared at the same events. In August 1963, the author was among the leaders who spoke before King gave his seminal "I Have a Dream" speech as part of the March on Washington. On that historic day, Baldwin struck a hopeful chord, saying, "For the first time in history, the Negro is becoming aware of his value as a human being and is no longer at the mercy of what the white people imagine him to be."[54]

Baldwin's activism continued after President Kennedy was assassinated and Lyndon B. Johnson moved into the White House. Unlike many Americans, the author wasn't satisfied with the civil rights initiatives that LBJ enacted. "What is crucial," Baldwin told a *New York Times* reporter in 1965, "is that none of these slogans—'War on Poverty,' 'The Great Society'—means anything unless there are basic changes in the redistribution of wealth and power."[55]

Lucien Happersberger supported Baldwin's activism in concrete ways. When the author was inundated with speaking invitations, the artist put his painting aside and served as Baldwin's business manager. This meant that Baldwin channeled all requests to Happersberger, who evaluated them and decided which ones the author/activist accepted. Happersberger then made his partner's travel arrangements and also accompanied him on many of the trips. When both men were at home in New York, they sometimes lived together but other times lived apart.[56]

RETURNING TO THE WRITING LIFE

Baldwin was so disillusioned after King's assassination in 1968 that he ceased his activist role in the civil rights movement and shifted his top priority back to writing. He also left the United States and moved to a farmhouse in the south of France.[57]

Baldwin was, by this stage in his life, in a very different place emotionally than he'd been earlier in his life. That is, now having published two critically acclaimed novels and two best sellers, he no longer depended as heavily on the emotional stability that he'd earlier been so desperate to find in his outlaw marriage with Happersberger.[58]

The author's productivity remained steady throughout the next decade, as he wrote four books between 1972 and 1979. While the quantity was impressive, many reviewers criticized the quality of Baldwin's writing during this period, saying none of the books rose to the standard he'd achieved with his earlier ones.[59]

On a personal level, Baldwin struggled with two realities. First, he was saddened by how his mentor's life had spiraled downward. By the mid-1970s, Beauford Delaney, the man who had served as Baldwin's role model for three decades, was confined to an insane asylum where he eventually died.[60]

The second fact that weighed heavily on Baldwin's mind was why his relationship with Happersberger was successful only for limited lengths of time. The writer ultimately blamed himself, asking his brother, David, the rhetorical question: "How could anyone feel contentment in the arms of a tornado?" In other words, Baldwin concluded that Happersberger had repeatedly been frightened away by the intensity of the writer's need for emotional security.[61]

True to the pattern the couple had followed since the early 1950s, Baldwin and Happersberger lived together in the French farmhouse on and off during the 1970s and early 1980s, and they also traveled together to the United States on several occasions.[62]

LIFE COMING TO AN END

While living in the farmhouse in early 1987, Happersberger noticed that his lover wasn't as interested in conversation and good food as in the past. Only after repeated urgings did Baldwin finally see a doctor, who diagnosed him as suffering from stomach cancer.[63]

Baldwin's health continued to decline, and it was clear by Thanksgiving that he was near death. On his final day, he and Happersberger watched a television documentary about the life of Bessie Smith. The film included clips of her singing, which allowed the two men to relive their blissful days in the Swiss chalet where Baldwin had finished *Go Tell It on the Mountain*. When the writer took his last breath that night, Happersberger was at his bedside.[64]

America's leading newspapers placed the news of Baldwin's death on their front pages. The *Boston Globe* praised him as "one of the most important writers of his generation," and the *Los Angeles Times* credited him with "awakening the consciousness of American whites to the plight of American blacks." The *New York Times* wrote in its obituary, "Mr. Baldwin's literary achievements and his activism made him a world figure," and then continued in a tribute, "Few writers so define a movement or a moment as did James Baldwin. In the 1950s and 1960s, he gave passionate voice to the emerging civil rights movement. His writing roused Americans, black and white, to attack the terrible legacy of racism."[65]

None of the obituaries or tributes mentioned Lucien Happersberger or the role he'd played in the author's life during the previous four decades.[66]

Happersberger stayed in France when his partner's body was returned to the United States where Baldwin's family, friends, and admirers celebrated his life and work with an enormous memorial service—four thousand people attended, and speakers included writers Maya Angelou and Toni Morrison—at the Cathedral of St. John the Divine in Manhattan. The Swiss artist then continued to avoid the public eye.[67]

Chapter 13

Robert Rauschenberg & Jasper Johns

1954–1962

Expanding the Definition of Art

...

Robert Rauschenberg and Jasper Johns revolutionized the art world. By incorporating popular imagery into their works, they pioneered what amounted to a new category of visual media. The two men questioned the authority of either an artist or the art establishment—particularly the abstract expressionists who'd held sway during the first half of the twentieth century—to dictate meaning. By celebrating images from contemporary culture, Rauschenberg and Johns challenged the fixed attitudes toward what could be considered art and invited individual viewers, by drawing from their own emotions and life experiences, to find an infinite variety of meanings in the artworks they were exposed to.

Critics say that Rauschenberg and Johns created their finest pieces between 1954 and 1962 when they worked and lived together as artists and lovers. Although this eight-year period represented only a fraction of their long careers, there's no question that their time as a same-sex couple contributed enormously to the hundreds of their works that enriched the visual arts, in America and throughout the world.

Milton Rauschenberg was born in Port Arthur, Texas, in 1925. His father was a lineman for the local power company, and his mother worked as a telephone operator.[1]

During his childhood, Milton filled notebooks with his own versions of comic book characters—Mickey Mouse, Dick Tracy, and Popeye were his favorites. He first put his drawing talent to practical use when he served in the U.S. Navy, sketching portraits of his fellow sailors that the young men then sent home to their families.[2]

Rauschenberg used GI Bill benefits to pay his tuition to the Académie Julian in Paris and then Black Mountain College in North Carolina. By this point he'd become Robert, changing his name to mark his rebirth as an artist. He'd also married fellow art student Susan Weil.[3]

The first exhibition of Rauschenberg's art came in 1951 after he and his wife had settled in New York City. No one who came to the gallery bought any of his works, which consisted of flat white paint applied to canvas.[4]

By 1953, Rauschenberg had divorced his wife and was romantically involved with artist Cy Twombly. That fall, Rauschenberg had his second exhibition at a New York gallery, this time the works consisting of solid black paintings. He again didn't sell anything, and a reviewer for *Arts and Architecture* magazine said of his work, "There is less than meets the eye."[5]

Jasper Johns was born in Augusta, Georgia, in 1930. His parents, who were farmers, divorced and abandoned their son when he was two years old. He was then shunted back and forth among various relatives living in the rural South.[6]

After graduating from high school, Jasper attended the University of South Carolina for three semesters and a commercial art school in New York City for six months, dropping out after being told he had no talent. He was then drafted into the U.S. Army and served for two years.[7]

In 1954, Johns returned to the Big Apple and worked as a clerk at a bookstore. He spent a good deal of time reading and began thinking about becoming a writer, but he also enjoyed drawing. "I had no focus. I was vague and rootless," he recalled many years later.[8]

CREATING AN OUTLAW MARRIAGE

Robert Rauschenberg and Jasper Johns met on a winter night early in 1954 on the corner of Madison Avenue and Fifty-seventh Street. Johns was walking home from his job at the bookstore, and Rauschenberg was with a friend who knew both men and introduced them.[9]

They were immediately attracted to each other, but it was Rauschenberg, his relationship with Twombly having ended, who made the first move. This happened partly because Rauschenberg was five years older and considerably more comfortable with his sexuality.[10]

After they met, Rauschenberg urged Johns to quit his bookstore job so they could work together creating window displays. This freelancing arrangement would give them time to paint, doing the displays only when they needed to pay the rent and buy food. Rauschenberg had been designing windows for various stores, and he was eager to collaborate on the work with Johns. "Bob and I began to get jobs together," Johns later recalled. "I realized I could do what he did—work only when I was broke and needed money. So I quit my regular job."[11]

Rauschenberg suggested that they move in together, but Johns said he wasn't ready to take that step. So they rented two loft apartments in the same building but on different floors. They generally slept at Johns's place because he had a refrigerator, while Rauschenberg didn't.[12]

MOVING OUT FROM ABSTRACT EXPRESSIONISM

By the spring of 1954, Rauschenberg and Johns were supporting each other's creative efforts. "Jasper and I literally traded ideas," Rauschenberg recalled years later. "He would say, 'I've got a terrific idea for you,' and then I'd return the favor by finding one for him."[13]

This sharing of ideas was critically important to the pair of artists because they faced the Herculean task of breaking away from the style of painting that dominated the art world at the time. Rauschenberg and Johns would get out of bed in the morning and immediately begin talking about what each of them planned to paint that day. "Jasper and I used to start each day," Rauschenberg said, "by having to move out from abstract expressionism."[14]

Artists at the center of that powerful movement applied their paint rapidly and with force, striving to create works in which they expressed emotions that they believed viewers could understand—if they looked long enough and hard enough. Brush strokes typically were large, and paint sometimes was even thrown onto the canvases. Leaders of the movement such as Willem de Kooning and Jackson Pollock made no effort to represent their subject matter, arguing that the spontaneity of the painting process released the creativity of their unconscious minds.

JOHNS SUPPORTING RAUSCHENBERG

The support Rauschenberg received from Johns gave him the confidence to experiment with new techniques. His paintings now were no longer flat but included shapes extending out from the surface. He created these textural elements—often two or three inches thick—by tearing newspaper pages into strips, adhering many layers of them to the canvas, and then painting over the protrusions.[15]

Johns's unequivocal support then gave Rauschenberg the confidence to take another step and begin incorporating objects into his paintings. He liked having another surface to work on besides the canvas, and he also liked that a picture reached out toward the person looking at it. The results were three-dimensional and sometimes free-standing, placing them somewhere between paintings and sculptures, thereby prompting Rauschenberg to coin a new term to describe his works: combines.[16]

He began with small objects such as a necktie and a pad of steel wool, and then he gradually moved on to larger items. One day he was walking past a taxidermist shop on Sixth Avenue and saw a stuffed Plymouth Rock hen that he couldn't resist—it reminded him of his childhood pets. The hen found its way into a free-standing combine. Another memorable piece consisted of three empty Coke bottles standing upright and inside a wooden frame that was flanked by wings on the two sides.[17]

An example of Johns helping his partner involved a stuffed goat. Because of the animal's size, Rauschenberg knew the work it became part of would have to sit on the floor rather than be mounted on the wall, but he struggled with how to make the goat look like it belonged in a painting. Johns suggested that Rauschenberg construct a platform that would extend out from the canvas and serve as a stylized pasture, the proper setting for such an animal. Rauschenberg instantly took his lover's advice. The work became one of the artist's signature pieces, as well as one that critics labeled a "seminal" work of the 1950s.[18]

RAUSCHENBERG SUPPORTING JOHNS

The support Johns received from Rauschenberg was even more significant. "Before that time, when anybody asked me what I did," Johns later recalled, "I said I was *going to become* an artist. Now that I was with Bob, I decided to stop *becoming* an artist and to *be* an artist."[19]

Johns's first step was to destroy all the paintings he'd created before beginning his outlaw marriage. He told a reporter many years later, "I got rid of everything because I wanted to change the form of my thought and the content of my work." The artist then stopped painting for a few months, waiting for inspiration.[20]

Rauschenberg helped him recognize that inspiration when it finally came. One morning in 1954, Johns casually mentioned to his partner that he'd had a "crazy" dream the previous night. When Rauschenberg asked for details,

Johns replied, "I was painting the American flag." Rauschenberg didn't think the dream was crazy at all, telling his partner, "That's a really great idea." And so Johns immediately went to his studio and began work on his first flag painting.[21]

Based on the image of an American flag stretched across a canvas with the paint extending all the way to the edge with no border, Johns's work appeared to be simple. On another level, though, it was complex: was it a flag or did it just *look like* a flag? Should viewers who see it stand up and recite the Pledge of Allegiance, or should they approach it as pure abstraction, a rectangle holding bands of color and a cluster of stars? Like many of the pieces Johns did after it, the painting blurred the line between artwork and the object it depicted, raising fundamental questions about reality and perception.[22]

After creating several paintings that featured flags and hearing enthusiastic words of support from Rauschenberg, Johns moved on to other subjects. He created works featuring the alphabet, then archery targets, and then the numbers 0 through 9. What all these items had in common, Johns later said, was that they were "things which are seen but not looked at."[23]

JOHNS BECOMING A SENSATION

Leo Castelli, who owned a Manhattan art gallery, had known Rauschenberg casually for several years. On a rainy Sunday afternoon in 1957, he climbed the stairs to the artist's fourth-story loft to look at his combines.[24]

After Castelli saw Rauschenberg's work, the artist insisted upon taking him down one flight so he could see what Johns had been doing. The gallery owner later recalled his first reaction. "I saw evidence of the most incredible genius—entirely fresh and new and not related to anything else," Castelli said. "It was like the sensation you feel when you see a very beautiful girl for the first time, and after five minutes you want to marry her." Castelli instantly offered to do a one-man show for Johns, though he didn't extend such an offer to Rauschenberg.[25]

Johns's show in January 1958 hit the art world like a meteor. The city's most important art patrons came to see the works and quickly bought paintings to add to their private collections. Meanwhile, the editor of *Art News,* one of the country's most respected journals in the field, placed one of the works, *Target with Four Faces,* on his cover. Most important of all, the director of collections from the Museum of Modern Art chose four of Johns's paintings to go on permanent display at America's foremost institution dedicated to modern art. By the time the show closed, every work had been purchased. One art historian would later write, "It was the most successful debut anyone could remember, and the repercussions were felt almost immediately, from Milan to Tokyo."[26]

There were two reasons why the paintings sparked such an extraordinary response. First was Johns's choice of subjects. "Unlike the abstract expressionists," wrote a critic from the *New York Times,* "Johns has no interest in lofty strivings or romantic ideals or heroic quests for the sublime. The only emotion suggested by his work is a cool, astringent irony." That reviewer also said, "Johns's work is an ingenious negation of abstract expressionism. His flags, targets and stenciled numbers are emptied of all illusion or grandeur, and they make viewers wonder whether a painting, like a cup or a chair, isn't just an ordinary material object."[27]

The second point that observers made about Johns's pieces had to do with the technique he used when creating them. "He paints his images with such elegance and control that they absolutely demand to be looked at," another *New York Times* critic said. "He lavishes great care on their execution." Because of the great care Johns took, his surfaces had a dense, sensuous look. He also used narrow, sensitive brushstrokes that were a striking contrast to those of the abstract expressionists.[28]

After Castelli had organized the one-man show for Johns, Rauschenberg went to the gallery owner's wife, Ileana, and asked her to cajole her husband into doing one for him, too. In dramatic contrast to the success of Johns's show, Rauschenberg's event was a complete failure. Critics opted not to review the show, and only a single painting was sold. One visitor commented on Rauschenberg's work through an act of vandalism. That is, when no one was looking, he scrawled two words across one of the combines: "Fuck You."[29]

AN OUTLAW MARRIAGE SURVIVING A MAJOR CHALLENGE

By the summer of 1958, the Rauschenberg/Johns outlaw marriage was in a very good place. The two men moved to a studio where they lived and worked together, pooling their money while providing unwavering support for each other's creativity. "We were just living and working, and our world was very much limited to each other," Johns later recalled. "We were very dependent on one another."[30]

The best moment of each artist's day came when he showed his partner what he was working on, Johns said. "The kind of exchange we had was stronger than talking. It's nice to have verbal ideas about painting, but it's much better to express them through the medium itself." When the men needed a break, they drove their secondhand white Jaguar to East Hampton for a few days of relaxation.[31]

Perhaps most laudable about the partnership at this stage was that it had weathered the kind of major shift that destroys many marriages. That is, when the two men had become a couple in 1954, Rauschenberg had been an established artist, already having had his own shows, while Johns was still struggling to decide if he wanted to be a writer or a painter. But now, four years later, Johns was the big success, having become a sensation in the art world, while Rauschenberg was still creating works that art critics and patrons either ignored or mocked. And yet, despite this dramatic change in their roles, the partnership was thriving.[32]

TAKING THEIR ART IN NEW DIRECTIONS

In 1959, Rauschenberg undertook a project to prove that he was a serious artist. Setting his combines aside, he created a series of illustrations based on Dante's *Inferno,* one drawing for each of the thirty-four cantos in the epic poem. The pieces blended Rauschenberg's own drawings with clippings he took from contemporary magazines. His modern-day Hell was populated with gas-masked National Guardsmen and athletes cut from the pages of *Sports Illustrated.*[33]

The year and a half that Rauschenberg devoted to the project was well spent. For when the series was exhibited, critics loved it. *Arts and Architecture* magazine wrote, "Rauschenberg attacks the problems of illustration with a classicist's sobriety," and the *New York Times* went so far as to say that the artist's visual depiction of Dante's poem was comparable in quality and impact to Michelangelo's *Last Judgment.*[34]

Johns also took his art in a new direction during the late 1950s. Still committed to focusing on subjects with the literal qualities of the flags and targets he'd been painting but now moving into sculpture, he created pieces that depicted everyday items such as flashlights and lightbulbs. He liked these objects, he told a reporter, because, "I can retain a great deal of what they are but still alter them." When Leo Castelli displayed the sculptures in his gallery, he had no problem finding buyers.[35]

The success that Castelli had with Johns's new works angered abstract expressionist Willem de Kooning, who bitterly joked about the gallery owner, "You could give that son of a bitch two beer cans and he could sell them." When Johns heard the comment, he turned the insult into inspiration. He created a piece consisting of two cans of Ballantine Ale, standing side by side, that he cast in bronze and painted so carefully that a viewer could easily mistake them for the real thing. When Castelli placed the work in his gallery, a collector bought it for $900. (When the collector put the piece up for auction in 1973, it sold for $900,000.)[36]

GOING SEPARATE WAYS

One of the illustrations that Rauschenberg created as part of his *Inferno* series showed Dante's description of the fate of sodomites. According to the poem, men who had sex with men were sentenced to run barefoot, for all of eternity, over hot sand. As part of his piece illustrating the punishment, Rauschenberg included a drawing of his own foot, outlined in red crayon. His public showing of this piece in 1960 marked the beginning of the end of his outlaw marriage.[37]

Specifically, the force that came between the two men was Johns's fear of being publicly identified as a homosexual. Rauschenberg including his foot in the illustration about sodomites was too explicit for his partner, creating a crack in the relationship that gradually grew larger. Johns objected to Rauschenberg using his own body part in an illustration about men who had sex with men, while Rauschenberg said the reference was too obscure to worry about.[38]

By 1961, various friends of the couple sensed there were problems, saying Johns often seemed guarded and withdrawn, sometimes bitterly sarcastic. Johns also bought a house on Edisto Island off the coast of South Carolina and began going there alone for lengthy periods.[39]

The final break came during the summer of 1962. At that point, Rauschenberg bought a house on Captiva Island off the coast of Florida. The split was painful for both men, and they had no contact whatsoever with each other for a full decade.[40]

Neither Rauschenberg nor Johns ever spoke publicly at any length about either their romantic relationship or their homosexuality. The most direct acknowledgment of their shared life came from Rauschenberg during a 1990 discussion with a writer from *Interview* magazine.

> RAUSCHENBERG: "I'm not frightened of the affection that Jasper and I had, both personally and as working artists. I don't see any sin or conflict in those days when each of us was the most important person in the other's life."
> INTERVIEWER: "Can you tell me why you parted ways?"
> RAUSCHENBERG: "Embarrassment about being well known."
> INTERVIEWER: "Embarrassment about being famous?"
> RAUSCHENBERG: "Socially. What had been tender and sensitive became gossip. It was sort of new to the art world that the two most well-known, up-and-coming studs were affectionately involved."[41]

Johns's fear about being identified as gay was fueled by the stigma that continued to be attached to homosexuality during the era. The nation's newspapers routinely referred to such men as "sex perverts" or "sex deviants," and law enforcement officials proactively worked to identify homosexuals. Any man who was found to have had sexual relations with another man was promptly fired and sent to jail.[42]

Throughout their careers, Rauschenberg and Johns avoided talking with reporters about any aspect of their personal lives, repeatedly saying they wanted their art to speak for itself. Johns was particularly reticent about granting interviews, agreeing to them only when a gallery owner or museum director insisted on such a session to promote an upcoming exhibition.[43]

RAUSCHENBERG WINNING GLOBAL ACCLAIM

The single Rauschenberg work that had sold during his one-man show at the Castelli Gallery in 1958 had been purchased by Alan Solomon, the curator of the Cornell University art museum in Ithaca, New York. Solomon's stature in the art world rose in 1963 when he was hired to direct the Jewish Museum on Manhattan's Upper East Side.[44]

To draw attention to the museum's recent expansion, Solomon organized fifty-five of Rauschenberg's works into a show that included examples of his art from the previous dozen years, including his austere white paintings as well as his combines and his *Inferno* illustrations. When critics and art patrons saw how Rauschenberg's art had evolved, their opinion about the artist instantly changed.[45]

The *Nation* called Rauschenberg's art "the most significant now being produced in the United States," and the *New York Times* observed, "His creations force a redefinition of what art is all about."[46]

In the wake of that triumph, officials at the Museum of Modern Art acknowledged Rauschenberg's stature by adding one of his combines to its permanent collection; the combine, which Rauschenberg had completed in 1961, includes an automobile tire as well as a license plate. Later in the year, officials at the museum also acquired his *Inferno* series.[47]

Rauschenberg's star soared even higher in the summer of 1964 when he became the first American ever to win the grand prize at the Venice Biennale, the international art world's highest honor. On the night the announcement was made, a crowd of revelers hoisted him onto their shoulders and carried him around St. Mark's Square like a conquering hero.[48]

ACHIEVING LEGENDARY STATUS

And so, by the mid-1960s, Rauschenberg and Johns were both major artists. Indeed, no museum anywhere in the world that claimed to have a first-class modern art collection could call its holdings complete unless it had several examples of each artist's work.

Still more acclaim came the men's way with the emergence of pop art, as observers credited them, because of their work in the 1950s, with being the godfathers of this new style of painting. Rauschenberg incorporating everyday objects into his pieces and Johns painting flags and targets, critics said, had laid the groundwork for artists such as Andy Warhol celebrating the Campbell's soup can and Roy Lichtenstein elevating comic book imagery into high art.[49]

Several Rauschenberg quotations reinforced that he and the pop artists had much in common. Among his most frequently repeated statements were "The strongest thing about my work, if I may say this, is that I chose to ennoble the ordinary," and "I really feel sorry for people who think things like soap dishes or mirrors or Coke bottles are ugly because they're surrounded by things like that all day long, and it must make them miserable."[50]

In the late 1990s and early 2000s, both men's names appeared in news stories reporting on the astronomical amounts of money institutions and individuals were spending to acquire their work. The Metropolitan Museum of Art paid $20 million for Johns's 1955 painting *White Flag,* the Museum of Modern Art paid $30 million for Rauschenberg's 1955 work *Rebus,* and a private collector bought Johns's 1959 painting *False Start* for a jaw-dropping $80 million—the largest amount ever paid for a work by a living artist.[51]

Despite the fact that Rauschenberg and Johns both continued to create new pieces into the beginning of the twenty-first century, critics repeatedly stated that their finest works—which also meant those that were the most valuable—were the ones they'd created during the period from 1954 to 1962 when they'd been a couple.[52]

KEEPING THEIR DISTANCE TO THE END

Although the breach between Rauschenberg and Johns never entirely healed, they made progress in that direction. By the early 1970s, they no longer avoided crossing paths, as they were both willing to attend the same exhibit openings. The two men were frequently spotted at these soirees chatting amiably with each other.[53]

Rauschenberg granted more interviews than Johns did, but one quotation from the more reticent of the two men received a great deal of attention. During a dinner party at the home of a leading art collector, the host expressed the opinion that Rauschenberg was the most influential figure in the history of American art. Suddenly realizing that his statement could be seen as a slight to Johns, the host quickly turned to the artist and said, "After you, of course, Jasper." Upon hearing the comment, Johns instantly smiled and said, "No, including me."[54]

With regard to the personal lives of the two men, biographers and journalists documented that Rauschenberg entered into a number of romantic relationships after he and Johns separated. These partners included a dancer in the 1960s and two artists, one in the 1970s and another in the early 2000s. Johns, by contrast, either didn't have other lovers or succeeded in keeping them out of the public eye.[55]

It's curious, in light of the fact that Johns's fear of the couple's sexuality becoming public was the reason they ended their relationship, that many news organizations reported on the outlaw marriage in the obituaries they published when Rauschenberg died in 2008. The *Los Angeles Times* said the two men had been "romantically linked," the *New York Times* mentioned the "intimacy of their relationship," and the Associated Press—in a story that was reprinted in newspapers around the world—stated: "Rauschenberg met Jasper Johns in 1954. He and the younger artist, who both became world-famous, became lovers and had important influence on each other's work."[56]

Chapter 14

Ismail Merchant & James Ivory

1961–2005

Turning Literary Works into Sumptuous Films

...

Merchant Ivory Productions was widely recognized, during the final decades of the twentieth century, for setting the gold standard when it came to adapting iconic novels into high-quality motion pictures. The company created films that are distinguished by their opulent sets, exquisite attention to period detail, and superb writing and acting. Two of Merchant Ivory's most highly lauded works are *A Room with a View* and *Howards End*—both movies won multiple Academy Awards.

The company was founded and led for more than four decades by same-sex couple Ismail Merchant and James Ivory. As producer, Merchant used his endless supply of energy and chutzpah to raise the money needed to make the films and his abundant charm to persuade such legendary performers as Anthony Hopkins, Maggie Smith, and Emma Thompson to star in them.

As director, Ivory brought to filmmaking a refined aesthetic style, ensuring that the movies were beautiful as well as sophisticated.

...

James Ivory was born into a middle-class family in 1928. His father owned a lumber company in the small town of Klamath Falls, Oregon, and his mother took care of James and his younger sister.[1]

The boy was fascinated, from an early age, with the world of filmmaking. "*Gone With the Wind* held me spellbound," he later wrote, "and I was old enough when it came out in 1939 to appreciate that it was something more than the usual." By the age of fourteen, he was already determined to carve out a career in the world of motion pictures.[2]

After high school, he enrolled at the University of Oregon, majoring in fine arts. He traveled to Europe between his junior and senior years, splitting his summer between France and Italy.[3]

Next came film school at the University of Southern California. As his master's thesis, Ivory made a documentary, titled *Venice: Theme and Variations,* which examined how artists of different time periods had viewed the beautiful Italian city.[4]

It was while studying Venetian art that Ivory became acquainted with Indian paintings. He was so taken by the works, in fact, that he made them the subject of his second film, *The Sword and the Flute.* The movie looked at Indian miniatures in the United States and was first screened at a party in New York City in early 1961.[5]

Ismail Noormohamed Abdul Rehman was born into an upper-class family in Bombay, India, in 1936. His father earned his living as a textile dealer, and his mother took care of her son and his six sisters.[6]

To ensure that Ismail received the best possible education, his parents sent him to private schools where his classes were taught in English. His flair for being a producer surfaced early, and he was already putting together variety shows while he was in secondary school.[7]

He continued his education at St. Xavier's College in Bombay, majoring in English literature while spending his free time staging more shows. It was during his undergraduate days that the young man fell in love with movies, setting his sights on relocating to America and producing films there.[8]

Ismail also proved, while still in college, that he had a talent for raising money. His profits from producing a variety show during his senior year were so substantial that they paid his tuition to New York University, where he earned a master's in business administration.[9]

By the time he finished graduate school, Ismail had changed his surname to Merchant, believing it was more cosmopolitan than his original one.[10]

In early 1961, one of Merchant's friends invited him to a party at a New

York City apartment where a film with an Indian theme was to be screened. The work was titled *The Sword and the Flute,* and it was directed by a young American filmmaker named James Ivory.[11]

CREATING AN OUTLAW MARRIAGE

Ivory and Merchant met at that New York screening. Recalling that evening many years later, Merchant said, "Conversation flowed," but Ivory politely disagreed, saying, "Not quite. Ismail kept popping up to telephone important people."[12]

Regardless of whether their initial chat was smooth or disjointed, the two men soon created a partnership that encompassed both their professional and personal lives. By late 1961, they'd not only founded a production company but also were living together as husband and husband.[13]

Merchant Ivory Productions chose *The Householder* as its first project. The film is a humorous coming-of-age story about a sheltered young man who's thrust into an arranged marriage. Most of the expenses to make the movie, which was shot in India, were paid by investors Merchant brought on board. Although critics praised the work, it didn't do well at the box office.[14]

The couple's next several releases were similar to the first one in that they feature Indian subjects but with a Western audience in mind. All of the films received praise from critics but didn't appeal to a broad viewership. They also shared the fact that their screenplays had been written by Ruth Prawer Jhabvala, who'd been born in Germany but was now living in India.[15]

CREATING A PROFESSIONAL PARTNERSHIP

As the various productions unfolded, it became clear that Ivory and Merchant, although they had very different personalities, complemented each other when it came to making movies.

Biographers who've written about James Ivory use adjectives such as "reserved," "withdrawn," "understated," and "genteel." An actress who worked with the director on his earliest films reinforced the same general theme when she described him as "retiring" and "not able to push himself on his own."[16]

Ismail Merchant's biographers, by contrast, opt for adjectives such as "extroverted," "ebullient," "brash," and "aggressive." One author described the producer as "a volatile man of quicksilver mood changes" who also was "extraordinarily self-disciplined and almost totally absorbed in his work" as well as one who was "intensely and deeply practical."[17]

When writing about Ivory's gifts as a filmmaker, biographers say he possesses "wonderful taste" that has manifested itself in "movies noted for the beauty and expert composition of their imagery. Ivory makes pictures that have atmosphere and resonance, and always a sense of style. It is often said that Ivory's films have his unique stamp on them—special qualities that enter into them: sophistication, tolerant affection, sharp wit, a feeling for place."[18]

With regard to Merchant's skills as a producer, one colleague created a vivid image of him by saying, "He's like an elephant outside the financier's door. You can see him through the glass, he won't go away, he is very patient, and there is always the chance that he will come crashing in." The demands on Merchant's ability to raise money grew significantly during the company's early years. In 1961, the couple's first film cost only $125,000 to make, but, by 1974, that figure had grown to $750,000.[19]

Merchant also developed a reputation as a producer who stretched a dollar as far as he could. For one film, Ivory wanted a cache of expensive jewelry that his partner knew they couldn't afford to buy. "I went to the Gem Palace, a wonderful jewelry shop in Jaipur," Merchant recalled, "and asked if I could perhaps borrow a bit of jewelry for the film. The owners filled up two briefcases with about $2 million worth of jewels and brought them, without any form of security, to the set."[20]

FOCUSING ON LITERARY WORKS

One night in the mid-1970s while Ivory and Merchant were at home watching TV, they saw a British-made film based on a book by American novelist Henry James. "I can do better than that," Ivory muttered. "Why should the English be doing this sort of thing and never the Americans?" The director meant his statement as a casual one, but Merchant took it to heart, saying that if his partner wanted to adapt literary works to the big screen, he'd find the money to do it. That conversation set the couple on the course that transformed their production company into the most highly regarded independent filmmaking enterprise in the world.[21]

For their first project in this new direction, Ivory and Merchant chose James's novel *The Europeans*. The film is a study of transatlantic manners and character that opens with the arrival of two siblings, who've been raised abroad, to a rural area near Boston in the 1840s. The brother, an artist, successfully woos and marries a wealthy young woman, but the sister, who is beautiful and fashionable but also opinionated and manipulative, is stymied in her effort to marry a socially prominent man when he concludes that her artful manners mean she can't be trusted.[22]

The Europeans, released in 1979, was embraced not only by critics, such as the one from the *Chicago Sun-Times* who praised it as "elegantly composed," but also by fans of art films. Encouraged by the success, the director took on a second work by Henry James, and the producer not only raised the money but also cast a star to lift the film to a higher level than any of the couple's previous ones.[23]

Set in the period immediately after the Civil War, *The Bostonians* focuses on American social reform efforts. The plot revolves around an unmarried suffragist who adopts a naive young inspirational speaker as her companion. Competing against the suffragist for the younger woman is a chauvinistic lawyer who's strikingly handsome.[24]

What set *The Bostonians* apart from other independent films was that the suffragist was played by Academy Award winner Vanessa Redgrave. For one of the nation's most honored actresses to star in a film that was the work of a production company outside the Hollywood studio system—and made for a modest $3 million—caused the motion picture world to stand up and take notice of Merchant Ivory Productions.[25]

An additional boost in stature for the company came when the film not only garnered positive reviews from the critics, with the *Los Angeles Times* describing it as "sumptuous" and the *Washington Post* saying, "It is a great movie," but also did relatively well at the box office.[26]

STRIKING GOLD WITH A ROOM WITH A VIEW

In 1973, the film magazine *Sight and Sound* had described James Ivory and Ismail Merchant as "two resilient, international optimists who continue to plan and organize in the belief that the best is yet to come. Ivory suggests, half jokingly, that Merchant is bound some day to have a really big financial success."[27]

A dozen years later, that success became reality when the same-sex couple adapted British novelist E. M. Forster's witty and engaging look at Edwardian manners into a huge hit.

A Room with a View revolves around an upper-class young woman named Lucy who travels to Italy under the watchful eye of her older cousin. When the women's room in their Florence pensione lacks good views of the city, they accept an offer from a man and his handsome and free-spirited son, a railway clerk named George, to switch rooms. A few days later on a trip into the Tuscan countryside, George kisses Lucy passionately, alarming the straitlaced cousin so severely that she cuts the holiday short. Back in England, Lucy agrees to marry a priggish but wealthy suitor. When George reappears, though, Lucy's heart joyfully triumphs over convention as she's drawn to his robust vitality. So she breaks her engagement and marries George.[28]

Ivory executed every element of the film with the utmost care. Among the memorable scenes is an early one in which Lucy plays a Beethoven piece on the piano, the nuanced movements of her body and the passion of her music subtly suggesting the romantic emotion in her nature that, later in the film, will be kindled into rebellion.[29]

A Room with a View's cast was one of its strengths. Academy Award winner Maggie Smith plays the archetype spinster—prim, anxious, and well-meaning—with hollow eyes that betray the human price she's paid for being inoffensive. Helena Bonham Carter's Lucy is girlishly appealing but also a young woman who possesses the courage to change her mind and refuse to marry a man she doesn't love. Julian Sands brings to his role as George an emotional fullness that communicates a healthy and irresistible manliness. Daniel Day-Lewis, who would go on to win two Academy Awards later in his career, plays the fiancé not merely as a foppish buffoon but also as a man with a vulnerability hidden beneath his starched collar.[30]

Critics who reviewed the film were unstinting in their praise. The *St. Louis Post-Dispatch* labeled it "superb," and the *Atlanta Constitution* called it "a scintillating and cherishable masterpiece." The *Washington Post* weighed in with the statement, "It is a lovely film," and the *Chicago Sun-Times* said, "The story moved slowly, it seemed, for the same reason you try to make ice cream last: because it's so good."[31]

When the Academy of Motion Picture Arts and Sciences announced its nominations for 1986, *A Room with a View* appeared on the list a stunning eight times, including nods to Ivory for best director and Merchant for best picture. By the end of the glamorous ceremony, the much-praised independent film had beaten out its competition from the major Hollywood studios in three categories, receiving golden statuettes for best costume design, best art direction, and best screenplay adaptation.[32]

The real game changer for Ivory and Merchant, however, came at the box office. For the men finally proved that they could create a cinematic work that pulled throngs of moviegoers into the neighborhood multiplex. They'd spent $3 million to create a film that produced gross revenues of $70 million.[33]

GOING PUBLIC WITH THEIR OUTLAW MARRIAGE

For the first quarter century of Ivory and Merchant's life together, only their closest friends and family members knew about their love for each other. They kept their outlaw marriage out of the public eye because they needed to raise money to make their films. That is, they feared that financial backing would be tough to come by if potential investors knew the two men weren't merely professional partners but also romantic ones.[34]

Those concerns faded dramatically after the financial success of *A Room with a View*. Merchant, in his role as producer, no longer had to worry about persuading people to invest in the films his partner directed, as the projects were now seen as surefire moneymakers. And so, the couple no longer felt a need to keep their personal relationship a secret.[35]

They went public with that aspect of their lives in a 1986 *New York Times* feature story. The headline read "Merchant and Ivory's Country Retreat," and the accompanying photo showed the two men posing between the Ionic columns on the front of a large house. The story identified the structure as the 1805 Hudson Valley country house where they'd been living together for the previous decade—their primary residence before that had been an apartment in Manhattan.[36]

Details in the story gave readers a sense of the dynamics of the couple's domestic partnership: Merchant did the cooking, Ivory did the decorating.

Among the producer's culinary triumphs were saffron and almond ice cream, according to the piece, which also quoted him as listing the ingredients in the Bloody Marys he served the reporter who came to the couple's home to interview them—the visitor gave the drink his seal of approval, pronouncing it "potent and throaty."[37]

As for Ivory's decorating, the *Times* characterized the director's style as "eclectic." The story reported that the central hallway in the house, which had twelve-foot ceilings, felt like "an informal museum" filled with objects the couple had collected while filming in locations around the world. The story pointed out that Ivory sometimes paired unlikely items with each other— such as placing an antique Chippendale settee near a stuffed deer head with massive antlers.[38]

The *Times* wasn't the only paper that helped the couple go public with their relationship, as stories about it soon appeared in the *Chicago Tribune* and *Washington Post* as well. In the *Tribune* piece, Merchant talked about the night twenty-five years earlier when he and Ivory met. "I asked him out for coffee after the screening," the producer recalled. "I think he was a bit taken aback by this brash young man, but he agreed." The reporter who did the *Post* piece tried her best to expose cracks in the couple's relationship, but her efforts failed, forcing her to write, "They won't divulge any big differences between them."[39]

STAYING TRUE TO THEIR ART

A Room with a View's success caused the major Hollywood studios, for the first time, to regard Ivory and Merchant as highly desirable filmmakers. In the eyes of the movers and shakers of the movie capital of the world, the couple had made a low-budget movie that had earned a great deal of money, and that meant the twosome was suddenly in great demand.

Ivory told a reporter, in 1986, that "truckloads of scripts" were arriving at his and Merchant's home. In other words, studio executives were trying to persuade the couple to take on projects they saw as likely moneymakers. "The projects have big budgets, and very often a star has said they want to do it. But it's not anything I'd want to make," Ivory said. "It's just rubbish."[40]

And so, despite receiving offers that most filmmakers would have jumped at the chance to make, the couple rejected them all. "The scripts were shallow," Merchant said. "None of them had any link to our methods of filmmaking. This was not how we saw ourselves."[41]

To show Hollywood exactly who they were as filmmakers, Ivory and Merchant chose as their next project a movie that they knew from the outset had no chance of drawing a huge audience or making a lot of money. Their choice did, however, reflect the men's new openness about their sexuality.

Maurice was adapted from E. M. Forster's novel about a young Englishman, during the Edwardian period, who gradually recognizes his homosexuality. He then must decide how to live his life—will he embrace his true nature and bear a stigma or will he suppress his feelings and move forward on a path toward conventional success? *Maurice* made a modest profit while earning positive reviews, such as the *New York Times* calling the film "deft" and "intelligent."[42]

STRIKING GOLD AGAIN WITH HOWARDS END

By the early 1990s, Ivory and Merchant had established such a sterling reputation that the most acclaimed actors in the world were eager to be associated with them, even if it meant earning a mere fraction of what the major Hollywood studios paid. Anthony Hopkins took that step in 1992 when, after winning an Academy Award a year earlier, he starred in the film that many critics would come to see as the greatest work Merchant Ivory Productions ever created.[43]

Howards End, which was adapted from E. M. Forster's novel of the same name, is set just before World War I and focuses on three families within the British class system. The Wilcoxes—Hopkins's character, Henry, is the family patriarch—earned their fortune through business ventures. The Schlegels inherited their wealth and are progressive thinkers committed to the arts and social reform. The Basts are struggling at a grim, much lower rung of society, fighting desperately to avoid being swallowed up by poverty.[44]

The central character is the older of the two Schlegel sisters, Margaret, and is played by Emma Thompson. Henry Wilcox's wife dies early in the film, and he then becomes attracted to Margaret, a somewhat flighty yet wonderfully compassionate soul—much like his deceased wife. When Margaret accepts Henry's marriage proposal, his greedy children and her headstrong sister are all dismayed. Meanwhile, the sister has befriended Leonard Bast, a down-on-his-luck clerk who aspires to a better life. The sister's relentless effort to help Leonard leads to a shocking moment of tragedy that takes one life and seriously damages several others.

Again, this film is distinguished by its attention to period detail. The

Wilcox mansion in London is the epitome of Edwardian opulence, the dark rooms made claustrophobic by the ubiquitous potted plants, porcelain figurines, and lace antimacassars. The Schlegel home feels more open because sunlight streams through the windows and paintings of landscapes dot the walls, which are painted a tasteful pale gray. The Bast apartment is dark and cramped, so small that there's barely room to move. Most striking of all is the Wilcox family's pastoral retreat, named Howards End, with its abundance of windows looking onto the colorful English garden—bursting with bright pink and yellow blossoms.[45]

Reviewers were exuberant about the film. The *Boston Globe* called it a "beautifully nuanced, richly textured masterpiece," and the *San Francisco Chronicle* said, "It's not only a feast for the eyes, but it's also a wise and thoughtful film." The *New York Times* pronounced the movie "a great pleasure" and also said, "It's time for legislation decreeing that no one be allowed to make a screen adaptation of a novel of any quality if James Ivory and Ismail Merchant are available and elect to do the job."[46]

The movie was nominated for nine Academy Awards, with Ivory making the list for director and Merchant for best picture. *Howards End* ultimately received the Oscars for best art direction, best screenplay adaptation, and best actress in a leading role—for Emma Thompson's tour de force performance as Margaret Schlegel.[47]

CREATING A THIRD MASTERPIECE

In 1993, Ivory and Merchant made what critics would come to see as the last of their great films. Many observers also saw the work as a triumph because it again starred Anthony Hopkins and Emma Thompson, but this time the filmmakers turned things upside down by casting the stars not as a wealthy couple but as a pair of servants.[48]

The Remains of the Day tells the story of a quintessential English butler, played by Hopkins, who uses the demands of his job to insulate himself from emotional risk. The other major character is a housekeeper, played by Thompson, who's generally sensible but sometimes irrepressibly passionate. She does her best to break through the armor that the butler has created to hide his feelings, but he remains stalwartly distant. The adaptation of a novel by writer Kazuo Ishiguro begins in the late 1930s and continues for twenty years, set in a majestic manor house appointed with leather-bound books and gleaming silver flatware.[49]

Reviews of the period piece overflowed with praise. The *New York Times* described it as "exquisite" and "spellbinding," the *Washington Post* called it "yet another jewel in the James Ivory and Ismail Merchant crown," and the

Boston Globe gushed that it was "impeccably crafted" and "one of the decade's most moving films." The movie gave Ivory his third Oscar nomination for best director and Merchant his third for best picture, although it ultimately didn't receive any Academy Awards.[50]

GOING IN NEW DIRECTIONS

After making *The Remains of the Day,* the couple decided they'd become too comfortable adapting literary works. So they set out to make other types of films. Among the projects they took on during the next several years were *Le Divorce,* a frothy comedy, and *Surviving Picasso,* a biography of the famous painter's mistress.[51]

It was while creating another movie during this period, *The Proprietor,* that Merchant reminded the world how far he'd go to make a film his partner wanted to make. Ivory had his heart set on shooting part of the movie inside the Trianon Palace hotel in Versailles, France, but the owners had a firm policy against allowing cameras on the premises. So Merchant dressed up in robes and a turban to pass himself off as the Maharaja of Jodhpur. The camera crew masqueraded as his entourage and, once inside, filmed the scenes Ivory wanted for the movie.[52]

DEATH ENDS A FORTY-YEAR OUTLAW MARRIAGE

In the spring of 2005, Ivory and Merchant were in London working on a project titled *The White Countess,* a love story set in 1930s Shanghai, when the producer began suffering severe pains in his abdomen. He underwent surgery for bleeding ulcers, and a day later he died, at the age of sixty-eight.[53]

Major newspapers around the country published obituaries summarizing Merchant's life and work, many of them acknowledging the contributions that he and Ivory had made to American filmmaking. The *San Francisco Chronicle,* for example, wrote, "Merchant Ivory came to symbolize scenes of rich décor and period atmosphere, castles and country houses of Europe, and lavish dinners and drawing room intrigue."[54]

Several of the obituaries spoke in broader terms about Ivory and Merchant's impact on the movie industry writ large. The *Chicago Tribune* stated, "Their hits—especially E. M. Forster's adaptations of 'A Room with a View' and 'Howards End'—helped revive the public's taste for well-made, emotionally literate period dramas," while the *Los Angeles Times* said, "They helped teach modern American audiences they need not fear period dramas."[55]

The *Times* was also among the news organizations that paid tribute to Ivory and Merchant's lengthy outlaw marriage. "In a business where professional marriages last hardly any longer than personal ones," the paper wrote, "the producer's association with Ivory, who was also Merchant's life partner, spanned more than 40 years."[56]

After Merchant died, Ivory sold the Hudson Valley house where the couple had lived and moved to an apartment in New York City. The director continued to make films, but they didn't compare in quality to the ones that he and Merchant had created together. In 2008, for example, Ivory's *The City of Your Final Destination* told the story of a doctoral student struggling to write a biography of a Latin American writer. Reviews were mixed, with the *New York Times* dismissing the film as "trivial."[57]

Chapter 15

Frances Clayton & Audre Lorde

1968–1988

Raising a Voice for Women of Color

...

Audre Lorde was a widely acclaimed writer who focused on a range of issues. Racism, sexism, and homophobia were the major themes in her early work. Like Martin Luther King Jr., Lorde insisted that issues of class and race be confronted in all movements for social change—including the women's liberation movement. Two of her seventeen books chronicled her experiences with cancer. Lorde received enormous praise as an effective voice both for women of color and for women who love women.

Lorde began her writing career in high school, when *Seventeen* magazine published the sixteen-year-old's first poem. It wasn't until she was in her mid-thirties, however, that Lorde published her first poetry collection. Before that point, she juggled several lives as wife, mother, librarian, and educator. Although she wrote every day during these years, she credited her same-sex partner of two decades, Frances Clayton, with making her life as an author and an activist possible.

...

Frances Louise Clayton was born in Elizabethtown, Illinois, in 1926. She was the youngest of seven children in a family headed by a Methodist minister who moved to a series of small churches throughout the Midwest. The blond-haired, blue-eyed Frances was shy and made few friends, partly because the family never stayed in one town for very long.[1]

A brilliant student, she received a scholarship to attend Indiana University and study behavioral psychologist in the program developed by the leader in the field, B. F. Skinner. After graduation, Clayton won fellowships to attend Brown University, where she earned her master's, and then the University of Minnesota, where she earned her PhD.[2]

Clayton joined the psychology faculty at Brown University in Providence, Rhode Island. She soon distinguished herself in the academic world because of her groundbreaking research on animal behavior, becoming the first woman in her department to achieve tenure.[3]

On a personal level, Clayton felt comfortable living alone and having serial relationships with women. Her teaching and laboratory work were highly satisfying to her, as was a sabbatical fellowship that took her to Cambridge University. By the late 1960s, and after having lived alone for a dozen years, however, she was open to new adventures.[4]

Audrey Geraldine Lorde was born in the Harlem neighborhood of New York City in 1934, the daughter of immigrants who'd left their native West Indies a decade earlier. When her father had first arrived in the United States, he'd peddled apples. But he later obtained a real estate license, and, after World War II, he owned an apartment building, which his wife helped him manage.[5]

A sense of the young Audrey's willfulness is captured by the fact that she dropped the "y" from her first name while she was still in elementary school. She didn't like the letter because it extended below the base line created by the other letters. Audre excelled academically but received low grades in conduct.[6]

By the age of twelve, she'd already fallen in love with poetry, memorizing any number of her favorite works. During her teens, Lorde began writing poems of her own, sharing them with a group of literary-minded friends.[7]

After graduating from Hunter College High School, Lorde worked as a nurse's aide to pay her living expenses while she attended then tuition-free Hunter College, a public institution in Manhattan. She earned her degree in English literature in 1959 and entered Columbia University's graduate program in library science, while continuing to create poems that she kept in her personal journal.[8]

Lorde's life wasn't limited to studying and writing, as she spent many nights drinking and dancing in Greenwich Village's various lesbian bars. She was often the only dark-skinned woman in the crowd.[9]

AUDRE LORDE FOCUSING ON BEING A WIFE AND MOTHER

In 1962, Lorde shocked many of her friends by marrying a legal aid attorney named Ed Rollins. Two factors made the pairing unusual. First, Lorde was black and Rollins was white. Second, Lorde was a lesbian and Rollins was a gay man—they both knew about the other's sexual orientation when they walked down the aisle.[10]

Lorde and Rollins were close and loving friends who both wanted children. They opted to marry each other—both for companionship and for "cover" in a world that didn't embrace gay or lesbian parents.[11]

By the time they married, Lorde had finished her master's and was working at a public library. Within three months after the wedding, she became pregnant and quit her job to devote all her time to preparing for the birth and then caring for Elizabeth Lorde-Rollins.[12]

The roles of wife and mother dominated Lorde's life during this period, while her writing was limited to jotting down an occasional phrase on a scrap of paper she shoved into her purse or diaper bag. The birth of a second child, Jonathan, in 1964 meant that the mother of two had even less time or energy to create poetry.[13]

Circumstances in the household changed when Ed Rollins lost his job. Lorde then returned to the workforce, becoming a librarian at an elementary school.[14]

In 1967, she received a phone call from a high school friend, poet Diane di Prima, who now headed a small publishing house and wanted to release a book containing some of the works Lorde had written in the 1950s.[15]

A few months after putting together that manuscript, Lorde received a second unexpected phone call. This one was from the National Endowment for the Arts, informing her that she'd been awarded a grant, based on a recommendation from di Prima, to serve as a poet-in-residence at Tougaloo College in Mississippi.[16]

CREATING AN OUTLAW MARRIAGE

When Lorde went to Mississippi for six weeks in early 1968, she was hoping to get a sense of what it would be like to teach full time. That aspect of her experience ultimately was eclipsed by another one she hadn't seen coming: she met the woman who changed her life.[17]

Frances Clayton also had come to Tougaloo College as a visiting professor, and she and Lorde were instantly attracted to each other. Clayton had been a committed anti-racism activist for many years when she accepted the position at Tougaloo. And so, in addition to chemistry, the two women shared values in working for racial justice and integration. One night when they were together, they experienced night riders terrorizing the campus. Lorde also admired Clayton's courage, as she was one of only six white professors on the Tougaloo faculty at the time.[18]

When Lorde returned to New York, she reinvented her life along the lines that Clayton envisioned for her. She left her job as a librarian and landed a job on the English faculty at the City University of New York. Lorde also told her husband she wanted a divorce.[19]

The changes that took place in Frances Clayton's life after she left Mississippi were significant as well. She'd previously been a focused and ambitious woman who'd succeeded at the highest level of the academic world, but now she reconsidered how much she was willing to sacrifice in order to spend her life with the woman she loved.[20]

BEGINNING A NEW LIFE

In 1970, Lorde separated from Ed Rollins so she could live with Clayton. A major factor influencing the location of the couple's shared home was a stipulation in Lorde's separation agreement, inserted by Rollins, that she couldn't move the children out of New York state. This detail propelled Clayton to resign from her tenured position and move to a house on Staten Island with Lorde and her children. Clayton said, many years later, "My top priority at that point was to live with Audre. The only way I could do that was to leave Brown, so that's what I did."[21]

Clayton had a tough time finding a new job in academe. Her credentials as a teacher and researcher were exemplary, but potential employers were suspicious about why she'd given up tenure at an Ivy League institution. When asked to explain her decision, Clayton wasn't willing to say she'd moved to New York to be with her lesbian lover—neither Clayton nor Lorde was yet willing to be publicly identified as gay. After several awkward interviews, she ended up teaching introductory psychology courses at Queens College, an institution that didn't support the cutting-edge research she'd been doing for the previous two decades.[22]

Lorde and Clayton's personal life during this period was very satisfying. Clayton focused on making it possible for Lorde to spend as much time as she could on her writing. Specific steps Clayton took included setting aside a room in the Staten Island house to be Lorde's study—it was strictly off limits to Elizabeth and Jonathan—and assuming the majority of the domestic chores for the family, such as the cooking and cleaning.[23]

AUDRE LORDE RISING IN THE PUBLISHING WORLD

Lorde's first collection of poems, titled *The First Cities,* had been reviewed only by the *Negro Digest,* which described the volume as a "quiet, introspective book." That critique had been enough to prompt another small press to publish a second collection of her poems, with the sole review this time being more critical, the journal *Poetry* stating, "Lorde writes free verse of no particular note."[24]

Broadside Press published two more collections of Lorde's poems. One, titled *From a Land Where Other People Live,* was nominated for a National Book Award in 1973; yet neither book was widely reviewed, which Lorde found discouraging.[25]

Frances Clayton wasn't familiar with the small presses that specialized in poetry, but her academic experience at a prestigious university made her knowledgeable about mainstream publishing. She and Lorde then discussed strategies and decided it was time to find a literary agent.[26]

After the couple researched which agents were working with feminist topics, Lorde contacted Charlotte Sheedy, who immediately agreed to represent her.[27]

AUDRE LORDE GAINING ACCLAIM AS A POET

During the late 1970s, Lorde's work received many positive critiques, establishing her as a gifted poet. Reviewers wrote their laudatory comments about two of her collections, both published by W. W. Norton.

The central metaphor driving the first book, titled *Coal,* was that the dark-skinned people of the world were like coal—dug from the earth to fuel the factories that gave industrialized societies their wealth. In the second book, titled *The Black Unicorn,* Lorde focused on the oppression that defined the black experience, with the initial poem stating:

> The black unicorn is restless
> the black unicorn is unrelenting
> the black unicorn is not
> free.[28]

Both books were reviewed in literary as well as general-interest publications. The journal *Choice* praised Lorde's poetry as "rich and startling in its speed and fervor," while the *Nation* pronounced her prose "brilliant and honest." The poetry journal *Parnassus* lauded Lorde's voice as "invigorating" and "powerful," going on to say that having her work released by a major publisher ranked as "a seminal event in the evolution of contemporary letters."[29]

These positive reviews combined with Lorde being one of the few published poets who was a lesbian—by this point, she and Clayton were both comfortable being identified as gay women—brought a stream of requests for her to give readings. And so, Lorde began traveling to university campuses and feminist bookstores across the country. She also represented the United States at a writing conference in Russia in 1976 and at an arts festival in Nigeria in 1977. And in the final year of the decade, she was a featured speaker at the rally following the historic March on Washington for Lesbian and Gay Rights in Washington, D.C.[30]

FRANCES CLAYTON REDEFINING HER LIFE

When Lorde made these trips, Clayton stayed at home and took care of Elizabeth and Jonathan, while also often paying the bulk of Lorde's travel expenses. It had been a challenge for Clayton, when she and Lorde started living together, to adjust to being part of a household with two children, as she'd never been around young people before. And now, only a few years later, she was taking sole responsibility for a pair of teenagers for as long as a month at a time.[31]

An even bigger change came in Clayton's career. After teaching at Queens College for three years, she decided to move into psychotherapy. It took her several years to make the transition, initially taking courses part-time while continuing to teach at Queens, and then being supervised by practicing psychotherapists.[32]

By the late 1970s, Clayton had established a private practice in Manhattan. As one of the first certified counselors in New York City who was openly lesbian, she soon had far more clients than she could fit into her schedule. Clayton also quickly gained a reputation as a highly principled professional who had a unique talent for working with other gay women. Elizabeth Lorde-Rollins said, many years later, "Frances provided an incredible service to any number of lesbians. Many women of that period were struggling to become comfortable with their sexuality, and Frances guided them through that process. Totally aside from what she did for my mother, she was an extraordinary woman in her own right."[33]

AUDRE LORDE TRIUMPHING AS A MEMOIRIST

In 1978, Clayton and Lorde's life was turned upside down when Lorde found what turned out to be a malignant lump in her right breast. She turned to Clayton for emotional support as well as help in learning about the disease and her options for fighting it, ultimately deciding to have a mastectomy.[34]

Lorde then wrote a memoir about her experience. In *The Cancer Journals,* she spoke candidly about the decision of whether to have reconstructive surgery so that it would look, to other people, like she still had two breasts. She rejected the idea, she wrote, because she didn't want to send the message that she was ashamed of what had happened to her. "Women have been programmed," Lorde said, "to view our bodies only in terms of how they look and feel to others, rather than how they feel to ourselves."[35]

Her memoir was extremely well received. Among the most high-profile reviews was one in *Ms.*, then at the height of its popularity. The feminist magazine praised the author for writing with a "shimmering urgency," going on to say, "Lorde describes how and why she came to reject the false comfort conventionally offered to the post-mastectomy woman and the lie embodied in the prosthetic breast: *You will be the same as before.*"[36]

Lorde's success with the memoir propelled her to write an experimental book in a genre she called biomythography. *Zami: A New Spelling of My Name* told of a young Audre coming of age as the daughter of West Indian immigrants—"zami" is a pejorative Caribbean word for lesbian. The book advised against dark-skinned girls trying to fit into the white world. Instead, *Zami* argued that home and culture are concepts that feminists don't have to define based solely on race or nationality but can find within communities of supportive women.[37]

Reviews of *Zami* reinforced Lorde's place as one of the country's preeminent women writers. The *New York Times* called *Zami* "an excellent and evocative autobiography." The paper continued, "Lorde's experiences are painted with exquisite imagery. Her West Indian heritage shows through most clearly in her use of word pictures that are sensual, steamy, at times near-tropical, evoking the colors, smells—repeatedly, the smells—shapes, textures that are her life."[38]

The consistently positive reviews led to a boost in Lorde's academic career. Now that her creative gifts were well documented, the English faculty at Hunter College recruited her to fill a position as a poet. Lorde began the job in September 1981.[39]

STRAINS IN THE OUTLAW MARRIAGE

While Lorde and Clayton both were soaring to new heights professionally, signs of trouble were beginning to emerge in their relationship.[40]

The problem had to do with a dramatic difference in how they approached their outlaw marriage. Clayton wanted them to be monogamous, but Lorde insisted on an open relationship. What's more, each woman expected the other one to change. Clayton felt hurt and betrayed by Lorde's outside life; Lorde felt constrained and misunderstood by Clayton's anger and discontent. This division in their perception and reality caused increasing unhappiness and discontent.[41]

AUDRE LORDE CREATING A FEMINIST CLASSIC

During the late 1970s and early 1980s, Lorde had published articles in several literary journals and had given speeches at numerous conferences. In 1984, she collected fifteen of these works—expanding some of them—into a book of essays that ultimately became a classic text that's since been read by generations of women's studies students.[42]

The most contentious argument in *Sister Outsider* was that the women's liberation movement was racist. Lorde argued that white feminists consistently denigrated women of color, supporting her charge with examples from her own personal experiences.[43]

She began one essay by describing how she'd asked a white woman, at the end of a weeklong conference on race, what she'd gained from the event. The woman had responded, "I feel black women really understand me a lot better now." Lorde reacted to that statement by writing, in an angry tone, "As if understanding *her* lay at the core of the race problem." In that same essay, Lorde recalled an instance in which a white poet had interrupted the reading of works by women of color to read her own poem and then rush off to participate in what she announced to the other women was an "important" panel.[44]

Because of such incidents, Lorde said women of color should be outraged at the racism that permeated the women's liberation movement. In a statement directed at white feminists, she said, "I cannot hide my anger to spare you guilt, for to do so insults and trivializes all our efforts." In another passage, she said, "We cannot allow our fear of anger to deflect us nor seduce us into settling for anything less than the hard work of excavating honesty."[45]

Critics gave *Sister Outsider* rave reviews. *Essence,* the widely circulated magazine aimed at African American women, applauded Lorde for writing "in a no-nonsense manner" and then said, "The works in the book add up to a personal, thought-provoking portrait of a multifaceted artist." The *Village Voice,* the country's leading alternative newspaper, described Lorde as an "erudite black lesbian feminist" and said of her book, "The provocative ideas of *Sister Outsider* will unsettle some readers, and that's just what Lorde intends."[46]

AUDRE LORDE SETTING OUT TO CHANGE THE WORLD

By the early 1980s, Lorde was widely known not only as a literary figure but also as a social and political activist who was fighting global injustice on any number of fronts.[47]

She had, for many years, been involved in the civil rights struggle in the United States. In 1963, for example, she'd traveled to the nation's capital to participate in the historic March on Washington. Sexism, racism, and homophobia also had been central themes in Lorde's poetry. And so, when she became a widely respected artist, she helped build and lead institutions and organizations committed to changing the world.[48]

In 1980, she joined half a dozen other women to found Kitchen Table: Women of Color Press. They created the publishing enterprise to ensure that the words being written by black, Latina, and Asian women found their way into print. Lorde played a key role in raising funds for Kitchen Table by speaking at numerous benefits. To strengthen the publisher's reputation, she had her next book, *I Am Your Sister,* released by the fledgling publisher rather than by Norton.[49]

Lorde's activism moved to the international stage in 1981 when she helped found Sisterhood in Support of Sisters in South Africa. The group's goal was to encourage personal bonds between black women living in the United States and in South Africa as a step toward ending apartheid. Again, Lorde's involvement included giving readings to raise money that financed the organization's work. By this point, she often concluded her presentations with a challenge to her audience: "Applause is easy. Go out and do something."[50]

MORE TROUBLE IN THE OUTLAW MARRIAGE

In mid-1984, Lorde began having problems digesting food. Her doctor, fearing the cancer in her breast from six years earlier had metastasized, conducted tests that found a tumor in her liver. Lorde rejected the possibility that the cancer had returned, continuing her rigorous schedule of writing, teaching, and traveling.[51]

Lorde and Clayton went to Vermont for a vacation after the school year ended, but the retreat didn't work for them. Lorde had become seriously involved with a woman named Gloria Joseph, and Clayton sensed the decline of their love during the vacation. Lorde experienced Clayton as being "negative" and longed to be with her lover. Clayton was equally miserable because she didn't understand, not knowing about her partner's other relationship, why Lorde was so distracted and distant.[52]

Gloria Joseph taught sociology at Hampshire College in Amherst, Massachusetts. She and Lorde had met in 1979 at a retreat for black feminists, and their paths had crossed again two years later when Lorde attended a symposium that Joseph, a native of the Virgin Islands, had hosted at her vacation home on the island of St. Croix. They soon realized how much they had in common—both were black women of West Indian heritage, both worked in academia, and both wrote about issues facing women of color.[53]

By 1984, the two women had become sexually intimate, and Lorde was traveling to St. Croix whenever she could. She often felt ill by this point, so she not only liked being with Joseph but also enjoyed luxuriating in the tropical weather of the Caribbean.[54]

Health problems became a priority for Lorde in 1985 when pain in her midsection became so intense that she had to seek medical attention. Tests found a second tumor in her liver, prompting her doctor to tell her she definitely had liver cancer.[55]

Frances Clayton accompanied her partner, during the break between semesters, to a private clinic in Switzerland where Lorde began taking herbal medications to strengthen her immune system. On an emotional level, Lorde leaned heavily on Clayton while at the clinic, with comments in her personal journal acknowledging that "Frances, good old trooper that she is," provided unconditional support.[56]

Despite Clayton's devotion during these difficult times, Lorde began the process of ending their relationship. Comments in her journal in early 1986 suggest that Lorde knew her action was selfish, considering all that Clayton had done for her, but was driven by her determination "to live the rest of my life with as much joy as possible." Her doctor told Lorde she had no more than five years to live.[57]

It isn't clear exactly when Lorde informed her partner that she'd fallen in love with someone else, but there's no question that Clayton was devastated by the news.[58]

By mid 1986, Lorde had resigned from her job at Hunter College and was living with Gloria Joseph on St. Croix. For the next two years, Lorde saw Clayton only briefly when she came to New York to deal with practical matters. The couple dated the official end of their relationship to 1988 when they sold the Staten Island house. The breakup was extremely painful for Clayton, who retired and moved to northern California in 1989.[59]

MAKING A MONUMENTAL CONTRIBUTION
TO WOMEN'S LITERATURE

The final half dozen years of Audre Lorde's life were defined by a mixture of physical pain and personal triumph. Her liver cancer caused constant discomfort, often to the point that she couldn't function. Lorde's medicine of choice was the restorative power that came from a life surrounded by the warmth, sunlight, and beauty of the Caribbean combined with the positive energy that emanated from her new partner. Professional accolades helped, too, as she published four more books, and was honored in 1991 as the official poet of New York State.[60]

Lorde died in 1992 on St. Croix, with Gloria Joseph at her bedside. America's leading newspapers reported the death, with the *Los Angeles Times* saying the fifty-eight-year-old literary icon's "drive for black female power dominated the best of her work," and the *Boston Globe* stating, "As a contributor to women's literature, her influence was monumental." None of the obituaries mentioned Frances Clayton, although the *New York Times* identified Gloria Joseph as Lorde's "companion."[61]

Lorde's two children organized a memorial service honoring their mother at New York City's Cathedral of St. John the Divine. More than four thousand people attended the event that celebrated Lorde's many achievements.[62]

Lorde's stature continued to rise after her death. Today she is regarded as one of the most important American women writers of the late twentieth century, and her literary works are incorporated into courses offered at colleges and universities around the world. Each year, thousands of new students are introduced to her powerful voice by reading either her books or samples of her shorter works that have been reprinted in dozens of anthologies. Typical of the statements summarizing Lorde's distinctive contributions is the following one from the book *New Black Feminist Criticism, 1985–2000*:

> Audre left for us words that many black women had been too afraid to speak. We had been taught that silence was golden, that it could protect you. Yet, as our daily lives and statistics proclaimed, we were steadily being attacked from within our homes as well as from without. Audre Lorde refused to be silenced, refused to be limited to any one category, insisted on being all that she was: poet, black, mother, lesbian, feminist, warrior, activist, woman.[63]

In 1998, Frances Clayton moved to Sun City, Arizona, where the climate helped ease her pain from arthritis. She continues to be in frequent contact with both Elizabeth Lorde-Rollins and Jonathan Rollins. "They are wonderful people," Clayton said in 2011, "who have enhanced my entire life."[64]

EPILOGUE

To make my final point in this book, I've chosen to violate one of the guiding principles I established in the prologue. That is, I'm going to talk about a same-sex couple who hasn't made a substantial contribution to the nation—merely a minor one. This final outlaw marriage is my own.

When I first became a college professor, I focused exclusively on teaching. I'd worked as a newspaper reporter and editor, and I wanted to share what I'd learned with the next generation of journalists. I hadn't done much academic research or writing, and I didn't intend to change that.

In my fourth year on the faculty, however, my colleagues at the university told me I was doing an excellent job of teaching but . . . if I didn't build a record of research in the next two years, I wouldn't be granted tenure. In short, I was about to perish because I hadn't published.

The day I heard that news, I went home in a rage. I had a new boyfriend at the time, and so I unloaded on him. "I became a *teacher* so I could *teach*," I screamed, "not so I could write articles for esoteric journals that nobody even reads! I'm not going to do it! I'm going to continue being a great teacher and that's that!"

My boyfriend heard me out and then said, in a soft voice, "But if you don't do the research, doesn't that mean you won't be *allowed* to teach after two more years?"

Those were words I didn't want to hear. I turned to him and asked (read: screeched), "So you're saying I shouldn't care about being a good teacher and I should only care about doing worthless research?"

He responded, "I'm not saying you shouldn't be a good teacher. But maybe you could try doing the research, too—at least for the next two years. Then you can teach forever." He paused for a moment before adding, "Who knows, maybe you'll even like doing the research."

I glared at him. "If I do any research, it will be the absolute *minimum* I have to do, I assure you of that." I then stomped out of the room.

It was only after a few more minutes of seething that I started thinking that, well, maybe he had a point.

That very tense conversation took place more than two decades ago.

Since then, I've published seven books. I've also published twenty-eight articles in academic journals, and I've presented thirty-four papers at academic conferences. Along the way, I was awarded tenure, promoted to full professor, and honored as American University's scholar/teacher of the year.

And so, as the final statement in my eighth book, I want to thank Tom Grooms, who set me on my path toward becoming a reasonably successful academic, as well as the guy who shared an outlaw marriage with me for twenty-eight years . . . until the District of Columbia approved same-sex marriage legislation last year and we then legally became husband and husband.

ACKNOWLEDGMENTS

A book with a scope as broad as this one—looking at the lives of thirty women and men from the mid-nineteenth century to the present day—must be built, at least partly, on the research of earlier biographers. The endnotes for the various chapters contain citations to the works these scholars provided me, but I also want to acknowledge their contributions here.

Because of the nature of *Outlaw Marriages,* some of these biographers were particularly helpful. One example that comes to mind is James Weber Linn, who wrote the 1968 book *Jane Addams: A Biography.* Linn explored the personal life of the legendary social worker and Nobel Peace Prize winner—who was also his aunt—with much more depth than previous biographers had, including making the statement that "Mary Smith became and always remained the highest and clearest note in the music that was Jane Addams's personal life." That sentence hinted at the hidden history of Jane Addams and Mary Rozet Smith's outlaw marriage, which I was then able to describe more fully after reading the women's correspondence and other papers at Swarthmore College and the University of Illinois.

Two more individuals I'm deeply indebted to made their contributions as I was writing the final chapter. During the early stages of my research on Audre Lorde and Frances Clayton, I was forced to rely heavily on the only biography that's been written about Lorde. Regrettably, that book contained only bits and pieces of information about Clayton, even though she'd been an enormous force in Lorde's life. I still remember how excited I was on the day that I contacted Lorde's daughter, Elizabeth Lorde-Rollins, and learned that she was eager not only to help me illuminate her mother's outlaw marriage but also to put me in touch with Clayton, who by this point was eighty-five years old and had retired to Arizona. That initial contact led to any number of e-mails, letters, and phone conversations between me and both Lorde-Rollins and Clayton that allowed me to include the details, in this book, that Lorde's biography had left untold.

After the previous paragraph, I need to explain that I wasn't, in fact, the person who tracked down Lorde-Rollins. That feat was accomplished by my dear and incredibly resourceful friend, Kim Gazella. As my final deadline for submitting this manuscript was approaching, I turned to Kim with a request (read: scream for help!). "I've signed a contract for my book, which is great," I told Kim, breathlessly, "but now I have to locate photos and get permission to use them, and, and, . . . I'm feeling totally overwhelmed . . . so I'm wondering if. . . ." Before I even finished asking her, Kim said, "I can help!" And help she did. With a level of energy, creativity, and persistence beyond anything I could have hoped for, Kim tracked down the photos that now add so very much to this book, and while doing all that, she also located Lorde-Rollins for me. Thank you, Kim.

I also want to express my gratitude to Gayatri Patnaik, executive editor at Beacon Press, for her invaluable role in shaping this book into its final form and to Howard Yoon, my literary agent, for finding precisely the right publisher for this project.

Finally, I want to thank my colleague at American University, Journalism Division director Jill Olmsted, for her unstinting support of my work and my former graduate assistant Matt Stevens for his wonderful help in conducting research at the Library of Congress.

NOTES

CHAPTER 1: WALT WHITMAN & PETER DOYLE, 1865–1892

1. On Whitman's early years, see David S. Reynolds, *Walt Whitman* (New York: Oxford University Press, 2005), 1–6; "Walt Whitman Dead," *Chicago Tribune*, March 27, 1892, 5; "Walt Whitman Dead," *Washington Post*, March 27, 1892, 1; "Walt Whitman's Career," *New York Times*, March 27, 1892, 10. Whitman's parents were Walter Whitman Sr. and Louisa Van Velsor Whitman.

2. "Walt Whitman Dead," *Chicago Tribune*, 5; "Walt Whitman Dead," *Washington Post*, 1; "Walt Whitman's Career," *New York Times*, 10.

3. Reynolds, *Walt Whitman*, 10–11.

4. Walt Whitman, *Complete Poetry and Collected Prose* (New York: Library of America, 1982), 40, 57.

5. David S. Reynolds, *Walt Whitman's America* (New York: Alfred A. Knopf, 1995), 341–42; Whitman, *Complete Poetry*, 1326.

6. *Leaves of Grass: A Textual Variorum of the Printed Poems / Walt Whitman*, Sculley Bradley, Harold W. Blodgett, Arthur Golden, and William White, eds. (New York: New York University Press, 1980), 1:262; Reynolds, *Walt Whitman*, 14–17; Whitman, *Complete Poetry*, 311.

7. *Whitman's Manuscripts: Leaves of Grass (1860)*, Fredson Bowers, ed. (Chicago: University of Chicago Press, 1955), 116.

8. "Walt Whitman's Career," *New York Times*, 10.

9. On Doyle's early years, see Henry Bryan Binns, *A Life of Walt Whitman* (New York: Haskell House, 1905), 230; Martin G. Murray, "'Pete the Great': A Biography of Peter Doyle," *Walt Whitman Quarterly* 12, no. 1 (Summer 1994): 1–3; Charley Shively, ed., *Calamus Lovers: Walt Whitman's Working-Class Camerados* (San Francisco: Gay Sunshine Press, 1987), 100. Doyle's parents were Peter Doyle Sr. and Catherine Nash Doyle.

10. Binns, *A Life*, 230; Murray, "'Pete the Great,'" 3–10; Shively, *Calamus Lovers*, 100.

11. Binns, *A Life*, 230; Murray, "'Pete the Great,'" 10–13; Reynolds, *Walt Whitman's America*, 487.

12. Richard Maurice Bucke, ed. *Calamus: A Series of Letters Written During the Years 1868–1880 by Walt Whitman to a Young Friend (Peter Doyle)* (Boston: Small, Maynard & Company, 1897), 23.

13. Bucke, *Calamus*, 23.

14. Ibid., 24–25; Murray, "'Pete the Great,'" 19, 27.

15. Murray, "'Pete the Great,'" 14; Shively, *Calamus Lovers*, 117.

16. Murray, "'Pete the Great,'" 27; *Walt Whitman: The Correspondence*, Edwin Haviland Miller, ed. (New York: New York University Press, 1961–1977), 2:84–85.

17. Murray, "'Pete the Great,'" 17–21; Reynolds, *Walt Whitman's America*, 487.

18. Bucke, *Calamus*, 26.

19. Murray, "'Pete the Great,'" 19; *Walt Whitman: Prose Works 1892*, Floyd Stovall, ed. (New York: New York University Press, 1963), 1:111.

20. John Burroughs, *The Writings of John Burroughs* (Boston: Houghton Mifflin, 1904), 3:220. See also, Binns, *A Life*, 301; Shively, *Calamus Lovers*, 117.

21. Shively, *Calamus Lovers*, 102.

22. Ibid., 100–101; Binns, *A Life*, 210; Murray, "'Pete the Great,'" 15.

23. Bucke, *Calamus*, 25–26.

24. Murray, "'Pete the Great,'" 15; *Walt Whitman: Notebooks and Unpublished Prose Manuscripts*, Edward F. Grier, ed. (New York: New York University Press, 1984), 2:821.

25. *Leaves of Grass: A Textual Variorum*, 2:488. Whitman used the personal name Jonathan in "A Boston Ballad," though the name did not represent a fictional hero but, instead, was intended to denote the average American.

26. Ibid., 2:482, 2:491, 2:507; Murray, "'Pete the Great,'" 16. The line "son of responding kisses" is in the poem "Vigil Strange I Kept on the Field One Night"; the line beginning "Many a soldier's" is in "The Dresser"; and the line beginning "more than all" is in "O Tan-Faced Prairie-Boy."

27. Florence Bernstein Freedman, *William Douglas O'Connor, Walt Whitman's Chosen Knight* (Athens: Ohio University Press, 1985), 198–200; Murray, "'Pete the Great,'" 17. The poems Whitman deleted were "Long I Thought that Knowledge Alone Would Suffice," "Hours Continuing Long," and "Who Is Now Reading This?"

28. Murray, "'Pete the Great,'" 21–28; Shively, *Calamus Lovers*, 101.

29. Shively, *Calamus Lovers*, 104; *Walt Whitman: The Correspondence*, 2:47.

30. *Walt Whitman: The Correspondence*, 2:67.

31. Ibid., 2:127, 2:62–63, 2:84–85; Shively, *Calamus Lovers*, 109.

32. *Walt Whitman: The Correspondence*, 2:47, 2:85.

33. Ibid., 2:110.

34. John Burroughs, "Walt Whitman and His 'Drum-Taps,'" *New York Galaxy*, December 1866; *Walt Whitman: The Correspondence*, 2:169.

35. Binns, *A Life*, 247–49; "Walt Whitman Dead," *Chicago Tribune*, 5.

36. Binns, *A Life*, 247–48; Bucke, *Calamus*, iii.

37. *Walt Whitman: The Correspondence*, 2:227.

38. Ibid., 2:265, 2:294, 2:296.

39. Shively, *Calamus Lovers*, 103; *Walt Whitman: The Correspondence*, 2:304.

40. *Walt Whitman: The Correspondence*, 2:308.

41. Murray, "'Pete the Great,'" 33; Reynolds, *Walt Whitman's America*, 524–26.

42. *Walt Whitman: The Correspondence*, 3:67.

43. Ibid., 3:87.

44. Ibid., 3:189.

45. *Critic,* November 5, 1881; "Literature," *Chicago Tribune,* November 26, 1881, 9; Reynolds, *Walt Whitman's America,* 544; "Walt Whitman Dead," *Chicago Tribune,* 5. The Boston publisher was James R. Osgood, and the Philadelphia publisher was Rees Welsh.

46. *Walt Whitman: The Correspondence,* 3:158–59.

47. Bucke, *Calamus,* iii.

48. J. Johnston, MD, and J. W. Wallace, *Visits to Walt Whitman in 1890–1891 by Two Lancashire Friends* (New York: Egmont Arens, 1918), 147; Murray, "'Pete the Great,'" 36.

49. Bucke, *Calamus,* 32–33.

50. Binns, *A Life,* 344; Murray, "'Pete the Great,'" 39.

51. "A Poet for Humanity," *Washington Post,* March 31, 1892, 1; "Walt Whitman's Career," *New York Times,* 10. On other obituaries and tributes that did not mention Doyle, see "Death of Walt Whitman," *New York Times,* 4; "Walt Whitman Dead," *Chicago Tribune,* 5; "Walt Whitman Dead," *Los Angeles Times,* March 27, 1892, 13; "Walt Whitman Dead," *San Francisco Chronicle,* March 27, 1892, 14; "Walt Whitman Dead," *Washington Evening Star,* March 28, 1892, 7; "Walt Whitman Dead," *Washington Post,* 1; "Whitman's Voice Forever Stilled," *Philadelphia Inquirer,* March 27, 1892, 1.

52. Shively, *Calamus Lovers,* 103.

53. Murray, "'Pete the Great,'" 34; Shively, *Calamus Lovers,* 115.

54. Bucke, *Calamus;* Murray, "'Pete the Great,'" 43.

55. Henry James, *Literature,* April 16, 1898; *Nation,* July 1, 1897.

56. Bucke, *Calamus,* 29.

57. Binns, *A Life;* Murray, "'Pete the Great,'" 43.

58. "Died," *Philadelphia Inquirer,* April 20, 1907, 7; "Died," *Washington Evening Star,* April 21, 1907, 5.

CHAPTER 2: MARTHA CAREY THOMAS & MAMIE GWINN, 1878–1904

1. On Thomas's early years, see "Carey Thomas, Noted Educator, Succumbs at 79," *Washington Post,* December 3, 1935, 6; Marjorie H. Dobkin, ed., *The Making of a Feminist: Early Journals and Letters of M. Carey Thomas* (Kent, OH: Kent State University Press, 1979), 5–15; Helen Lefkowitz Horowitz, *The Power and Passion of M. Carey Thomas* (Urbana: University of Illinois Press, 1994), 3–55; "Miss M. C. Thomas of Bryn Mawr Dies," *New York Times,* December 3, 1935, 25. Thomas's parents were James Thomas and Mary Whitall Thomas.

2. Horowitz, *Power and Passion,* 19, 37–49, 442; "M. Carey Thomas," Martha Carey Thomas Papers, Bryn Mawr College Archives.

3. Thomas to Hannah Whitall Smith, August 8, 1874, Thomas Papers.

4. Horowitz, *Power and Passion,* 74; "Miss M. C. Thomas," 25.

5. On Gwinn's early years, see "Biography of Alfred LeRoy Hodder and Mary Gwinn Hodder," Alfred and Mamie Gwinn Hodder Papers, Princeton University Li-

brary; Horowitz, *Power and Passion,* 92. Gwinn's parents were Charles J. M. Gwinn and Mathilda Gwinn, and her maternal grandfather was Reverdy Johnson.

6. "Alfred Hodder Dies at Forty," *New York Times,* March 4, 1907, 9; "Biography," Hodder Papers; "Deaths," *New York Times,* November 13, 1940, 23; Horowitz, *Power and Passion,* 1994), 92.

7. "Biography," Hodder Papers; Horowitz, *Power and Passion,* 92.

8. "Biography," Hodder Papers; Dobkin, *Making of a Feminist,* 156; Horowitz, *Power and Passion,* 92.

9. Martha Carey Thomas diary, February 2 and 22, 1878, Martha Carey Thomas Papers, Bryn Mawr College Archives.

10. Edith Finch, *Carey Thomas of Bryn Mawr* (New York: Harper & Brothers, 1947), 84; Mamie Gwinn Hodder, "Reminisces of M. Carey Thomas," Hodder Papers; Horowitz, *Power and Passion,* 93; Dell Richards, *Superstars: Twelve Lesbians Who Changed the World* (New York: Carroll & Graf, 1993), 85.

11. Thomas diary, February 24, 1879, Thomas Papers; Thomas to Gwinn, July 13, 1879, Simon Flexner Papers, American Philosophical Society Library, Philadelphia; Horowitz, *Power and Passion,* 102.

12. "Carey Thomas," 6; Finch, *Carey Thomas,* 88; Horowitz, *Power and Passion,* 102.

13. Horowitz, *Power and Passion,* 103.

14. Thomas diary, January 11, 1879, Thomas Papers.

15. Horowitz, *Power and Passion,* 105.

16. Ibid., 108; "Biography," Hodder Papers; Dobkin, *Making of a Feminist,* 155.

17. Horowitz, *Power and Passion,* 112–16; Thomas to Mary Whitall Thomas, February 1, 1880, Thomas Papers.

18. Thomas to Mary Whitall Thomas, November 13, 1880, and January 5, 1882, Thomas Papers.

19. Gwinn to Thomas, March 1882, Thomas Papers; Thomas diary, September 14, 1878, and October 12, 1878, Thomas Papers.

20. Horowitz, *Power and Passion,* 138; Richards, *Superstars,* 85.

21. Thomas to Richard Cadbury, April 4, 1880, Thomas Papers.

22. Horowitz, *Power and Passion,* 134.

23. Thomas to Mary Garrett, January 11, 1881, Thomas Papers.

24. "Carey Thomas," 6; Richards, *Superstars,* 76.

25. Horowitz, *Power and Passion,* 148.

26. Ibid., 148.

27. Ibid., 145–46, 153; Richards, *Superstars,* 76.

28. Horowitz, *Power and Passion,* 148–49; Richards, *Superstars,* 76.

29. Horowitz, *Power and Passion,* 150–51.

30. Ibid., 152, 154; Dobkin, *Making of a Feminist,* 19; "Miss M. C. Thomas," 25.

31. Horowitz, *Power and Passion,* 186, 195; "Miss M. C. Thomas," 25.

32. "A New College for Women," *New York Times,* March 17, 1884, 2.

33. "Biography," Hodder Papers; Horowitz, *Power and Passion,* 192–97; "M. Carey Thomas," Thomas Papers.

34. Horowitz, *Power and Passion,* 197.

35. Ibid., 201; Gwinn to Thomas, July 31, 1884, and May 2, 1884, Thomas Papers.

36. "M. Carey Thomas," Thomas Papers.

37. Ibid.; Horowitz, *Power and Passion,* 202–3; Richards, *Superstars,* 71.

38. "M. Carey Thomas," Thomas Papers.

39. Horowitz, *Power and Passion,* 219.

40. Gwinn to Thomas, March 1886, Thomas Papers.

41. Horowitz, *Power and Passion,* 244, 295; "M. Carey Thomas," Thomas Papers; Richards, *Superstars,* 82.

42. E. J. Edwards, "America's Leaders in the Higher Education of Women," *New York Times,* November 5, 1911, SM11; Horowitz, *Power and Passion,* 146–47.

43. Horowitz, *Power and Passion,* 262.

44. Ibid., 265; "Miss M. C. Thomas," 25.

45. Horowitz, *Power and Passion,* 324.

46. Ibid., 266–67, 300; "Biography," Hodder Papers; "M. Carey Thomas," Thomas Papers.

47. "Women Enjoy a Banquet," *New York Times,* May 6, 1896, 1.

48. Ibid.; Horowitz, *Power and Passion,* 320.

49. Edwards, "America's Leaders," SM11.

50. Thomas to Gwinn, 1896, Hodder Papers.

51. Horowitz, *Power and Passion,* 323–27; "M. Carey Thomas," Thomas Papers.

52. "Miss Mary Garrett Dead," *New York Times,* April 4, 1915, 8.

53. Gwinn to Thomas, April 4, 1884; April 5, 1884; and October 10, 1884, Hodder Papers.

54. Horowitz, *Power and Passion,* 263; Richards, *Superstars,* 88–89; Thomas to Gwinn, November 26, 1893, Thomas Papers.

55. "Biography," Hodder Papers; Thomas to Gwinn, March 2, 1901, Thomas Papers.

56. Dobkin, *Making of a Feminist,* 157; Horowitz, *Power and Passion,* 283.

57. "M. Carey Thomas," Thomas Papers; "Miss Mary Garrett," 8.

58. Gwinn to Thomas, August 1, 1899, Hodder Papers; Horowitz, *Power and Passion,* 355.

59. Horowitz, *Power and Passion,* 283–84.

60. Richards, *Superstars,* 71.

61. Dobkin, *Making of a Feminist,* 157; Horowitz, *Power and Passion,* 292–96; "News of Bryn Mawr College," *New York Times,* May 6, 1895, 9.

62. Horowitz, *Power and Passion,* 367; Thomas to Gwinn, February 3, 1894, Thomas Papers.

63. Horowitz, *Power and Passion,* 367; Richards, *Superstars,* 71, 89.

64. "Alfred Hodder Dies," 9.

65. Ibid.

66. "Miss Mary Garrett," 8.

67. "Garrett Millions to Miss Thomas," *New York Times,* April 9, 1915, 6; Horowitz, *Power and Passion,* 424; Richards, *Superstars,* 88–89.

68. "Twelve Greatest Women," *New York Times,* June 25, 1922, 21.

69. Katie Doyle Gaffney interview by Marjorie Housepian Dobkin, February 4, 1975, Katie Doyle materials, Bryn Mawr College Archives.

70. Horowitz, *Power and Passion,* 412–13, 440; Richards, *Superstars,* 90.

71. Hodder, "Reminisces," Hodder Papers; Horowitz, *Power and Passion,* 373.

72. Hodder, "Reminisces," Hodder Papers.

73. Ibid.; "Deaths," *New York Times,* November 13, 1940, 23; "Miss M. C. Thomas," 25; "Miss M. Thomas, Former Head of Bryn Mawr, Dies," *Chicago Tribune,* December 3, 1935, 16; "An Unconventional Daughter," *Washington Post,* December 5, 1935, 8.

CHAPTER 3: NED WARREN & JOHN MARSHALL, 1884–1927

1. David Sox, *Bachelors of Art: Edward Perry Warren & the Lewes House Brotherhood* (London: Fourth Estate, 1991), 254. For other statements about Marshall and Warren's collections being among the best ever assembled, see Stephen L. Dyson, *Ancient Marbles to American Shores: Classical Archaeology in the United States* (Philadelphia: University of Pennsylvania Press, 1998), 155; Douglass Shand-Tucci, *The Crimson Letter: Harvard, Homosexuality, and the Shaping of American Culture* (New York: St. Martin's, 2003), 92.

2. On Marshall's early years, see Sox, *Bachelors of Art,* 39–40.

3. Sox, *Bachelors of Art,* 39–40.

4. Ibid.

5. Ibid.

6. On Warren's early years, see "Edward Perry Warren," *New York Times,* December 30, 1928, 17; Martin Green, *The Warrens of Mount Vernon Street: A Boston Story, 1860–1910* (New York: Scribner's, 1989), 29–55; History Project, *Improper Bostonians* (Boston: Beacon Press, 1998), 93; Sox, *Bachelors of Art,* 3–14. Warren's parents were Samuel D. Warren and Susan Clarke Warren.

7. History Project, *Improper Bostonians,* 93; Sox, *Bachelors of Art,* 4–6.

8. Sox, *Bachelors of Art,* 4.

9. Ibid., 13; "Edward Perry Warren," 17; Osbert Burdett and E. H. Goddard, *Edward Perry Warren: The Biography of a Connoisseur* (London: Christopher, 1941), 32.

10. Shand-Tucci, *Crimson Letter,* 91–92; Sox, *Bachelors of Art,* 16.

11. Sox, *Bachelors of Art,* 16, 38–39. Warren's first lover was Arthur George Bainbridge West.

12. Ibid., 42.

13. Ibid., 29, 36; Green, *Warrens of Mount Vernon Street,* 92.

14. Sox, *Bachelors of Art,* 40.

15. Marshall to Warren, September 1889, Ashmolean Library, Oxford University; Shand-Tucci, *Crimson Letter,* 90.

16. Sox, *Bachelors of Art,* 45.

17. Green, *Warrens of Mount Vernon Street,* 168.

18. Sox, *Bachelors of Art,* 51.

19. Ibid., 51–52, 54; Shand-Tucci, *Crimson Letter,* 90.

20. Sox, *Bachelors of Art,* 50.

21. Ibid., 52–53; Green, *Warrens of Mount Vernon Street,* 125; Shand-Tucci, *Crimson Letter,* 90.

22. Dyson, *Ancient Marbles,* 143.

23. Sox, *Bachelors of Art,* 135; W. M. Whitehill, *The Museum of Fine Arts, Boston: A Centennial History* (Cambridge, MA: Harvard University Press, Belknap Press, 1970), 52, 148.

24. Green, *Warrens of Mount Vernon Street,* 174, 221; Sox, *Bachelors of Art,* 57–58, 173. The bust of the Roman woman became known as the *Bust of a Woman in High Relief.*

25. Green, *Warrens of Mount Vernon Street,* 136; Sox, *Bachelors of Art,* 95.

26. Dyson, *Ancient Marbles,* 145; Sox, *Bachelors of Art,* 64, 66–67.

27. Sox, *Bachelors of Art,* 126.

28. Ibid., 97; Whitehill, *Museum of Fine Arts,* 157; Shand-Tucci, *Crimson Letter,* 92.

29. Green, *Warrens of Mount Vernon Street,* 136.

30. Sox, *Bachelors of Art,* 70, 80.

31. Ibid., 70; Burdett and Goddard, *Edward Perry Warren,* 179, 226.

32. Burdett and Goddard, *Edward Perry Warren,* 226.

33. Ibid., 230.

34. Ibid.

35. Sox, *Bachelors of Art,* 77.

36. Ibid., 76.

37. Green, *Warrens of Mount Vernon Street,* 180.

38. On the jug, see the Metropolitan Museum of Art's Heilbrunn Timeline of Art History, http://www.metmuseum.org/.

39. On the cup and safety pin, see the Metropolitan Museum of Art's New Greek and Roman Galleries, http://www.metmuseum.org/, and on the plaques, see Aleksandr Leskov, "The Maikop Treasure," *Silk Road Foundation Newsletter,* http://www.silk-road.com/.

40. On the sandaled foot, see the Metropolitan Museum of Art's New Greek and Roman Galleries, http://www.metmuseum.org/.

41. Sox, *Bachelors of Art,* 77, 81.

42. Green, *Warrens of Mount Vernon Street,* 204.

43. Ibid., 127.

44. Burdett and Goddard, *Edward Perry Warren,* 302, 400; Green, *Warrens of Mount Vernon Street,* 127. On Warren using his collecting to advance the acceptance of homosexuality, see also Dyson, *Ancient Marbles,* 138.

45. For detailed analyses of the Warren Cup, see John R. Clarke, "The Warren Cup and the Context for Representations of Male-to-Male Lovemaking in Augustan and Early Julio-Claudian Art," *Art Bulletin* 75 (1993): 275–94; John Pollini, "The Warren Cup: Homoerotic Love and Symposial Rhetoric in Silver," *Art Bulletin* 81 (1999): 21–52.

46. On the vase, see History Project, *Improper Bostonians,* 93; the vase has been attributed to the Amasis Painter and is now owned by the Museum of Fine Arts in Boston. On the fragments, see John R. Clarke, *Looking at Lovemaking: Constructions*

of Sexuality in Roman Art, 100 B.C.-A.D. 250 (Berkeley: University of California Press, 1998), 73, 75; Pollini, "Warren Cup," 30–31.

47. Green, *Warrens of Mount Vernon Street*, 204.

48. Sox, *Bachelors of Art*, 253–54.

49. Michael Camille and Adrian Rifkin, *Other Objects of Desire: Collectors and Collecting Queerly* (Malden, MA: Blackwell), 86.

50. Sox, *Bachelors of Art*, 54, 65.

51. Ibid., 109.

52. Ibid.

53. Burdett and Goddard, *Edward Perry Warren*, 345; Shand-Tucci, *Crimson Letter*, 92.

54. Green, *Warrens of Mount Vernon Street*, 231; Sox, *Bachelors of Art*, 123, 127.

55. "Edward Perry Warren," 17; Sox, *Bachelors of Art*, 129.

56. "Edward Perry Warren," 17.

57. Sox, *Bachelors of Art*, 130.

CHAPTER 4: MARY ROZET SMITH & JANE ADDAMS, 1891–1934

1. On Addams's early years, see Robin K. Berson, *Jane Addams: A Biography* (Westport, CT: Greenwood, 2004), 1–19; "Jane Addams of Hull House Is Dead," *Chicago Tribune*, May 22, 1935, 1, 4; Cornelia Meigs, *Jane Addams: Pioneer for Social Justice* (Boston: Little, Brown), 1970), 1–46. Addams's parents were John Huy Addams and Sarah Weber Addams.

2. Meigs, *Jane Addams*, 21–30.

3. Ibid., 35–36.

4. Ibid., 43–44.

5. On Smith's early years, see James Weber Linn, *Jane Addams: A Biography* (New York: Greenwood, 1968), 147–48; Meigs, *Jane Addams*, 54–56. Smith's parents were Charles Mather Smith and Sarah Rozet Smith.

6. Linn, *Jane Addams*, 147–48; Meigs, *Jane Addams*, 54–55.

7. Linn, *Jane Addams*, 147–48; Meigs, *Jane Addams*, 54.

8. Jean Bethke Elshtain, *Jane Addams and the Dream of American Democracy* (New York: Basic Books/Perseus, 2002), 23; Linn, *Jane Addams*, 147; Meigs, *Jane Addams*, 54.

9. Meigs, *Jane Addams*, 44–45.

10. Ibid., 45–46.

11. Ibid., 49–50, 52.

12. Ibid., 60.

13. Ibid., 54–56; Linn, *Jane Addams*, 147; "Miss Mary Rozet Smith," *New York Times*, February 24, 1934, 14; "Pioneer Patron of Hull House, Mary Smith, Dies," *Chicago Tribune*, February 24, 1934, 20.

14. Meigs, *Jane Addams*, 55–56.

15. Elshtain, *Jane Addams*, 289; "Miss Mary Rozet Smith," *New York Times*, 14; "Pioneer Patron," *Chicago Tribune*, 20.

16. Elshtain, *Jane Addams*, 23; Linn, *Jane Addams*, 147.

17. For the quote, see Linn, *Jane Addams,* 147. See also Lillian Faderman, *Odd Girls and Twilight Lovers: A History of Lesbian Life in Twentieth-Century America* (New York: Penguin, 1991), 25–28; Katherine Joslin, *Jane Addams, a Writer's Life* (Urbana and Chicago: University of Illinois Press, 2004), 11; Dell Richards, *Superstars: Twelve Lesbians Who Changed the World* (New York: Carroll & Graf, 1993), 97–98.

18. Meigs, *Jane Addams,* 54–55.

19. For the quote, see Elshtain, *Jane Addams,* 289. On Smith taking Addams to her home to keep her from overexerting herself, see also Allen F. Davis, *American Heroine: The Life and Legend of Jane Addams* (New York: Oxford University Press, 1973), 87; Louise W. Knight, *Citizen: Jane Addams and the Struggle for Democracy* (Chicago: University of Chicago Press, 2005), 214.

20. Faderman, *Odd Girls,* 25; Lillian Faderman, *To Believe in Women: What Lesbians Have Done for America—A History* (Boston: Houghton Mifflin, 1999), 126; Richards, *Superstars,* 106.

21. Faderman, *Odd Girls,* 26; Meigs, *Jane Addams,* 145.

22. Addams to Smith, January 20, 1897, and Smith to Addams, September 3, 1933, Jane Addams Personal Papers, University of Illinois, Chicago; Faderman, *To Believe,* 130.

23. Addams to Smith, May 26, 1902, Addams Personal Papers; Davis, *American Heroine,* 89; Joslin, *Jane Addams,* 11.

24. Kathryn Kish Sklar, "Who Funded Hull-House?" in Kathleen D. McCarthy, *Lady Bountiful Revisited: Women, Philanthropy, and Power* (New Brunswick, NJ: Rutgers University Press, 1990), 101.

25. Davis, *American Heroine,* 85; Faderman, *Odd Girls,* 26.

26. Faderman, *Odd Girls,* 26; Sklar, "Who Funded," 95, 100–101.

27. Linn, *Jane Addams,* 129, 209; Meigs, *Jane Addams,* 140; "Miss Mary Rozet Smith," *New York Times,* 14; "Pioneer Patron," *Chicago Tribune,* 20; Sklar, "Who Funded," 100–101, 106.

28. Joslin, *Jane Addams,* 248; Fred J. Koch to Jane Addams, February 26, 1934, Jane Addams Papers, Swarthmore College Peace Collection.

29. Addams to Smith, August 15, 1895, Addams Personal Papers; Linn, *Jane Addams,* 148.

30. "Miss Mary Rozet Smith," *New York Times,* 14; "Pioneer Patron," *Chicago Tribune,* 20; Richards, *Superstars,* 93, 105.

31. Berson, *Jane Addams,* 33; Richards, *Superstars,* 93, 105.

32. Berson, *Jane Addams,* 32; Richards, *Superstars,* 93, 105; Sklar, "Who Funded," 105, 107.

33. Elshtain, *Jane Addams,* 150.

34. Ibid., 289; Faderman, *Odd Girls,* 25.

35. Elshtain, *Jane Addams,* 213–15; Linn, *Jane Addams,* 291; Meigs, *Jane Addams,* 145–46; "Pioneer Patron," *Chicago Tribune,* 20.

36. Elshtain, *Jane Addams,* 151; Richards, *Superstars,* 107. The resident's name was Gertrude Barnum.

37. Faderman, *To Believe,* 132; Linn, *Jane Addams,* 353.

38. Addams to Smith, March 22, 1904, and undated letter from 1904, Addams Personal Papers; Richards, *Superstars*, 107.

39. Davis, *American Heroine*, 86. Addams and Smith traveled to the Middle East in 1913, to Mexico in 1925, and to the West Indies in 1926.

40. Elshtain, *Jane Addams*, 217–18.

41. Berson, *Jane Addams*, 72, 74.

42. "Jane Addams Chronology," Jane Addams Papers, Swarthmore College Peace Collection; Knight, *Citizen*, 391.

43. Berson, *Jane Addams*, 78. The Dutch feminist was Aletta Jacobs.

44. Davis, *American Heroine*, 222, 233.

45. Berson, *Jane Addams*, 112; Elshtain, *Jane Addams*, 213; Joslin, *Jane Addams*, 166.

46. Berson, *Jane Addams*, 78–79.

47. Ibid., 79–84.

48. Ibid., 84–88, 90.

49. Ibid., 98; Linn, *Jane Addams*, 345; Joslin, *Jane Addams*, 241.

50. Berson, *Jane Addams*, 110–11; "Pioneer Patron," *Chicago Tribune*, 20; Richards, *Superstars*, 112.

51. Berson, *Jane Addams*, 109–10.

52. Linn, *Jane Addams*, 390.

53. Davis, *American Heroine*, 289.

54. "Miss Mary Rozet Smith," *New York Times*, 14; "Pioneer Patron," *Chicago Tribune*, 20.

55. Davis, *American Heroine*, 289.

56. Elshtain, *Jane Addams*, 247–48.

57. "Death Ends Career of Jane Addams," *Baltimore Sun*, May 22, 1935, 1; "Death Takes Jane Addams," *Boston Globe*, May 22, 1935, 1; "Founder of Hull House, Jane Addams, Succumbs," *Los Angeles Times*, May 22, 1935, 1; "Jane Addams Dies in Her 75th Year," *New York Times*, May 22, 1935, 1; "Jane Addams Dies; Won Wide Acclaim as Social Worker," *Philadelphia Inquirer*, May 22, 1935, 1; "Jane Addams, Famous Social Worker, Dies," *San Francisco Chronicle*, May 22, 1935, 1; "Jane Addams," *Chicago Tribune*, 1; "Jane Addams, Peace Crusader, and Foe of Slums, Dead at 74," *Washington Post*, May 23, 1935, 1.

CHAPTER 5: BESSIE MARBURY & ELSIE DE WOLFE, 1892–1933

1. On Marbury's early years, see "Elisabeth Marbury Dead," *Washington Post*, January 23, 1933, 3; "Elisabeth Marbury Dies in 77th Year," *New York Times*, January 23, 1933, 14; Elisabeth Marbury, *My Crystal Ball* (New York: Boni and Liveright, 1923), 9–57. Marbury's parents were Francis F. Marbury and Elizabeth McCoun Marbury.

2. Marbury, *My Crystal Ball*, 10, 12.

3. Ibid., 13, 24.

4. Nina Campbell and Caroline Seebohm, *Elsie de Wolfe: A Decorative Life* (New York: Panache, 1992), 30.

5. On de Wolfe's early years, see "Lady Mendl Dies in France at 84," *New York*

Times, July 13, 1950, 25; Jane S. Smith, *Elsie de Wolfe: A Life in the High Style* (New York: Atheneum, 1982), 5–16. De Wolfe's parents were Stephen de Wolfe and Georgiana Copeland de Wolfe.

6. "Lady Mendl Dies," 25; Smith, *Elsie de Wolfe,* 5–16.

7. "Lady Mendl Dies," 25.

8. Marbury, *My Crystal Ball,* 57–58.

9. Smith, *Elsie de Wolfe,* 29.

10. Ibid., 12–13, 25.

11. Ruby Ross Goodnow, "The Story of Elsie de Wolfe," *Good Housekeeping,* June 1913, 762.

12. Ibid.; Smith, *Elsie de Wolfe,* 38–39.

13. Smith, *Elsie de Wolfe,* 49.

14. Ibid., 57.

15. Ibid.; "After the Matinee," *Town Topics,* December 15, 1887.

16. Smith, *Elsie de Wolfe,* 63.

17. Ibid.

18. Ibid.

19. Alice-Leone Moats, "The Elsie Legend," *Harper's Bazaar,* May 1949, 171.

20. "'The Other Girl' Scores," *New York Times,* December 30, 1903, 2; Smith, *Elsie de Wolfe,* 90.

21. Smith, *Elsie de Wolfe,* 96.

22. Campbell and Seebohm, *Elsie de Wolfe,* 49.

23. Penny Sparke, *Elsie de Wolfe: The Birth of Modern Interior Decoration* (New York: Acanthus, 2005), 38–39.

24. Ibid., 39.

25. Ibid., 41.

26. Elsie de Wolfe, *The House in Good Taste* (New York: Century, 1913), 96; Goodnow, "Story of Elsie de Wolfe," 764.

27. "Can Women Appreciate a Club?" *Los Angeles Times,* April 14, 1907, G2; "Colony Club Finds Midsummer Pleasures in the City," *New York Times,* July 7, 1907, X5; "New Club for Women," *Washington Post,* March 12, 1907, 12.

28. Sparke, *Elsie de Wolfe,* 45, 111.

29. Ibid., 49.

30. Ibid., 67, 75; "Mellody Farm," *Harper's Bazaar,* August 1918, 34–35.

31. Sparke, *Elsie de Wolfe,* 114.

32. Ibid., 165–66.

33. Ibid., 13.

34. de Wolfe, *House,* 48.

35. "American Homes," *New York Times,* November 9, 1913, BR611.

36. Smith, *Elsie de Wolfe,* 142–43, 166.

37. Ibid., 197.

38. Ibid., 135; Elsie de Wolfe, "What Every Woman Wants to Know," *New York Times,* February 1, 1914, X11.

39. Smith, *Elsie de Wolfe,* 114, 216.

40. Ibid., 203–4.

41. Campbell and Seebohm, *Elsie de Wolfe,* 92.

42. "Elisabeth Marbury Dead in New York," *Boston Globe,* January 23, 1933, 15.

43. Smith, *Elsie de Wolfe,* 193–94.

44. Ibid., 194.

45. Campbell and Seebohm, *Elsie de Wolfe,* 92.

46. Smith, *Elsie de Wolfe,* 211.

47. Ibid., 201–2.

48. "Elisabeth Marbury Dead," 15; "Smith's Nomination Sure," *New York Times,* January 12, 1927, 1; "Trend to Roosevelt Strong," *New York Times,* January 10, 1932, 1.

49. Smith, *Elsie de Wolfe,* 223.

50. Ibid., 222.

51. Ibid., 223–24.

52. Campbell and Seebohm, *Elsie de Wolfe,* 96–97.

53. Ibid., 96.

54. "Lady Mendl at Home," *House and Garden,* May 1941, 50; Sparke, *Elsie de Wolfe,* 275–76.

55. Smith, *Elsie de Wolfe,* 252.

56. "Elisabeth Marbury Dies," 14; "Elisabeth Marbury Dead," 15; "Woman Stage Producer Dies," *Los Angeles Times,* January 23, 1933, 2.

57. "Lady Mendl at Home," 50; Smith, *Elsie de Wolfe,* 288–91.

58. Tony Duquette, "Elsie de Wolfe," *Architectural Digest,* September 1996, 139.

59. "Lady Mendl Dies," 25; Sparke, *Elsie de Wolfe,* 270–72.

60. Smith, *Elsie de Wolfe,* 304, 306, 308.

61. Ibid., 324; "Lady Mendl Dies," 25.

62. Duquette, "Elsie de Wolfe," 139; Smith, *Elsie de Wolfe,* 327.

63. "Death Comes to Lady Mendl of Party Fame," *Los Angeles Times,* July 13, 1950, 17; Hedda Hopper, "Gay Set Mourns Brilliant Hostess," *Los Angeles Times,* July 13, 1950, 17; "Lady Mendl, 84, Noted Hostess, Dies in France," *Chicago Tribune,* July 13, 1950, 18; "Lady Mendl Dies," 25; "Lady Mendl, Ex-Actress, Dies in France," *Washington Post,* July 13, 1950, B2; "Lady Mendl: International Hostess, Actress, Style Leader," *Boston Globe,* July 13, 1950, 16.

CHAPTER 6: J. C. LEYENDECKER & CHARLES BEACH, 1901–1951

1. On Leyendecker's early life, see Laurence S. Cutler and Judy Goffman Cutler, *J. C. Leyendecker* (New York: Abrams, 2008), 19–36; "J. C. Leyendecker, Noted Artist, 77," *New York Times,* July 26, 1951, 20; Michael Schau, *J. C. Leyendecker* (New York: Watson-Guptill, 1974), 14–27; Kent Steine and Frederic B. Taraba, *The J. C. Leyendecker Collection* (Portland, OR: Collectors Press, 1996), 6–8. Leyendecker's parents were Peter Leyendecker and Elizabeth Ortseifen Leyendecker.

2. Schau, *Leyendecker,* 14.

3. "Keeping Posted," *Saturday Evening Post,* October 15, 1938, 108.

4. Ibid.; "J. C. Leyendecker Dies at Age of 77," *(New Rochelle, NY) Standard-Star,* July 26, 1951, 1; Carole Turbin, "Fashioning the American Man: The Arrow Collar Man, 1907–1931," *Gender & History* 14, no. 3 (November 2002), 474.

5. On Beach's early years, see Cutler and Cutler, *Leyendecker,* 36–37; Schau, *Leyendecker,* 30, 32–33; Turbin, "Fashioning," 475, 479.

6. Cutler and Cutler, *Leyendecker,* 36–37; Schau, *Leyendecker,* 30, 32–33; Turbin, "Fashioning," 475, 479.

7. Cutler and Cutler, *Leyendecker,* 36–38; Schau, *Leyendecker,* 30, 32–33; Turbin, "Fashioning," 475, 479.

8. *The Century,* cover, August 1896.

9. "Leyendecker Dies," *Standard-Star,* 1.

10. Schau, *Leyendecker,* 20–21.

11. Ibid., 21.

12. Ibid., 24.

13. "Leyendecker Dies," *Standard-Star,* 1.

14. Cutler and Cutler, *Leyendecker,* 36.

15. Ibid.

16. Ibid.; Schau, *Leyendecker,* 30–32; Turbin, "Fashioning," 475.

17. Cutler and Cutler, *Leyendecker,* 36; Norman Rockwell, *My Adventures as an Illustrator* (New York: Abrams, 1988), 167.

18. Cutler and Cutler, *Leyendecker,* 1, 36, 40; Gary Kriss, "The Father of the New Year's Baby," *New York Times,* December 27, 1998, WE13; Rockwell, *My Adventures,* 168; Schau, *Leyendecker,* 18.

19. Cutler and Cutler, *Leyendecker,* 36, 38.

20. Ibid., 36; Virginia Clair, "Leyendecker Remembered as Perfectionist," July 26, 1951, *Standard-Star,* 1.

21. Rockwell, *My Adventures,* 167; Turbin, "Fashioning," 470–91.

22. *Collier's,* cover, September 6, 1902; *Collier's,* cover, June 4, 1904.

23. Rockwell, *My Adventures,* 167.

24. Ibid.; Clair, "Leyendecker Remembered," 1; Emmanuel Cooper, *The Sexual Perspective: Homosexuality and Art in the Last 100 Years in the West* (New York: Routledge, 1986), 132; "Noted Artist," *New York Times,* 20; Kriss, "Father," WE13; Schau, *Leyendecker,* 25, 32–33; Steine and Taraba, *Leyendecker Collection,* 10.

25. "The American Holiday," *Saturday Evening Post,* February 21, 1903, 12; Clair, "Leyendecker Remembered," 1; Cutler and Cutler, *Leyendecker,* 67; Schau, *Leyendecker,* 25; Steine and Taraba, *Leyendecker Collection,* 9.

26. *Saturday Evening Post,* covers, November 30, 1912; July 6, 1918; May 31, 1919.

27. Cutler and Cutler, *Leyendecker,* 67.

28. Clair, "Leyendecker Remembered," 1; "Noted Artist," *New York Times,* 20; David Rowland, "Leyendecker: Sunlight and Stone," *Saturday Evening Post,* May–June 1973, 56; Schau, *Leyendecker,* 25; Steine and Taraba, *Leyendecker Collection,* 10.

29. Clair, "Leyendecker Remembered," 1; Cooper, *Sexual Perspective,* 132; Rowland, "Leyendecker," 56; Schau, *Leyendecker,* 25, 33, 45; Steine and Taraba, *Leyendecker Collection,* 10.

30. Cutler and Cutler, *Leyendecker,* 40; Schau, *Leyendecker,* 39; Steine and Taraba, *Leyendecker Collection,* 8.

31. Clair, "Leyendecker Remembered," 1; Cutler and Cutler, *Leyendecker,* 35, 71–73.

32. Cutler and Cutler, *Leyendecker*, 75; "Noted Artist," *New York Times*, 20; Schau, *Leyendecker*, 23.

33. Schau, *Leyendecker*, 28.

34. Ibid.; Turbin, "Fashioning," 471–72.

35. For reproductions of the 1922 image, see Cutler and Cutler, *Leyendecker*, cover and 78.

36. For reproductions of the ads, see Cutler and Cutler, *Leyendecker*, 76, 99.

37. On the Arrow Collar Man becoming the country's first male sex symbol, see Cutler and Cutler, *Leyendecker*, 73–74; Schau, *Leyendecker*, 30; Turbin, "Fashioning," 471–75.

38. Schau, *Leyendecker*, 30.

39. On admirers not knowing that Beach was gay, see David B. Boyce, "Coded Desire in 1920s Advertising," *Gay & Lesbian Review* 7, no. 1 (Winter 2000): 26–32; Richard Martin, "Gay Blades: Homoerotic Content in J. C. Leyendecker's Gillette Advertising Images," *Journal of American Culture* 18, no. 2 (Summer 1995): 75–82.

40. Cutler and Cutler, *Leyendecker*, 36.

41. On Leyendecker and Beach keeping their relationship out of the public eye, see Boyce, "Coded Desire," 26–32; Kriss, "Father," WE13; Martin, "Gay Blades," 75–82.

42. Cutler and Cutler, *Leyendecker*, 38.

43. Ibid.

44. "Leyendecker Dies," *Standard-Star*, 1.

45. Ibid.

46. Cutler and Cutler, *Leyendecker*, 46; Steine and Taraba, *Leyendecker Collection*, 10–11.

47. Clair, "Leyendecker Remembered," 1; Cutler and Cutler, *Leyendecker*, 75; Rowland, "Leyendecker," 56; Steine and Taraba, *Leyendecker Collection*, 10–11.

48. Cooper, *Sexual Perspective*, 132; Cutler and Cutler, *Leyendecker*, 44; Rockwell, *My Adventures*, 171; Schau, *Leyendecker*, 39.

49. Clair, "Leyendecker Remembered," 1; "Leyendecker Dies," *Standard-Star*, 1; "Noted Illustrator Dies," *Standard-Star*, April 19, 1924, 1; Rockwell, *My Adventures*, 171.

50. Clair, "Leyendecker Remembered," 1.

51. Cutler and Cutler, *Leyendecker*, 46.

52. Ibid.

53. Ibid., 47.

54. "Keeping Posted," 108; Rockwell, *My Adventures*, 172; Schau, *Leyendecker*, 36; Steine and Taraba, *Leyendecker Collection*, 11.

55. Cooper, *Sexual Perspective*, 131; "Keeping Posted," 108; Steine and Taraba, *Leyendecker Collection*, 12.

56. Cooper, *Sexual Perspective*, 132; Cutler and Cutler, *Leyendecker*, 50; Kriss, "Father," WE13; Steine and Taraba, *Leyendecker Collection*, 12–13.

57. Cutler and Cutler, *Leyendecker*, 50; Steine and Taraba, *Leyendecker Collection*, 13.

58. "Leyendecker Dies," *Standard-Star*, 1; "Noted Artist," *New York Times*, 20.

59. "'Model' Inherits $30,000," *New York Times,* August 14, 1951, 25. Mary Leyendecker died in 1957.

60. Beach died on August 28, 1952.

61. Clair, "Leyendecker Remembered," 1; "Noted Artist," *New York Times,* 20.

CHAPTER 7: ALICE B. TOKLAS & GERTRUDE STEIN, 1907-1946

1. On Stein's early years, see Lucy Daniel, *Gertrude Stein* (London: Reaktion, 2009), 11–23; "Gertrude Stein Dies in France," *New York Times,* July 28, 1946, 40. Stein's parents were Daniel Stein and Amelia Keyser Stein.

2. Daniel, *Gertrude Stein,* 22.

3. Ibid., 28.

4. Ibid., 41.

5. Ibid., 47, 49; Janet Hobhouse, *Everybody Who Was Anybody: A Biography of Gertrude Stein* (New York: Putnam, 1975), 19–20; Linda Simon, *The Biography of Alice B. Toklas* (New York: Doubleday, 1977), 146–47. Stein's young female lover was named May Bookstaver.

6. On Toklas's early years, see Simon, *Alice B. Toklas,* 3–44. Toklas's parents were Ferdinand Toklas and Emma Levinsky Toklas.

7. Simon, *Alice B. Toklas,* 8, 11.

8. Ibid., 26.

9. Ibid., 15.

10. Ibid., 21.

11. Daniel, *Gertrude Stein,* 56–57; James R. Mellow, *Charmed Circle: Gertrude Stein and Company* (New York: Praeger, 1974), 4.

12. Daniel, *Gertrude Stein,* 57.

13. Mellow, *Charmed Circle,* 97.

14. Daniel, *Gertrude Stein,* 69.

15. Ibid., 94. The girl was Annette Rosenshine.

16. Shari Benstock, *Women of the Left Bank: Paris, 1900–1940* (Austin: University of Texas Press, 1986), 166; Daniel, *Gertrude Stein,* 94–95.

17. Daniel, *Gertrude Stein,* 95.

18. Benstock, *Women of the Left Bank,* 157; Simon, *Alice B. Toklas,* 70; Gertrude Stein, *As Fine as Melanctha* (New Haven, CT: Yale University Press, 1954), 231, 234–35, 247.

19. Benstock, *Women of the Left Bank,* 164, 169; Daniel, *Gertrude Stein,* 96, 103, 109, 159; Hobhouse, *Everybody Who Was,* 93, 144; Janet Malcolm, *Two Lives: Gertrude and Alice* (New Haven, CT: Yale University Press, 2007), 156–57; Simon, *Alice B. Toklas,* 68, 72, 76, 84, 115, 132.

20. Benstock, *Women of the Left Bank,* 152; Daniel, *Gertrude Stein,* 58.

21. Benstock, *Women of the Left Bank,* 156–57, 162–63, 175; Daniel, *Gertrude Stein,* 95; Hobhouse, *Everybody Who Was,* 93; Simon, *Alice B. Toklas,* 99–102, 107–8.

22. Simon, *Alice B. Toklas,* 99.

23. Ibid., 100–101. The quotations were published in Stein's "If You Had Three Husbands," in *Geography and Plays* (Boston: Four Seasons, 1922), 382.

24. Simon, *Alice B. Toklas,* 107. The quotations were published in Stein's "Lifting Belly" in *Bee Time Vine and Other Pieces* (New Haven, CT: Yale University Press, 1953), 80.

25. Daniel, *Gertrude Stein,* 96; Gertrude Stein, *Three Lives* (New York: Grafton, 1909); "Three Lives," *Nation,* January 20, 1910, 65.

26. Benstock, *Women of the Left Bank,* 168; Simon, *Alice B. Toklas,* 111; Gertrude Stein, *Tender Buttons* (New York: Claire Marie, 1914).

27. "Futurist Essays," *Los Angeles Times,* August 9, 1914, IIIA3; "Public Gets Peep at Extreme Cubist Literature in Gertrude Stein's 'Tender Buttons,'" *Chicago Tribune,* June 5, 1914, 15.

28. Lillian Faderman, *Surpassing the Love of Men* (New York: William Morrow, 1981), 404; Simon, *Alice B. Toklas,* 115.

29. G. E. K., "Miss Stein Applies Cubism to Defenseless Prose," *Baltimore Sun,* August 25, 1923; Stein, *Geography and Plays.*

30. Daniel, *Gertrude Stein,* 147; Hobhouse, *Everybody Who Was,* 157–58; Simon, *Alice B. Toklas,* 134–35.

31. "Gertrude Stein's Solemn Quest for Genial Obscurity," *Philadelphia Public Ledger,* January 5, 1929; "Hogarth Essays," *New Orleans Times-Picayune,* March 17, 1926.

32. Simon, *Alice B. Toklas,* 146.

33. Ibid., 149; Gertrude Stein, "Stanzas in Meditation," *Stanzas in Meditation and Other Poems* (New Haven, CT: Yale University Press, 1956), 90.

34. Simon, *Alice B. Toklas,* 148–49.

35. Benstock, *Women of the Left Bank,* 170–71; Simon, *Alice B. Toklas,* 149; Gertrude Stein, *The Autobiography of Alice B. Toklas* (New York: Harcourt, Brace and Company, 1933), 265; Alice B. Toklas, *Staying on Alone: Letters of Alice B. Toklas,* Edward Burns, ed. (New York: Liveright, 1973), 91.

36. Daniel, *Gertrude Stein,* 156; Simon, *Alice B. Toklas,* 150.

37. Stein, *Autobiography,* 43, 78, 153, 246.

38. Simon, *Alice B. Toklas,* 150.

39. Theodore Hall, "Miss Stein Looks Homeward," *Washington Post,* October 8, 1933, SM10; Paul Jordan-Smith, "I'll Be Judge You Be Jury," *Los Angeles Times,* September 10, 1933, A5; "Stein's Way," *Time,* September 11, 1933, 57.

40. Simon, *Alice B. Toklas,* 169.

41. Ernest Kirschten, "Stein Smile Wins Radcliffe," *Boston American,* November 20, 1934; "Miss Stein Returns to Her Native Land," *Nation,* November 7, 1934, 521.

42. Gertrude Stein, *Everybody's Autobiography* (New York: Random House, 1937), 289.

43. Daniel, *Gertrude Stein,* 161; Simon, *Alice B. Toklas,* 161.

44. Ellen Alix DuPoy, "New Poem of Gertrude Stein Given Praise," *Chicago Tribune,* October 21, 1933, 15.

45. Daniel, *Gertrude Stein,* 131; Sherwood Anderson, "Four American Impressions: Gertrude Stein," *New Republic,* October 11, 1922, 171. On Stein influencing Anderson, see also Gilbert A. Harrison, "Gertrude Stein and the Nay-Sayers," *New Republic,* March 18, 1957, 18; "Stein's Way," 57.

46. Daniel, *Gertrude Stein,* 131. On Stein influencing Hemingway, see also Fanny Butcher, "Gertrude Stein Writes a Book in Simple Style," *Chicago Tribune,* September 2, 1933, 8; Harrison, "Gertrude Stein," 18; "Stein's Way," 57; Edmund Wilson, "Autobiography of Alice B. Toklas," *New Republic,* October 11, 1933. Ernest Hemingway was awarded the Nobel Prize for Literature in 1954.

47. Alice B. Toklas, *What Is Remembered* (New York: Holt, Rinehart and Winston, 1963), 117. On Stein influencing Fitzgerald, see also Harrison, "Gertrude Stein," 18; "Stein's Way," 57.

48. Hobhouse, *Everybody Who Was,* 185; Simon, *Alice B. Toklas,* 165. On Stein influencing Wilder, see also Harrison, "Gertrude Stein," 18; "Stein's Way," 57.

49. Simon, *Alice B. Toklas,* 176.

50. Ibid., 182–85.

51. Ibid., 188–89.

52. "Gertrude Stein Dies in France," *New York Times,* July 28, 1946; "Gertrude Stein Dies in Paris," *Los Angeles Times,* July 28, 1946, 1; "Gertrude Stein Dies in Paris," *San Francisco Chronicle,* July 28, 1946, 9; "Gertrude Stein Dies in Paris," *Washington Post,* July 28, 1946, 1; "Gertrude Stein, Famed Author, Dies in France," *Chicago Tribune,* July 28, 1946, 26.

53. Malcolm, *Two Lives,* 161.

54. Simon, *Alice B. Toklas,* 217.

55. Ibid., 208, 217.

56. Ibid., 217.

57. Ibid., 218–19; Alice B. Toklas, *The Alice B. Toklas Cook Book* (New York: Harper & Brothers, 1954), 173.

58. "Briefly Noted," *New Yorker,* February 5, 1955, 116; "A Dish Is a Dish Is a Dish," *Time,* November 22, 1954, 10; Toklas, *Cook Book,* 42–43.

59. "Alice B. Toklas, 89," *Washington Post,* March 8, 1967, B4; "Alice B. Toklas Dies," *San Francisco Examiner,* March 7, 1967, 41; "Alice B. Toklas Is Dead in Paris," *San Francisco Chronicle,* March 8, 1967, 27; "Alice Toklas, Companion of Gertrude Stein," *Boston Globe,* March 8, 1967, 38; "Alice Toklas Dies," *Chicago Tribune,* March 8, 1967, D7; "Alice Toklas, 89, Is Dead in Paris," *New York Times,* March 8, 1967, 45.

CHAPTER 8: JANET FLANNER & SOLITA SOLANO, 1919-1975

1. On Solano's early years, see "Biographical Note: Solita Solano," Janet Flanner and Solita Solano Papers, Manuscript Division, Library of Congress, Washington, D.C., 4–5; "Solita Solano, Novelist, 86," *New York Times,* November 26, 1975, 32; Brenda Wineapple, *Genêt: A Biography of Janet Flanner* (Lincoln: University of Nebraska Press, 1989), 48–49. Solano's father was Almadus Wilkinson.

2. "Biographical Note: Solano," Flanner and Solano Papers, 5; Wineapple, *Genêt,* 49.

3. "Biographical Note: Solano," Flanner and Solano Papers, 5; "Solita Solano," *New York Times,* 32; Wineapple, *Genêt,* 49–50.

4. "Biographical Note: Solano," Flanner and Solano Papers, 5; Wineapple, *Genêt,* 47, 50–51.

5. On Flanner's early years, see "Biographical Note: Janet Flanner," Flanner and Solano Papers; Phil Casey, "The Lady Known as Genêt," *Washington Post,* July 2, 1972, F1, F5; Mary McCarthy, "Conversation Piece," *New York Times Book Review,* November 21, 1965, BR5, BR88–91; Alden Whitman, "Janet Flanner, Reporter in Paris for The New Yorker, Dies at 86," *New York Times,* November 8, 1978, B10; Wineapple, *Genêt,* 1–39. Flanner's parents were Frank Flanner and Mary Hockett Flanner.

6. McCarthy, "Conversation Piece," BR90; Wineapple, *Genêt,* 18, 20.

7. McCarthy, "Conversation Piece," BR5.

8. Janet Flanner, "Impressions in the Field of Art," *Indianapolis Star,* April 14, 1918, F38.

9. Wineapple, *Genêt,* 32, 38.

10. Ibid., 47; Jane Grant, *Ross, The New Yorker, and Me* (New York: Reynal, 1968), 223.

11. Wineapple, *Genêt,* 51–53.

12. Ibid., 53; William Murray, *Janet, My Mother, and Me: A Memoir of Growing Up with Janet Flanner and Natalia Danesi Murray* (New York: Simon & Schuster, 2000), 38.

13. Ronald Weber, *News of Paris: American Journalists in the City of Light Between the Wars* (Chicago: Ivan R. Dee, 2006), 226; Wineapple, *Genêt,* 54–56.

14. Solita Solano, *National Geographic,* "Constantinople Today," June 1922, 647, and "Vienna: A Capital Without a Nation," January 1923, 76–102; Wineapple, *Genêt,* 57.

15. Janet Flanner, *Paris Was Yesterday, 1925–1939* (New York: Viking Press, 1962), vii; Weber, *News of Paris,* 226.

16. Flanner and Solano to Carlos Baker, December 27, 1966, Flanner and Solano Papers.

17. Solano to Hildegarde Flanner Monhoff, December 5, 1923, Flanner and Solano Papers; Wineapple, *Genêt,* 70.

18. Grant to Flanner, June 1925, Jane Grant Papers, University of Oregon, Eugene, Oregon.

19. Mary Blume, "The Enduring Journalism of Janet Flanner," *Los Angeles Times,* November 26, 1978, Q68.

20. Weber, *News of Paris,* 226.

21. Ibid., 227–28.

22. Ibid., 227, 230, 232; Grant, *Ross, The New Yorker,* 11; Wineapple, *Genêt,* 49, 102.

23. Grant, *Ross, The New Yorker,* 11; Murray, *Janet, My Mother, and Me,* 42; Weber, *News of Paris,* 227, 229; Wineapple, *Genêt,* 100.

24. Murray, *Janet, My Mother, and Me,* 41–43; Weber, *News of Paris,* 230, 232; Wineapple, *Genêt,* 49, 102.

25. Genêt, "Paris Letter," *New Yorker,* October 10, 1925, 28, 30; Wineapple, *Genêt,* 98.

26. Grant, *Ross, The New Yorker,* 8–9.

27. Genêt, "Paris Letter," *New Yorker,* April 3, 1926, 51; April 16, 1927, 95.

28. Genêt, "Paris Letter," *New Yorker,* September 25, 1926, 66.

29. Genêt, "Paris Letter," *New Yorker,* October 10, 1925, 28; April 17, 1926, 61.

30. Murray, *Janet, My Mother, and Me,* 42–43; Weber, *News of Paris,* 230; Wineapple, *Genêt,* 103.

31. Flanner to Mary Hockett Flanner, November 17, 1927, Flanner and Solano Papers; Janet Flanner, *New Yorker,* "Profiles: Isadora," January 1, 1927, 17–19, and "Profiles: The Egotist," October 29, 1927, 23–25.

32. "Paris in the Twenties," The Twentieth Century, CBS television program, April 17, 1960; "Two Get Divorce in Paris," *New York Times,* April 1, 1926, 6; Wineapple, *Genêt,* 122.

33. Solita Solano, *The Uncertain Feast* (New York: G. P. Putnam's Sons, 1924); Solita Solano, *The Happy Failure* (New York: G. P. Putnam's Sons, 1925); Solita Solano, *This Way Up* (New York: G. P. Putnam's Sons, 1927); Wineapple, *Genêt,* 80.

34. Genêt, "Letter from Paris," *New Yorker,* July 7, 1934, 67–68; Ralph Ingersoll, *Fortune,* August 1934, 97.

35. Janet Flanner, "Letter from Berlin," *New Yorker,* August 1, 1936, 40; August 15, 1936, 39–41; and August 22, 1936, 64–67; Genêt, "London Letter," *New Yorker,* December 12, 1936, 71–72.

36. Janet Flanner, *New Yorker,* "Come as Somebody Else," November 25, 1933, 24–27; "Her Majesty, The Queen," May 4, 1935, 20–24, and May 11, 1935, 28–32; "One-Man Group," December 9, 1939, 32–37; "Perfume and Politics," May 3, 1930, 22–25; "Russian Firebird," January 5, 1935, 23–28.

37. Janet Flanner, "Fuehrer," *New Yorker,* February 29, 1936, 20–24; March 7, 1936, 27–31; and March 14, 1936, 22–26; Flanner letter to Mary Hockett Flanner, October 27, 1937, Flanner and Solano Papers.

38. Murray, *Janet, My Mother, and Me,* 45.

39. Ibid., 74; Janet Flanner, *New Yorker,* "A Reporter at Large: Paris, Germany," December 7, 1940, 58; "A Reporter at Large: Soldats de France, Debout," February 1, 1941, 20; "A Reporter at Large: Le Nouvel Ordre," March 15, 1941, 38–47; "A Reporter at Large: Blitz by Partnership," June 7, 1941, 42–54; and "A Reporter at Large: So You're Going to Paris," June 21, 1941, 36–48.

40. Murray, *Janet, My Mother, and Me,* 35, 129.

41. Wineapple, *Genêt,* 181–82, 252.

42. Janet Flanner, *New Yorker,* "Annals of Crime: The Beautiful Spoils," February 22, 1947, 31–48; March 1, 1947, 33–49; and March 8, 1947, 38–55; "Letter from Nuremberg," March 16, 1946, 92–94; March 23, 1946, 78, 80–84; and March 30, 1946, 76–82.

43. James Johnson Sweeney, "Masters in Profile," *New York Times,* March 24, 1957, 253.

44. Wineapple, *Genêt,* 267.

45. Flanner to Solano, February 1, 1966, and March 17, 1966, Flanner and Solano Papers.

46. Wineapple, *Genêt,* 269.

47. Flanner to Solano, March 1, 1963; September 21, 1964; and October 26, 1964, Flanner and Solano Papers; Murray, *Janet, My Mother, and Me,* 257–77.

48. Flanner to Solano, March 1, 1963; May 6, 1963; and September 21, 1964, Flanner and Solano Papers.

49. Benjamin Bradlee, "Paragon of Correspondents Provides Excellent History," *Washington Post,* November 16, 1965, A18; Janet Flanner, *Paris Journal: 1944–1965* (New York: Atheneum, 1965); Glenway Wescott, "The Tri-Colored Rainbow," *New York Herald Tribune,* December 19, 1965, 8.

50. Harry Gilroy, "Book Awards Go to 4 U.S. Writers," *New York Times,* March 16, 1966, A42.

51. Wineapple, *Genêt,* 286–89.

52. Casey, "Lady Known as Genêt," F1; Janet Flanner, *Paris Journal: 1965–1971* (New York: Atheneum, 1971); Flanner, *Paris Was Yesterday;* Janet Flanner, *London Was Yesterday, 1934–1939* (New York: Viking, 1975); "Paris Journal," *Saturday Review,* November 27, 1971, 40; Richard C. Wald, "Letters from London," *Chicago Tribune,* June 1, 1975, G3.

53. Flanner to Solano, January 31, 1974, Flanner and Solano Papers; "Solita Solano," *New York Times,* 32.

54. Genêt, "Letter from Paris," *New Yorker,* September 29, 1975, 110; "N. Danesi Murray," *New York Times,* June 13, 1994, D10.

55. "Died," *Newsweek,* November 20, 1978, 134; Whitman, "Janet Flanner," B10.

56. Blume, "Enduring Journalism," *Los Angeles Times,* Q68; "Janet Flanner, 86, Writer," *Philadelphia Inquirer,* November 9, 1978, C7. "Janet Flanner, 86, Wrote on Paris for New Yorker," *Boston Globe,* November 9, 1978, 83; "New Yorker's 'Genêt,' Janet Flanner, Is Dead," *Chicago Tribune,* November 9, 1978, C21; J.Y. Smith, "Janet Flanner, of New Yorker, Dies," *Washington Post,* November 8, 1978, B3.

CHAPTER 9: GRETA GARBO & MERCEDES DE ACOSTA, 1931–1960

1. On de Acosta's early years, see "Mercedes de Acosta, 75, Dies," *New York Times,* May 10, 1968, 44; Barry Paris, *Garbo: A Biography* (New York: Knopf, 1995), 255–57; Robert A. Schanke, *"That Furious Lesbian": The Story of Mercedes de Acosta* (Carbondale: Southern Illinois University Press, 2003), 1–99. De Acosta's parents were Ricardo de Acosta and Micaela Hernandez de Alba y de Alba.

2. Schanke, *Furious Lesbian,* 22–26.

3. Ibid., 41–42, 56–66; Diana McClellan, *The Girls: Sappho Goes to Hollywood* (New York: St. Martin's, 2000), 36–37, 83–84.

4. "Miss De Acosta Wed to Abram Poole," *New York Times,* May 12, 1920, 11; Schanke, *Furious Lesbian,* 50–51.

5. Schanke, *Furious Lesbian,* 56–60, 122–23.

6. Ibid., 43, 68, 74–75, 87. De Acosta's two plays staged on Broadway were *Sandro Botticelli,* about the painting *The Birth of Venus,* in 1923, and *Jacob Slovak,* about anti-Semitism, in 1927; de Acosta's play staged in Paris was *Jehanne d'Arc,* about Joan of Arc, in 1925.

7. Percy Hammond, "The Theaters," *New York Tribune,* March 27, 1923; Schanke, *Furious Lesbian,* 69, 75–76, 88.

8. Schanke, *Furious Lesbian,* 102.

9. On Garbo's early years, see Paris, *Garbo,* 3–77; Karen Swenson, *Greta Garbo: A Life Apart* (New York: Lisa Drew/Scribner, 1997), 24–84. Garbo's parents were Karl Gustafsson and Anna Karlsson Gustafsson.

10. Paris, *Garbo,* 21–26.

11. Ibid., 33–37. The director was Erik Petschler, and the film was *Peter the Tramp.*

12. Paris, *Garbo,* 46–49. The director was Mauritz Stiller.

13. Swenson, *Greta Garbo,* 76.

14. Jane Ellen Wayne, *The Golden Girls of MGM: Greta Garbo, Joan Crawford, Lana Turner, Judy Garland, Ava Gardner, Grace Kelly and Others* (New York: Carroll & Graf, 2003), 80–81.

15. Paris, *Garbo,* 83.

16. Ibid., 568; Swenson, *Greta Garbo,* 99.

17. For the quote, see Paris, *Garbo,* 111. See also Wayne, *Golden Girls,* 81.

18. Paris, *Garbo,* 129.

19. Ibid., 127.

20. Ibid., 129.

21. Ibid., 178.

22. Ibid., 179.

23. Ibid., 257–58; Mercedes de Acosta, *Here Lies the Heart* (New York: Reynal, 1960), 213–14; Schanke, *Furious Lesbian,* 103–5.

24. de Acosta, *Here Lies the Heart,* 215–16; Paris, *Garbo,* 257.

25. de Acosta, *Here Lies the Heart,* 219.

26. Ibid., 219–20; Paris, *Garbo,* 259; Schanke, *Furious Lesbian,* 104–5.

27. de Acosta, *Here Lies the Heart,* 222; Paris, *Garbo,* 260; Schanke, *Furious Lesbian,* 105.

28. de Acosta, *Here Lies the Heart,* 224, 226.

29. Paris, *Garbo,* 262–63.

30. Ibid., 255; McClellan, *The Girls,* 128.

31. Hollis Alpert, "Saga of Greta Gustafsson," *New York Times Magazine,* September 5, 1965, 57; de Acosta, *Here Lies the Heart,* 214; McClellan, *The Girls,* 128; Paris, *Garbo,* 259; Swenson, *Greta Garbo,* 260.

32. de Acosta, *Here Lies the Heart,* 127; McClellan, *The Girls,* 128; Paris, *Garbo,* 217, 265; Swenson, *Greta Garbo,* 258.

33. de Acosta, *Here Lies the Heart,* 219; McClellan, *The Girls,* 128; Paris, *Garbo,* 262–63.

34. de Acosta, *Here Lies the Heart,* 251.

35. Paris, *Garbo,* 284.

36. McClellan, *The Girls,* 343; Swenson, *Greta Garbo,* 285.

37. Paris, *Garbo,* 217.

38. Ibid., 128–29, 218; de Acosta, *Here Lies the Heart,* 227–28; McClellan, *The Girls,* 128.

39. Paris, *Garbo,* 218, 221.

40. de Acosta, *Here Lies the Heart,* 251; Paris, *Garbo,* 289.

41. Paris, *Garbo,* 304.

42. Schanke, *Furious Lesbian,* 109.

43. Paris, *Garbo,* 324.

44. "Garbo, Going Home, Leads Wild Chase in New York," *Los Angeles Times,*

July 26, 1932, 1; Garbo to de Acosta, September 19, 1935, folder 23, Mercedes de Acosta Collection, Rosenbach Museum and Library, Philadelphia; Paris, *Garbo*, 311.

45. Schanke, *Furious Lesbian*, 109.

46. Ibid.; Gayelord Hauser to de Acosta, November 9, 1939, de Acosta Collection.

47. Schanke, *Furious Lesbian*, xxi, 73.

48. "At the Picture Theaters," *New York Herald Tribune*, January 9, 1927, F3; "Best Performances in Current Pictures," *Los Angeles Times*, January 31, 1927, C1; Mordaunt Hall, "The Screen," *New York Times*, December 27, 1933, 23.

49. Bart Barnes, "Greta Garbo Dies at Age 84," *Washington Post*, April 16, 1990, A10.

50. McClellan, *The Girls*, 163–68, 246–47; Schanke, *Furious Lesbian*, 113–17.

51. Paris, *Garbo*, 374.

52. "Bans Garbo Film at Providence, R.I.," *New York Times*, November 26, 1941, 29; Nelson B. Bell, "Two-Faced Woman Stars a Duplex Garbo," *Washington Post*, December 5, 1941, 13; "Garbo Tries Comedy Way Second Time," *Los Angeles Times*, December 6, 1941, A9.

53. de Acosta, *Here Lies the Heart*, 315; Paris, *Garbo*, 381.

54. Schanke, *Furious Lesbian*, 109–10.

55. Ibid., 144–46.

56. Paris, *Garbo*, 405; Schanke, *Furious Lesbian*, 152; Hugo Vickers, *Loving Garbo: The Story of Greta Garbo, Cecil Beaton, and Mercedes de Acosta* (New York: Random House, 1994), 114. Garbo made the statement to Cecil Beaton.

57. Paris, *Garbo*, 386–431; Schanke, *Furious Lesbian*, 132–50.

58. Garbo to de Acosta, August 15, 1949, folder 23, and Ram Gopal to de Acosta, May 16, 1965, folder 11, de Acosta Collection; de Acosta, *Here Lies the Heart*, 398.

59. Paris, *Garbo*, 411–17; Frederick Sands and Sven Broman, *The Divine Garbo* (New York: Grosset and Dunlap, 1979), 193–95.

60. Paris, *Garbo*, 440.

61. Schanke, *Furious Lesbian*, 162.

62. Ibid., 171; Garbo to de Acosta, June 7, 1952, and December 22, 1954, folder 23, de Acosta Collection; McClellan, *The Girls*, 370; Vickers, *Loving Garbo*, 243.

63. Arthur Todd, "The Place Cards Read Like an All-Star Cast at a Benefit," *New York Times*, May 29, 1960, BR6.

64. Garbo to de Acosta, undated, folder 23, de Acosta Collection; Schanke, *Furious Lesbian*, 168.

65. Paris, *Garbo*, 510; Schanke, *Furious Lesbian*, 167.

66. de Acosta to Richard Buckle, April 22, 1961, and de Acosta to William McCarthy, October 1964, folder 7, de Acosta Collection.

67. "Mercedes de Acosta," *New York Times*, 44.

68. Gray Horan, "Garbo's Refuge," *New York Times*, September 2, 1990, SM30.

69. Barnes, "Greta Garbo Dies," A1, A10; Michael Blowen, "Greta Garbo, Film Star of '20s, '30s, Dies at 84," *Boston Globe*, April 16, 1990, 1, 47; Peter B. Flint, "Greta Garbo, 84, Screen Icon Who Fled Her Stardom, Dies," *New York Times*, April 16, 1990, A1, D11; Burt A. Folkart, "Greta Garbo, Alluring but Aloof Film Star, Dies at

84," *Los Angeles Times,* April 16, 1990, A1, A24, A25; Jack Larson, "Garbo: Outtakes of a Life," *Washington Post,* April 22, 1990, B2; Tom Shales, "The Glory That Was Garbo," *Washington Post,* April 16, 1990, B1.

CHAPTER 10: AARON COPLAND & VICTOR KRAFT, 1932–1976

1. David Patrick Stearns, "Appreciation; Copland Captured Sounds of a Nation," *USA Today,* December 3, 1990, D1.

2. On Copland's early years, see Howard Pollack, *Aaron Copland: The Life and Work of an Uncommon Man* (New York: Henry Holt, 1999), 15–29; John Rockwell, "Copland, the Dean of U.S. Music, Dies at 90," *New York Times,* December 3, 1990, A1; Marc E. Vargo, *Noble Lives: Biographical Portraits of Three Remarkable Gay Men— Glenway Wescott, Aaron Copland, Dag Hammarskjold* (New York: Harrington Park Press, 2005), 46–49. Copland's parents were Harris Morris Copland and Sarah Mittenthal Copland.

3. Pollack, *Aaron Copland,* 30–56; Rockwell, "Copland," A1; Vargo, *Noble Lives,* 48–51.

4. Pollack, *Aaron Copland,* 50, 52–53.

5. On Kraft's early years, see Pollack, *Aaron Copland,* 239; Carol J. Oja and Judith Tick, *Aaron Copland and His World* (Princeton, NJ: Princeton University Press, 2005), 152–54. Kraft's parents were Samuel Etler and Bella Etler.

6. "Music Week Medals Won by Many Youths," *New York Times,* April 29, 1925, 24; Pollack, *Aaron Copland,* 239.

7. Pollack, *Aaron Copland,* 239.

8. Ibid., 121; Aaron Copland and Vivian Perlis, *Copland: 1900 Through 1942* (Boston: Faber and Faber, 1984), 106; Rockwell, "Copland," A1.

9. Lawrence Gilman, "Music," *New York Herald Tribune,* January 12, 1925; Pollack, *Aaron Copland,* 156.

10. "Concerts," *New York Times,* March 4, 1932, 16; Virgil Thomson, "Aaron Copland," *Modern Music* 9, no. 2 (1932): 67.

11. Pollack, *Aaron Copland,* 235.

12. Ibid., 3; David Denby, "The Gift to Be Simple," *New Yorker,* December 13, 1999, 102.

13. Pollack, *Aaron Copland,* 179–80.

14. Ibid., 182–185; Vargo, *Noble Lives,* 56.

15. Copland and Perlis, *Copland: 1900 Through 1942,* 213; Pollack, *Aaron Copland,* 217.

16. Copland and Perlis, *Copland: 1900 Through 1942,* 213; Pollack, *Aaron Copland,* 217.

17. Pollack, *Aaron Copland,* 239.

18. Ibid., 239–40.

19. Copland and Perlis, *Copland: 1900 Through 1942,* 213.

20. Pollack, *Aaron Copland,* 239; Vargo, *Noble Lives,* 56–57.

21. Pollack, *Aaron Copland,* 239–40.

22. Copland and Perlis, *Copland: 1900 Through 1942,* 216.

23. Ibid.

24. Ibid., 213–16; Oja and Tick, *Aaron Copland,* 152–54; Pollack, *Aaron Copland,* 224, 277–78.

25. Copland and Perlis, *Copland: 1900 Through 1942,* 245; Pollack, *Aaron Copland,* 299.

26. Copland and Perlis, *Copland: 1900 Through 1942,* 246, 268; Pollack, *Aaron Copland,* 240, 303.

27. "Bravos Hail Peerce at Bowl," *Los Angeles Times,* August 18, 1939, A11; Compton Pakenham, "Recent Phonograph Recordings," *New York Times,* April 23, 1939, 132; Jay Walz, "Vienna Boys Sing Album of Easter Music," *Washington Post,* April 2, 1939, 77.

28. *Time,* June 5, 1939.

29. Pollack, *Aaron Copland,* 343.

30. Copland and Perlis, *Copland: 1900 Through 1942,* 252; Vargo, *Noble Lives,* 57.

31. Copland and Perlis, *Copland: 1900 Through 1942,* 229.

32. Pollack, *Aaron Copland,* 102; Vargo, *Noble Lives,* 57.

33. Pollack, *Aaron Copland,* 359–60.

34. Denby, "Gift to Be Simple," 102; Hans Kindler, "Handel Suite Symphony's Forte Today," *Washington Post,* January 21, 1945, S5; Pollack, *Aaron Copland,* 360; "Stokowski Offers Christmas Music," *New York Times,* December 19, 1944, 26.

35. For the quote, see Michael Tilson Thomas, music director of the San Francisco Symphony, in "Copland and the American Sound," a video recording directed and produced in 2006 by David Kennard and Joan Saffa. Pollack, *Aaron Copland,* 361–62.

36. Copland and Perlis, *Copland: Since 1943* (New York: St. Martin's, 1989), 77; Pollack, *Aaron Copland,* 237.

37. For the quote, see Pollack, *Aaron Copland,* 225. Pollack, *Aaron Copland,* 375.

38. Copland and Perlis, *Copland: Since 1943,* 62.

39. Edwin Denby, "The Dance: Appalachian Spring," *New York Herald Tribune,* May 15, 1945, 14; Pollack, *Aaron Copland,* 47.

40. "Pulitzer Awards for 1944 Revealed," *New York Times,* May 8, 1945, A1.

41. Pollack, *Aaron Copland,* 346, 383, 432.

42. Ibid., 240; Copland and Perlis, *Copland: Since 1943,* 19.

43. Pollack, *Aaron Copland,* 235.

44. Ibid., 236, 246–48.

45. Copland and Perlis, *Copland: Since 1943,* 174; Vargo, *Noble Lives,* 57–58.

46. Pollack, *Aaron Copland,* 241–42; Vargo, *Noble Lives,* 58.

47. Copland and Perlis, *Copland: Since 1943,* 87, 135, 293, 334; Pollack, *Aaron Copland,* 96, 240.

48. Pollack, *Aaron Copland,* 236–37.

49. Ibid., 243.

50. Ibid., 242; Copland and Perlis, *Copland: Since 1943,* 309.

51. Pollack, *Aaron Copland,* 242–43.

52. Copland to Phillip Ramey, October 12, 1972, Aaron Copland Collection, Music Division, Library of Congress, Washington, D.C.

53. Ernest A. Lotito, "30 to Receive Freedom Medals," *Washington Post,* July 4, 1964, A1; Pollack, *Aaron Copland,* 476.

54. Copland and Perlis, *Copland: Since 1943,* 359, 383.

55. Ibid., 401; Pollack, *Aaron Copland,* 244; Vargo, *Noble Lives,* 58.

56. Pollack, *Aaron Copland,* 244; Vargo, *Noble Lives,* 58.

57. Copland and Perlis, *Copland: Since 1943,* 387.

58. Pollack, *Aaron Copland,* 244; Vargo, *Noble Lives,* 58.

59. Pollack, *Aaron Copland,* 244.

60. Richard F. Shepard, "TV: 'Kennedy Center Honors' Celebrates the Performing Arts," *New York Times,* December 29, 1979, 42; Lon Tuck, "12 to Receive Arts Medals," *Washington Post,* July 8, 1986, D3.

61. Vargo, *Noble Lives,* 58.

62. For the quote, see Rockwell, "Copland," A1. "Aaron Copland Dies; Music Found the American Mood," *Los Angeles Times,* December 3, 1990, A1; Bart Barnes, "Eminent American Composer Aaron Copland Dies at 90," *Washington Post,* December 3, 1990, A1; "Composer Copland Dies," *Chicago Tribune,* December 3, 1990, A1; Richard Dyer, "Composer Aaron Copland Dies," *Boston Globe,* December 3, 1990, A1.

CHAPTER 11: FRANK MERLO & TENNESSEE WILLIAMS, 1948–1963

1. On Williams's early years, see Donald Spoto, *The Kindness of Strangers: The Life of Tennessee Williams* (Boston: Little, Brown, 1985), 1–66; Dakin Williams and Shepherd Mead, *Tennessee Williams: An Intimate Biography* (New York: Arbor House, 1983), 13–45; Tennessee Williams, *Memoirs* (New York: New Directions, 1972), 1–51. Williams's parents were Cornelius Williams and Edwina Dakin Williams.

2. John J. Goldman, "Tennessee Williams, 71, Playwright, Dies in N.Y.," *Los Angeles Times,* February 26, 1983, A19.

3. Ibid.

4. Williams, *Memoirs,* 24, 36.

5. Richard Christiansen, "Tennessee Williams Killed by Bottle Cap," *Chicago Tribune,* February 27, 1983, B11.

6. Williams and Mead, *Tennessee Williams,* 64.

7. J. Y. Smith, "Tennessee Williams Is Dead at Age 71," *Washington Post,* February 26, 1983, B6.

8. On Merlo's early years, see Spoto, *Kindness,* 152–54; Williams and Mead, *Tennessee Williams,* 169–80.

9. Spoto, *Kindness,* 244–45.

10. Ibid.

11. Williams and Mead, *Tennessee Williams,* 73.

12. Spoto, *Kindness,* 69.

13. Richard Christiansen, "Last Curtain Falls for Dramatist Tennessee Williams, Dead at 71," *Chicago Tribune,* February 26 1983, 1, 2.

14. Goldman, "Tennessee Williams," A20.

15. Claudia Cassidy, "Fragile Drama Holds Together in Tight Spell," *Chicago Tri-*

bune, December 27, 1944, 11; "Glass Menagerie Is Best Play of Year, Drama Critics Decide," *New York Times,* April 11, 1945, 18; Leonard Lyons, "Broadway Glossary," *Washington Post,* May 12, 1945, 8.

16. Frank S. Adams, "Pulitzer Prizes Go to 'Streetcar' and Michener's Stories of Pacific," *New York Times,* May 4, 1948, A1; Howard Barnes, "O'Neill Status Won by Author of Streetcar," *New York Herald Tribune,* December 14, 1947, E1; Wolcott Gibbs, "Theater," *New Yorker,* December 13, 1947, 50.

17. Spoto, *Kindness,* 141, 145–46.

18. Ibid., 139.

19. Ibid., 145; Williams, *Memoirs,* 139; Williams to Paul Bigelow, January 7, 1948, Rare Books and Manuscript Library, Columbia University, New York.

20. Spoto, *Kindness,* 149; Williams to Elizabeth Schauffler and Audrey Wood, January 1948, Harry Ransom Humanities Research Center, University of Texas, Austin.

21. Williams and Mead, *Tennessee Williams,* 153; Williams to Elizabeth Schauffler and Audrey Wood, January 1948, Harry Ransom Humanities Research Center; Williams to Elia Kazan, January 25, 1948, Wesleyan University Cinema Archives, Middletown, Connecticut.

22. Ronald Hayman, *Tennessee Williams: Everyone Else Is an Audience* (New Haven, Connecticut: Yale University Press, 1993), 125.

23. Williams journal entry May 29, 1949, reprinted in Margaret Bradham Thornton, ed., *Notebooks: Tennessee Williams* (New Haven, CT: Yale University Press, 2006), 485.

24. Williams and Mead, *Tennessee Williams,* 146.

25. Williams, *Memoirs,* 155.

26. Ibid.; Williams and Mead, *Tennessee Williams,* 146.

27. Williams journal entries May 29, 1949, and December 30, 1953, reprinted in Thornton, *Notebooks,* 501, 607.

28. Williams and Mead, *Tennessee Williams,* 241, 244.

29. Ibid., 169.

30. Spoto, *Kindness,* 153, 258; Thornton, *Notebooks,* 486.

31. Williams, *Memoirs,* 189.

32. Hayman, *Tennessee Williams,* 136; Williams and Mead, *Tennessee Williams,* 171; Williams, *Memoirs,* 162.

33. Spoto, *Kindness,* 165; Williams to Paul Bigelow, August 3, 1950, and to Carson McCullers, April 1950, Special Collections Library, Duke University, Durham, North Carolina; Williams to Cheryl Crawford, June 9, 1950, Billy Rose Theatre Collection, New York Public Library for the Performing Arts, Lincoln Center, New York.

34. Brooks Atkinson, "At the Theatre," *New York Times,* February 5, 1951, 33; Claudia Cassidy, "'Rose Tattoo' a Stimulating Drama in Bud," *Chicago Tribune,* December 31, 1950, 5; Hayman, *Tennessee Williams,* 137.

35. Williams to Audrey Wood, March 27, 1950, Harry Ransom Humanities Research Center.

36. Spoto, *Kindness,* 195; Williams to Cheryl Crawford, June 1954, Billy Rose Theatre Collection; Williams to Cheryl Crawford, August 23, 1954, Harry Ransom Humanities Research Center.

37. Hayman, *Tennessee Williams*, 165–66; Spoto, *Kindness*, 179, 193; Williams and Mead, *Tennessee Williams*, 248.

38. Brooks Atkinson, "Theatre: Tennessee Williams' 'Cat,'" *New York Times*, March 25, 1955, 18; John Chapman, "Acting Excellent, but Williams Play Lacks Purpose," *Chicago Tribune*, March 26, 1955, 13; Walter Winchell, "The Broadway Lights," *Washington Post*, March 14, 1955, 35.

39. Charles Grutzner, "Pulitzer Winners," *New York Times*, May 3, 1955, 1; "Williams' Drama Cited by Critics," *New York Times*, April 13, 1955, 33.

40. Williams, *Memoirs*, 188.

41. Spoto, *Kindness*, 239.

42. John Chapman, "Theatre Reviews," *New York Daily News*, December 29, 1961, 44; T. E. Kalem, "The Angel of the Odd," *Time*, March 9, 1962, 53; Dorothy Kilgallen, "New York's a Winter Playground," *Washington Post*, January 28, 1962, G6.

43. For articles about Williams's personal life that do not talk about his sexuality, see Brooks Atkinson, "His Bizarre Images Can't Be Denied," *New York Times*, November 26, 1961, BR1; Richard L. Coe, "It's Williams in a Nutshell," *Washington Post*, November 11, 1961, A13; Robert Kirsch, "Two Studies of Tennessee Williams," *Los Angeles Times*, December 27, 1961, A5; "Tennessee Williams Seeks New Subjects," *Los Angeles Times*, August 4, 1962, A8.

44. Sam Zolotov, "'Iguana' Is Cited by Critics Circle," *New York Times*, April 11, 1962, 46.

45. Spoto, *Kindness*, 162; Williams journal entry August 12, 1954, reprinted in Thornton, *Notebooks*, 651; Williams to Gore Vidal, August 13, 1951, Houghton Library, Harvard University, Cambridge, MA.

46. Jed Horne, "A Playwright Lives His Greatest Drama," *People Weekly*, May 26, 1975, 37; Williams and Mead, *Tennessee Williams*, 241, 244; Williams to Carson McCullers, July 15, 1953, Harry Ransom Humanities Research Center.

47. Spoto, *Kindness*, 242; Margaret A. Van Antwerp, "Unbeastly Williams," *Newsweek*, June 17, 1960, 96.

48. Spoto, *Kindness*, 242.

49. Williams, *Memoirs*, 183.

50. Ibid., 183.

51. Horne, "Playwright Lives," 37; Williams and Mead, *Tennessee Williams*, 247.

52. Williams, *Memoirs*, 193.

53. Ibid., 194.

54. Michiko Kakutani, "Tennessee Williams," *New York Times*, August 13, 1981, C17; T. E. Kalem, "The Angel of the Odd," *Time*, March 9, 1962, 53.

55. Spoto, *Kindness*, 264, 291; Williams and Mead, *Tennessee Williams*, 241. The poet was Frederick Nicklaus, and the paid companion was William Glavin.

56. Clive Barnes, "Theater: 'In the Bar of a Tokyo Hotel,'" *New York Times*, May 12, 1969, 54; "Torpid Tennessee," *Time*, May 23, 1969, 75.

57. Goldman, "Tennessee Williams," A20.

58. Carla Hall and Mary Battiata, "Celebrating the Celebrated," *Washington Post*, December 8, 1980, B1; Richard F. Shepard, "TV: 'Kennedy Center Honors' Celebrates the Performing Arts," *New York Times*, December 29, 1979, 42.

59. Christiansen, "Tennessee Williams," B11.

60. Goldman, "Tennessee Williams," A1; Mel Gussow, "Tennessee Williams Is Dead Here at 71," *New York Times,* 1; Smith, "Tennessee Williams," B6. The seven plays listed in the tribute were *The Glass Menagerie, A Streetcar Named Desire, Summer and Smoke, The Rose Tattoo, Cat on a Hot Tin Roof, Sweet Bird of Youth,* and *The Night of the Iguana.*

61. For the quote, see Goldman, "Tennessee Williams," A19. For other obituaries and tributes that referred to Merlo, see Christiansen, "Last Curtain," 2; Barbara Kantrowitz, "Tennessee Williams Is Dead," *Philadelphia Inquirer,* February 26, 1983, A1, A4; Smith, "Tennessee Williams," B6; "Tennessee Williams Found Dead at 71," *San Francisco Chronicle,* February 26, 1983, 1, 12.

CHAPTER 12: JAMES BALDWIN & LUCIEN HAPPERSBERGER, 1949–1987

1. On Baldwin's early years, see James Campbell, *Talking at the Gates: A Life of James Baldwin* (Berkeley: University of California Press, 1991), 3–45; David Leeming, *James Baldwin: A Biography* (New York: Knopf, 1994), 3–55. Baldwin's mother was Emma Berdis Jones, and his stepfather was David Baldwin.

2. Leeming, *James Baldwin,* 26, 37–42.

3. Ibid., 33.

4. James Baldwin, "The Harlem Ghetto," *Commentary,* February 1948, 165–70; James Baldwin, "Maxim Gorki as Artist," *Nation,* April 12, 1947, 427–28; Robert Coles, "James Baldwin Back Home," *New York Times,* July 31, 1977, BR1.

5. Campbell, *Talking at the Gates,* 50–57; Leeming, *James Baldwin,* 56.

6. Campbell, *Talking at the Gates,* 50–57.

7. Ibid., 60–61; Leeming, *James Baldwin,* 74–79; W. J. Weatherby, *James Baldwin: Artist on Fire* (New York: Donald I. Fine, 1989), 90–92.

8. Campbell, *Talking at the Gates,* 60–61; Leeming, *James Baldwin,* 74–79; Weatherby, *James Baldwin,* 90–92.

9. Campbell, *Talking at the Gates,* 60.

10. Ibid., 60–61; Leeming, *James Baldwin,* 74–79; Weatherby, *James Baldwin,* 90–92.

11. Leeming, *James Baldwin,* 75.

12. Campbell, *Talking at the Gates,* 61; Weatherby, *James Baldwin,* 90.

13. *James Baldwin: The Price of the Ticket* documentary, directed by Karen Thorsen, California Newsreel, 1990.

14. Leeming, *James Baldwin,* 79.

15. *Price of the Ticket* documentary.

16. Campbell, *Talking at the Gates,* 75; Leeming, *James Baldwin,* 75, 79.

17. Leeming, *James Baldwin,* 75–76, 322.

18. Campbell, *Talking at the Gates,* 61.

19. Leeming, *James Baldwin,* 76.

20. Ibid., 80.

21. Ibid.; Campbell, *Talking at the Gates,* 61; Weatherby, *James Baldwin,* 98.

22. Leeming, *James Baldwin,* 80.

23. James Baldwin, *Go Tell It on the Mountain* (New York: Knopf, 1953).

24. "Lord, Hold My Hand," *Time*, May 18, 1953, 126; Anthony West, "Books," *New Yorker*, June 20, 1953, 93.

25. Leeming, *James Baldwin*, 91, 322; Weatherby, *James Baldwin*, 102.

26. Leeming, *James Baldwin*, 94–95.

27. Ibid., 95, 100. James Baldwin, *Notes of a Native Son* (Boston: Beacon, 1955).

28. Campbell, *Talking at the Gates*, 94–95; Leeming, *James Baldwin*, 99.

29. Campbell, *Talking at the Gates*, 95; Leeming, *James Baldwin*, 99; Weatherby, *James Baldwin*, 108.

30. Campbell, *Talking at the Gates*, 104–5; Weatherby, *James Baldwin*, 111.

31. James Baldwin, *Giovanni's Room* (New York: Dial, 1956).

32. Leeming, *James Baldwin*, 99, 154–55.

33. D. B., "Giovanni's Room," *San Francisco Chronicle*, December 2, 1956, 24; Katherine Gauss Jackson, "Books in Brief," *Harper's*, November 1956.

34. For articles about Baldwin that did not mention his sexuality, see Esther Greenberg, "Skip Size, Shape and Shrinkage in Choosing Fiction," *Washington Post*, November 25, 1956, E7; Granville Hicks, "Tormented Triangle," *New York Times*, October 14, 1956, BR3; "A Sophisticated Fare for Trained Appetites," *Washington Post*, October 14, 1956, E7.

35. Leeming, *James Baldwin*, 154–55.

36. Ibid., 119–20.

37. James Baldwin, *Nobody Knows My Name: More Notes of a Native Son* (New York: Dial, 1961), 13.

38. Leeming, *James Baldwin*, 180.

39. Ibid., 287; Campbell, *Talking at the Gates*, 170.

40. Weatherby, *James Baldwin*, 171–72, 245.

41. Ibid., 189.

42. James Baldwin, *Another Country* (New York: Dial, 1962).

43. William Barrett, "Weight of the City," *Atlantic Monthly*, July 1962, 110; "New York Cacophony," *Time*, June 29, 1962, 76; Charles Poore, "Books of the Times," *New York Times*, June 26, 1962, 31.

44. Henry Raymont, "Publishers Fight Baldwin Book Ban," *New York Times*, June 30, 1963, 47; Weatherby, *James Baldwin*, 191.

45. Leeming, *James Baldwin*, 116.

46. Ibid., 197.

47. Ibid.; Campbell, *Talking at the Gates*, 153.

48. Campbell, *Talking at the Gates*, 61.

49. James Baldwin, *The Fire Next Time* (New York: Dial, 1963).

50. William Barrett, "Reader's Choice," *Atlantic Monthly*, March 1963, 156; R. J. Dwyer, "I Know about the Negroes and the Poor," *National Review*, December 17, 1963, 517; Saul Maloff, "Love: The Movement Within," *Nation*, March 2, 1963, 181.

51. Bart Barnes, "James Baldwin, Playwright, Novelist, Dies," *Washington Post*, December 2, 1987, A1.

52. *New York Times*, "Kennedy Blamed by Baldwin," *New York Times*, May 13,

1963, 25; Layhmond Robinson, "Robert Kennedy Consults Negroes Here About North," May 25, 1963, 1; Layhmond Robinson, "Robert Kennedy Fails to Sway Negroes at Secret Talks Here," May 26, 1963, 1; Anthony Lewis, "Robert Kennedy Confers Today with Theater Men on Race Issue," May 27, 1963, 1; "3 Negro Speakers on TV Hold Kennedy Leadership Inadequate," June 25, 1963, 13.

53. "At the Root of the Negro Problem," *Time,* May 17, 1963, 26.

54. Bernard Gavzer, "Rides Crest of Historic Wave," *Los Angeles Times,* June 30, 1963, B1, B11; M. S. Handler, "James Baldwin Rejects Despair Despite Race 'Drift and Danger,'" *New York Times,* June 3, 1963, A1, A19; James Reston, "'I Have a Dream . . . ,'" *New York Times,* August 29, 1963, 1.

55. Nat Hentoff, "James Baldwin Gets 'Older and Sadder,'" *New York Times,* April 11, 1965, X1.

56. Campbell, *Talking at the Gates,* 189; Leeming, *James Baldwin,* 233.

57. Barnes, "James Baldwin," A1.

58. Leeming, *James Baldwin,* 322.

59. James Baldwin, *No Name in the Street* (New York: Dial, 1972); *If Beale Street Could Talk* (New York: Dial, 1974); *The Devil Finds Work* (New York: Dial, 1976); *Just Above My Head* (New York: Dial, 1979). On Baldwin's early books being stronger than his later ones, see Peter S. Prescott, "The Dilemma of a Native Son," *Newsweek,* December 14, 1987, 86.

60. Leeming, *James Baldwin,* 331–32.

61. Ibid., 334; Baldwin to David Baldwin, October 3, 1975, James Baldwin Papers, Schomburg Center for Research in Black Culture, New York.

62. Leeming, *James Baldwin,* 355–56.

63. Ibid., 372.

64. Ibid., 385.

65. "James Baldwin's Fire," *New York Times,* December 2, 1987, A34; Lee Daniels, "James Baldwin, the Writer, Dies in France at 63," *New York Times,* December 1, 1987, D27; Mark Feeney, "James Baldwin Dies," *Boston Globe,* December 2, 1987, A1; "Novelist James Baldwin Dies in France at 63," *Los Angeles Times,* December 1, 1987, A1.

66. On obituaries and tributes that did not mention Happersberger, see Barnes, "James Baldwin," A1; Daniels, "James Baldwin," D27; Mark Feeney, "James Baldwin Dies," *Boston Globe,* December 2, 1987, A1; "James Baldwin's Fire," *New York Times,* December 2, 1987, A34; "Novelist James Baldwin Dies in France at 63," *Los Angeles Times,* December 1, 1963, A1; Peter Prescott, "The Dilemma of a Native Son," *Newsweek,* December 14, 1987, 86.

67. Campbell, *Talking at the Gates,* 232; Lee Daniels, "Friends Gather to Celebrate Baldwin's Gifts," *New York Times,* December 9, 1987, B1; Marianne Yen, "An Emotional Farewell to Baldwin," *Washington Post,* December 9, 1987, B3.

CHAPTER 13: ROBERT RAUSCHENBERG & JASPER JOHNS, 1954–1962

1. On Rauschenberg's early years, see Mary Lynn Kotz, *Rauschenberg: Art and Life* (New York: Abrams, 2004), 47–85; Calvin Tomkins, *Off the Wall: Robert Rauschenberg and the Art World of Our Time* (Garden City, NY: Doubleday, 1980), 14–34. Rauschenberg's parents were Ernest Rauschenberg and Dora Matson Rauschenberg.

2. Kotz, *Rauschenberg,* 56.

3. Ibid., 60–61, 69, 71.

4. Ibid., 74.

5. Ibid., 71, 82; James Fitzsimmons, "Art," *Arts and Architecture,* October 1953, 33–34.

6. On Johns's early years, see Grace Glueck, "'Once Established,' Says Jasper Johns, 'Ideas Can Be Discarded,'" *New York Times,* October 16, 1977, B1, B31; Deborah Solomon, "The Unflagging Artistry of Jasper Johns," *New York Times Magazine,* June 19, 1988, 20–23, 63–65; Tomkins, *Off the Wall,* 110–11. Johns's parents were William Jasper Johns and Jean Riley Johns.

7. Glueck, "'Once Established,'" B31.

8. Jonathan Katz, "The Art of Code: Jasper Johns and Robert Rauschenberg," in Whitney Chadwick and Isabelle de Courtivron, eds., *Significant Others: Creativity & Intimate Partnership* (New York: Thames Hudson, 1993), 191; Solomon, "Unflagging Artistry," 23; Tomkins, *Off the Wall,* 111.

9. Barbaralee Diamonstein Spielvogel, *Inside the Art World: Conversations with Barbaralee Diamonstein* (New York: Rizzoli, 1994), 116.

10. Tomkins, *Off the Wall,* 111.

11. Glueck, "'Once Established,'" B31.

12. Jo Ann Lewis, "Jasper Johns, Personally Speaking," *Washington Post,* May 16, 1990, F6.

13. Tomkins, *Off the Wall,* 118.

14. Katz, "Art of Code," 197.

15. Kotz, *Rauschenberg,* 76.

16. Tomkins, *Off the Wall,* 134.

17. Ibid., 135. The piece with the hen is *Untitled,* and the piece with the Coke bottles is *Coca Cola Plan.*

18. Kotz, *Rauschenberg,* 91; Matt Schudel, "Innovative Mind Found Art in the Unwanted," *Washington Post,* May 14, 2008, A1; Tomkins, *Off the Wall,* 136. The piece with the goat is *Monogram.*

19. Leo Steinberg, "Jasper Johns: The First Seven Years of His Art," in *Other Criteria: Confrontations with Twentieth-century Art* (New York: Oxford University Press, 1972), 27.

20. Solomon, "Unflagging Artistry," 63.

21. Ibid.

22. The piece is *Flag.*

23. Jasper Johns interview with Walter Hopps, *Artforum,* March 1965.

24. Solomon, "Unflagging Artistry," 63.

25. Tomkins, *Off the Wall,* 141–142.

26. Ibid., 144; Solomon, "Unflagging Artistry," 63. The four paintings purchased by the museum were *Flag, Green Target, White Numbers,* and *Target with Four Faces.*

27. Solomon, "Unflagging Artistry," 63.

28. Ibid.; Glueck, "'Once Established,'" B1.

29. Tomkins, *Off the Wall,* 142–43, 145.

30. Ibid., 133–34.

31. Glueck, "'Once Established,'" B31; Tomkins, *Off the Wall,* 187.

32. Kotz, *Rauschenberg,* 98.

33. Ibid., 99.

34. Dore Ashton, "Rauschenberg's Illustrations for Dante's Inferno," *Arts and Architecture,* February 1961, 4; Roberta Smith, "Art: Drawings by Robert Rauschenberg, 1958–68," *New York Times,* October 31, 1986, C28.

35. Glueck, "'Once Established,'" B31; Tomkins, *Off the Wall,* 184.

36. Tomkins, *Off the Wall,* 184.

37. Katz, "Art of Code," 202; Smith, "Art: Drawings," C28.

38. Martin Duberman, "Is There Room for Privacy on Canvas?" *New York Times,* September 7, 1997, H89; Katz, "Art of Code," 189; John Russell, "Rauschenberg and Johns: Mr. Outside and Mr. Inside," *New York Times,* February 15, 1987, H33, H34; Smith, "Art: Drawings," C28.

39. Tomkins, *Off the Wall,* 197–98.

40. Ibid., 198, 224, 291–92.

41. Paul Taylor, "Robert Rauschenberg: 'I can't even afford my works anymore,'" *Interview,* December 1990, 146.

42. John D'Emilio, *Sexual Politics, Sexual Communities: The Making of a Homosexual Minority in the United States, 1940–1970* (Chicago: University of Chicago Press, 1983), 40–53.

43. Lewis, "Jasper Johns," F6; Solomon, "Unflagging Artistry," 65.

44. Tomkins, *Off the Wall,* 206.

45. Ibid., 208.

46. Max Kozloff, *Nation,* December 7, 1963; Brian O'Doherty, "Robert Rauschenberg," *New York Times,* April 28, 1963, X13.

47. Tomkins, *Off the Wall,* 160, 209. The first work acquired by the museum was *First Landing Jump.*

48. Kotz, *Rauschenberg,* 110; "Venice Prize Goes to Rauschenberg," *New York Times,* June 20, 1964, 23.

49. Robert Levinson, "Gemini and the Rebirth of Graphics," *Los Angeles Times,* January 24, 1971, U24; Solomon, "Unflagging Artistry," 20–23, 64; Jean M. White, "USIA Venice Exhibition Will Lean to 'Pop Art,'" *Washington Post,* April 3, 1964, A3.

50. Michael Kimmelman, "Robert Rauschenberg, American Artist, Dies at 82," *New York Times,* May 14, 2008, A1; Schudel, "Innovative Mind," A16.

51. *New York Times,* Alan Riding, "A Debut in Venice for a Coveted Art Collection, Originally Bound for Paris," May 1, 2006, E3; Carol Vogel, "Met Buys Its First Painting by Jasper Johns," October 29, 1998, E1; Carol Vogel, "Works by Johns and de Kooning Sell for $143.5 Million," October 22, 2006, E1.

52. Blake Gopnik, "Robert Rauschenberg, Alchemist of the Mundane," *Washington Post,* May 14, 2008, C1; Kimmelman, "Robert Rauschenberg," A1; Kotz, *Rauschenberg,* 190; Smith, "Art: Drawings," C28.

53. Tomkins, *Off the Wall,* 300.

54. Ibid.; Schudel, "Innovative Mind," A16.

55. Kimmelman, "Robert Rauschenberg," A1; Schudel, "Innovative Mind," A16; Tomkins, *Off the Wall,* 213–14, 289.

56. Kimmelman, "Robert Rauschenberg," A1; Christopher Knight, "Robert Rauschenberg, 1925–2008," *Los Angeles Times,* May 14, 2008, A1; Mitch Stacy, "Pop Artist Robert Rauschenberg Dead at 82," *Seattle Times,* May 14, 2008, A1 (distributed by the Associated Press).

CHAPTER 14: ISMAIL MERCHANT & JAMES IVORY, 1961–2005

1. On Ivory's early years, see Robert Emmet Long, *The Films of Merchant Ivory* (New York: Harry N. Abrams, 1999), 27–30; John Pym, *The Wandering Company: Twenty-one Years of Merchant Ivory Films* (London: British Film Institute, 1999), 18–23. Ivory's parents were Edward Ivory and Hallie DeLoney Ivory.

2. Pym, *Wandering Company,* 20.

3. Ibid.; James Morrison, "James Ivory," in *International Dictionary of Films and Filmmakers,* vol. 2: *Directors,* Sara Pendergast and Tom Pendergast, eds. (Detroit: St. James Press, 2000), 469–72.

4. Morrison, "James Ivory," 469–72; Long, *Films of Merchant Ivory,* 29.

5. Long, *Films of Merchant Ivory,* 30; David Noh, "Enjoying a Golden Partnership," *Washington Blade,* May 18, 2001, 39.

6. On Merchant's early years, see Philip Kemp, "Ismail Merchant," in *International Dictionary of Films and Filmmakers,* vol. 2: *Directors,* Sara Pendergast and Tom Pendergast, eds. (Detroit: St. James Press, 2000), 590–91; Long, *Films of Merchant Ivory,* 12–16; Pym, *Wandering Company,* 14–17. Merchant's parents were Noormohamed Rehman and Hazrabi Rehman.

7. Long, *Films of Merchant Ivory,* 14.

8. Kemp, "Ismail Merchant," 590–91; Long, *Films of Merchant Ivory,* 14.

9. Kemp, "Ismail Merchant," 590–91; Long, *Films of Merchant Ivory,* 14.

10. Adam Bernstein, "Ismail Merchant, of Merchant-Ivory Films, Dies," *Washington Post,* May 26, 2005, B6; Vibhuti Patel, "Ismail Merchant, 1936–2005," *Newsweek,* June 6, 2005, 95.

11. Long, *Films of Merchant Ivory,* 16.

12. Noh, "Enjoying a Golden Partnership," 39; Pym, *Wandering Company,* 18.

13. Noh, "Enjoying a Golden Partnership," 39; Pym, *Wandering Company,* 18.

14. Long, *Films of Merchant Ivory,* 40–44; Noh, "Enjoying a Golden Partnership," 39; Pym, *Wandering Company,* 13.

15. Pym, *Wandering Company,* 23–29.

16. Nigel Farndale, "Interview with Film Director James Ivory," *FilmLife,* April 18, 2010; Carla Hall, "Merchant Ivory, Making Beautiful Films Together," *Washington Post,* October 25, 1987, F5; Long, *Films of Merchant Ivory,* 18, 32. The actress who made the statement was Madhur Jaffrey.

17. Farndale, "Interview"; Noh, "Enjoying a Golden Partnership," 39; Long, *Films of Merchant Ivory,* 13, 18, 32.

18. Long, *Films of Merchant Ivory,* 18, 30.

19. Ibid., 18, 41, 83.

20. Ibid., 18.

21. Ibid., 96; Noh, "Enjoying a Golden Partnership," 39.

22. *The Europeans* was released in 1979.

23. Roger Ebert, "The Europeans," *Chicago Sun-Times,* February 22, 1980; Long, *Films of Merchant Ivory,* 130.

24. *The Bostonians* was released in 1984.

25. Vanessa Redgrave won her Academy Award for best supporting actress in 1977's *Julia.*

26. Sheila Benson, "'Bostonians,'" *Los Angeles Times,* December 6, 1984, K1; Joseph McLellan, "Literate & Likable," *Washington Post,* September 22, 1984, D1.

27. Long, *Films of Merchant Ivory,* 145.

28. *A Room with a View* was released in 1986.

29. Long, *Films of Merchant Ivory,* 141–42.

30. Daniel Day-Lewis won Academy Awards for best actor in 1989's *My Left Foot* and 2007's *There Will Be Blood.*

31. Harper Barnes, "A Room with a View," *St. Louis Post-Dispatch,* April 4, 1986, G3; Scott Cain, "E. M. Forster's Fops Are Tops in 'Room,'" *Atlanta Constitution,* April 25, 1986, P7; Roger Ebert, "A Room With a View," *Chicago Sun-Times,* April 4, 1986; Rita Kempley, "A Well-Designed Room," *Washington Post,* April 4, 1986, W29.

32. Tom Shales, "'Hannah' and 'Room with a View' Take 3 Awards Each," *Washington Post,* March 31, 1987, C1. The best costume design award went to Jenny Beavan and John Bright, the best art direction award went to Gianni Quaranta, Brian Ackland-Snow, Brian Savegar, and Elio Altamura, and the best screenplay adaptation award went to Ruth Prawer Jhabvala.

33. Farndale, "Interview."

34. Long, *Films of Merchant Ivory,* 145.

35. Ibid.

36. Joseph Giovannini, "Merchant and Ivory's Country Retreat," *New York Times,* April 3, 1986, C1, C8.

37. Ibid., C8.

38. Ibid.

39. Julia Cameron, "Producer Ismail Merchant Plays Hunches into Cinematic Success," *Chicago Tribune,* April 3, 1986, D7; Hall, "Merchant Ivory," F5.

40. Cameron, "Producer Ismail Merchant," F5.

41. Long, *Films of Merchant Ivory,* 145.

42. John Gross, "'Maurice' Brings a Small Book into Sharp Relief," *New York Times,* October 4, 1987, H39.

43. Bernstein, "Ismail Merchant," B6. Anthony Hopkins won his best actor Academy Award for 1991's *The Silence of the Lambs.*

44. Long, *Films of Merchant Ivory,* 192.

45. Jay Carr, "Merchant-Ivory 'Howards End,'" *Boston Globe,* April 24, 1992, 81, 86; Janet Maslin, "Finding Realities to Fit the Illusions of 'Howards End,'" *New York Times,* March 12, 1992, C1.

46. Vincent Canby, "A Drawing-Room War with Edwardian Grace," *New York Times,* March 13, 1992, C1, C15; Carr, "Merchant-Ivory," 86; Edward Guthmann, "A Classy 'Howards End,'" *San Francisco Chronicle,* April 17, 1992, C1.

47. Carla Hall, "Eastwood, 'Unforgiven' Take Top Oscars," *Washington Post,*

March 30, 1993, E1. The best art direction award went to Luciana Arrighi and Ian Whittaker, and the best screenplay adaptation award went to Ruth Prawer Jhabvala.

48. Farndale, "Interview"; Rita Kempley, "In a Class by Itself," *Washington Post*, November 5, 1993, G1; Morrison, "James Ivory," 469–72.

49. Noh, "Enjoying a Golden Partnership," 39.

50. Vincent Canby, "Blind Dignity: A Butler's Story," *New York Times*, November 5, 1993, C1; Jay Carr, "'Remains,'" *Boston Globe*, November 5, 1993, 33; Kempley, "Class by Itself," G1.

51. Noh, "Enjoying a Golden Partnership," 39. *Le Divorce* was released in 2003, and *Surviving Picasso* was released in 1996.

52. Bernstein, "Ismail Merchant," B6; Warren Hoge, "Ismail Merchant, Producer of Sumptuous and Literate Films, Dies at 68," *New York Times*, May 26, 2005, C18; *The Proprietor* was released in 1996.

53. Hoge, "Ismail Merchant, Producer," C18.

54. Warren Hoge, "Ismail Merchant—Collaborator on Award-Winning Films," *San Francisco Chronicle*, May 26, 2005, B6.

55. "Half of Merchant-Ivory Film Duo Behind Oscar-Winning Dramas," *Chicago Tribune*, May 26, 2005, B9; John Horn, "Ismail Merchant, 68," *Los Angeles Times*, May 26, 2005, B12.

56. Horn, "Ismail Merchant," B12.

57. Stephen Holden, "Genteel Lives Unsettled in Uruguay," *New York Times*, April 16, 2008.

CHAPTER 15: FRANCES CLAYTON & AUDRE LORDE, 1968–1988

1. On Clayton's early years, Alexis De Veaux, *Warrior Poet: A Biography of Audre Lorde* (New York: W. W. Norton, 2004), 97; Rodger Streitmatter telephone interview with Frances Clayton, July 22, 2011. Clayton's parents were the Reverend James Madison Clayton and Georgia Frances Myra Mae Blessing Clayton.

2. De Veaux, *Warrior Poet*, 97; Streitmatter interview with Clayton.

3. De Veaux, *Warrior Poet*, 97; Streitmatter interview with Clayton.

4. De Veaux, *Warrior Poet*, 97; Streitmatter interview with Clayton.

5. On Lorde's early years, see Blanche Wiesen Cook and Clare M. Coss, "Audre Lorde," in *Notable American Women: A Biographical Dictionary Completing the Twentieth Century*, Susan Ware, ed. (Cambridge, MA: Belknap Press of Harvard University Press, 2004), 394–96; De Veaux, *Warrior Poet*, especially 11–13; Joan Wylie Hall, ed., *Conversations with Audre Lorde* (Jackson: University of Mississippi Press, 2004), xix-xxv. Lorde's parents were Frederick Byron Lorde and Linda Gertrude Belmar Lorde.

6. Hall, *Conversations*, xix.

7. Karla M. Hammond, "Audre Lorde: Interview," in Hall, *Conversations*, 34.

8. De Veaux, *Warrior Poet*, 62; Hall, *Conversations*, xix-xx.

9. Hall, *Conversations*, xx; Margaret Homan, "Audre Lorde," in Darlene Clark Hine, ed., *Black Women in America: An Historical Encyclopedia* (Brooklyn, NY: Carlson, 1993), 732.

10. De Veaux, *Warrior Poet*, 77.

11. De Veaux, *Warrior Poet*, 73–75; Streitmatter interview with Blanche Wiesen Cook and Clare M. Coss, October 29, 2011.

12. Ibid., 80; Hall, *Conversations*, xx.

13. De Veaux, *Warrior Poet*, 81–84; Hall, *Conversations*, xx.

14. De Veaux, *Warrior Poet*, 88, 93.

15. Ibid., 94; Hall, *Conversations*, xx.

16. De Veaux, *Warrior Poet*, 94–95; Hall, *Conversations*, xx.

17. Cook and Coss, "Audre Lorde," 395; De Veaux, *Warrior Poet*, 96; Hall, *Conversations*, xx.

18. De Veaux, *Warrior Poet*, 97; Hammond, "Audre Lorde: Interview," 33; Homan, "Audre Lorde," 732; Streitmatter interview with Cook and Coss; Adrienne Rich, "An Interview with Audre Lorde," in Hall, *Conversations*, 56.

19. De Veaux, *Warrior Poet*, 102–106; Hall, *Conversations*, xx. Lorde initially taught at City College and then moved to Herbert H. Lehman College and later to John Jay College of Criminal Justice; all three colleges are part of the City University of New York system.

20. De Veaux, *Warrior Poet*, 113; Hall, *Conversations*, 58.

21. The quote is from Streitmatter interview with Clayton. See also De Veaux, *Warrior Poet*, 113, 121–22.

22. De Veaux, *Warrior Poet*, 125.

23. Ibid., 123, 126.

24. Audre Lorde, *The First Cities* (New York: Poets Press, 1968); Dudley Randall, *Negro Digest* 17 (1968): 13; Audre Lorde, *Cables to Rage* (London: Paul Breman, 1970); Mike Doyle, "Made in Canada," *Poetry*, March 1972, 357.

25. De Veaux, *Warrior Poet*, 153; Audre Lorde, *From a Land Where Other People Live* (Detroit: Broadside Press, 1973); Audre Lorde, *New York Head Shop and Museum* (Detroit: Broadside Press, 1974).

26. De Veaux, *Warrior Poet*, 156; Hall, *Conversations*, xxi, 57.

27. De Veaux, *Warrior Poet*, 156–57.

28. Audre Lorde, *The Black Unicorn: Poems* (New York: W. W. Norton, 1978), 3; Audre Lorde, *Coal* (New York: W. W. Norton, 1976).

29. "The Black Unicorn," *Choice*, March 1979, 80; Hayden Carruth, "A Year's Poetry," *Nation*, December 23, 1978, 712; R. B. Stepto, "The Phenomenal Woman and the Severed Daughter," *Parnassus*, Fall-Winter 1979, 312.

30. De Veaux, *Warrior Poet*, 161, 163, 172; Hall, *Conversations*, xxii.

31. Joseph F. Beam, "An Interview with Audre Lorde," in Hall, *Conversations*, 128; De Veaux, *Warrior Poet*, 126, 163, 322; Dagmar Schultz, "Audre Lorde on Her Cancer Illness," in Hall, *Conversations*, 137; Streitmatter interview with Clayton.

32. Streitmatter interview with Clayton.

33. Streitmatter telephone interview with Elizabeth Lorde-Rollins, July 20, 2011.

34. De Veaux, *Warrior Poet*, 188–91, 223; Hall, *Conversations*, xxi; Schultz, "Audre Lorde," 132.

35. Audre Lorde, *The Cancer Journals* (San Francisco: Spinsters Ink, 1980), 64–65.

36. Susan McHenry, "The Cancer Journals," *Ms.,* April 1981, 42.

37. Audre Lorde, *Zami: A New Spelling of My Name* (Boston: Persephone Press, 1982).

38. Rosemary Daniel, "The Poet Who Found Her Own Way," *New York Times,* December 19, 1982, BR12.

39. De Veaux, *Warrior Poet,* 279, 291.

40. Ibid., 301, 323, 356.

41. Streitmatter interview with Cook and Coss.

42. Homan, "Audre Lorde," 733.

43. Audre Lorde, *Sister Outsider* (Trumansburg, NY: Crossing Press, 1984), 124–33.

44. Lorde, *Sister Outsider,* 125–26.

45. Ibid., 128, 130.

46. Thulani Davis and Cheryl Everette, "Books," *Essence,* August 1984, 48; Kate Walter, "Outside In," *Village Voice,* September 4, 1984, 52.

47. Cook and Coss, "Audre Lorde," 394.

48. Ibid., 395; De Veaux, *Warrior Poet,* 80.

49. Cook and Coss, "Audre Lorde," 395; Audre Lorde, *I Am Your Sister: Black Women Organizing Across Sexualities* (New York: Kitchen Table: Women of Color Press, 1985).

50. Cook and Coss, "Audre Lorde," 395; Matthew Rothschild, "Adrienne Rich: 'I happen to think poetry makes a huge difference,'" *Progressive,* January 1994.

51. De Veaux, *Warrior Poet,* 337–38.

52. Streitmatter interview with Cook and Coss.

53. Cook and Coss, "Audre Lorde," 395; De Veaux, *Warrior Poet,* 242, 279.

54. Cook and Coss, "Audre Lorde," 395; Alexis De Veaux, "Just Between Us," *Village Voice Literary Supplement,* April 1993, 14; De Veaux, *Warrior Poet,* 322, 338; Hall, *Conversations,* xxiii.

55. De Veaux, *Warrior Poet,* 352.

56. Ibid., 355; Lorde journal entry, December 20, 1985, Audre Lorde Papers.

57. Lorde journal entry, January 3, 1986, Audre Lorde Papers; De Veaux, *Warrior Poet,* 358.

58. Alexis De Veaux, "Searching for Audre Lorde," *Callaloo* 23, no. 1 (2000): 66.

59. De Veaux, "Searching," 66; De Veaux, *Warrior Poet,* 361.

60. Hall, *Conversations,* xxv; Audre Lorde, *Our Dead Behind Us: Poems* (New York: W. W. Norton, 1986); *A Burst of Light: Essays* (Ithaca, NY: Firebrand Books, 1988); *Undersong: Chosen Poems, Old and New* (New York: W. W. Norton, 1992); *The Marvelous Arithmetics of Distance: Poems 1987–1992* (New York: W. W. Norton, 1993).

61. "Audre Lorde, 58," *Boston Globe,* November 19, 1992, 57; "Audre Lorde, 58, A Poet, Memoirist and Lecturer Dies," *New York Times,* November 20, 1992, A23; "Audre Lorde; Feminist Poet Who Wrote of Discrimination," *Los Angeles Times,* November 19, 1992, A30. See also "Audre Lorde, New York's Feminist Poet Laureate," *Chicago*

Tribune, November 19, 1992, C20; "Audre Lorde, Poet," *Washington Post,* November 19, 1992, C4.

62. Nadine Brozan, "Chronicle," *New York Times,* January 13, 1993, B4.

63. Barbara Christian, *New Black Feminist Criticism, 1985–2000* (Urbana: University of Illinois Press, 2007), 164; Homan, "Audre Lorde," 733.

64. Streitmatter interview with Clayton.

PHOTOGRAPHY/ILLUSTRATION CREDITS

Walt Whitman and Peter Doyle, 1865; courtesy of the Library of Congress.

Martha Carey Thomas and Mamie Gwinn, 1879; courtesy of Bryn Mawr College Archives.

Edward Perry Warren and John Marshall, 1895; photo by Edward Reeves, courtesy of Edward Reeves Photographer, printed with permission.

Mary Rozet Smith and Jane Addams, 1896; courtesy of the Jane Addams Collection, Swarthmore College Peace Collection.

Bessie Marbury and Elsie de Wolfe, from *My Crystal Ball*, 1923.

J. C. Leyendecker, 1920; Leyendecker illustration of Charles Beach, 1922; both courtesy of the National Museum of American Illustration.

Alice B. Toklas and Gertrude Stein, 1934; courtesy of Photofest.

Janet Flanner, 1921; Solita Solano, c. 1920; both courtesy of the Library of Congress.

Greta Garbo, 1930s; courtesy of Photofest. Mercedes de Acosta, 1920s; courtesy of Rosenbach Museum and Library.

Aaron Copland, c. 1925; courtesy of Photofest. Victor Kraft, 1935; courtesy of the Library of Congress.

Frank Merlo and Tennessee Williams; photo, Richard Leavitt Collection of Tennessee Williams, MS.2065, University of Tennessee Libraries, Knoxville, Special Collections; courtesy of Richard E. Leavitt Estate.

James Baldwin and Lucien Happersberger, 1953; courtesy of David Leeming.

Robert Rauschenberg and Jasper Johns, 1955; photo by Rachel Rosenthal, courtesy of Rachel Rosenthal Company.

Ismail Merchant and James Ivory, 1984; courtesy of Photofest.

Frances Clayton and Audre Lorde, 1979; courtesy of Blanche W. Cook.